Endorsements for *The Invitation*

As a thirty-year career Army Infantry Officer and current Field Staff Member for Officer's Christian Fellowship (OCF), I give my strongest recommendation to this book, *The Invitation*. OCF encourages officers to integrate their faith with their profession. This book is ideal for all who seek to practically apply scripture in any setting: job, family, community, as well as for personal growth. Each devotional shares an interesting story with a simple message and Bible verse that invites the reader to join God's family. Denny has the knack for taking ordinary experiences and drawing on scripture to provide a biblical basis for life lessons. This is a perfect devotional for a year-long journey of discovery. It is a book that provides hope, offers practical biblical truths, and challenges us to examine God's promises and claims found in the Bible.

Stephen A. Shambach
Colonel, U.S. Army (ret)

The Invitation by Dennis Bilter is just that, an invitation to meet Jesus, as though from a friend. What both impresses and encourages me in this devotional is that it meets us precisely where we live in everyday life through stories, anecdotes, and simple, practical truths. In each day's offering, one encounters Jesus in fresh ways that challenge, not with weighty guilt, but with deep conviction and gospel joy. Bilter draws the reader in with winsomeness and hopeful expectation. I was blessed to read *The Invitation*, and you will be as well!

Mike Khandjian
Sr. Pastor, Chapelgate Presbyterian Church
Author of *A Sometimes Stumbling Life*

The Invitation by Dennis Bilter is a wonderful devotional. The uniting theme running throughout the 366 daily devotionals is that "Jesus Christ loves you; come and see." Each of these stories is poignant, concise, biblically sound, and practical. The Holy Spirit speaks through these devotionals because they are relevant, reassuring, and uplifting. I added these devotionals to my daily quiet time and will use them for years to come. Thank you, Denny, and thank You, Lord.

Ted Davis
Doctor of Strategic Leadership (DSL)
LTC (Retired) US Army
Owner, Grace Strategic Services, Inc

Denny Bilter's daily meditations are right on target for us who live in turbulent times subject to the push and pull of many cultural currents! In this time of spiritual unrest, his meditations situate us on the firm foundation of the Rock of the Living God! His reflections place us in the certainty of Our Loving God's Living Word! Highly recommended!

Father Jerry Deponai
Chaplain (MAJ) Retired, USMA 1974
Pastor, St. Anthony's Catholic Church, Nanuet, New York

After years of journaling his spiritual walk and daily experiences with the Lord, Denny is now inviting all of us to read his inner thoughts, questions, and understanding of God. With his background as a professional soldier, successful businessman, devoted family man, and salt-of-the-earth Christian, Denny shows us how to observe the world and to see and apply God's truth in any circumstance, all the time. His daily devotions are neither theoretical nor theological, but they are surely uplifting, inspiring, and theologically correct.

Greg Dabel
Founder, Kids for the Kingdom

I have known Denny for over forty years. He is my mentor, Bible teacher, and I am honored to call him my friend. *The Invitation* that is extended to you is one that you cannot refuse. It will change your life. While reading this powerful daily devotional, you will become intimately acquainted with Our Savior, Jesus Christ. Every day you will be inspired, feel hopeful about the future, grow in knowledge of God's word, and experience our Lord's unconditional love.

Patti Quartuccio, R.N.
Retired Executive Director of a pregnancy resource center in Connecticut

Having known the author very well for three decades and watching him walk through life's often-unexpected twists and turns, this devotional contains real-life examples of a real faith in Christ, clung to and lived by a real person. This is a genuine picture of accepting the invitation to walk with Jesus Christ.

Ron Colantonio
Served 27 years in local law enforcement as a detective and policeman

I heartily recommend Denny Bilter's book, *The Invitation,* as it has something for everyone and everything for someone! It is practical, interesting, relatable, challenging, and doctrinally sound. Knowing the author as my friend and his life's testimony makes the book's contents just that much more believable and special! You'll find it an easy read with lasting results!

John F. Fletcher
Retired Pastor
Ambassador-at-large, Pioneers

This devotional is almost like having a conversation with Denny Bilter. The Bible verses and accompanying messages are clear and easy to understand. Denny loves God, encourages others to grow in their faith, and looks for ways to share his faith. I was able to see these characteristics in Denny when I accompanied him on 6 mission trips—and there is no better way to get to know a person's character than to accompany him on an overseas mission trip with high school students! He is the real deal, and this devotional comes from his heart.

Patricia E. Hayden
Friend, RN, and CRNP

When I first met Denny more than 30 years ago, he was teaching a Bible study for young married couples. He was an excellent teacher—he could tell the stories of the Bible well. He could also explain difficult concepts in a simple way. Then, he would practically apply them to our daily lives. You always left his class feeling more hopeful for the week ahead because you grew in your understanding of God and cultivated a deeper relationship with Him. Needless to say, the

Bible study grew significantly. Through the years, Denny and Faith have also been great friends. As we all do, they have experienced great mountaintops of life and some deep, deep valleys. Through it all, I have observed Denny's faithful application of God's Word to encourage his heart, to glean understanding in difficult circumstances, and to take the next step. For Denny, biblical truth is not just a subject to teach but also the only truth to live by. I am thankful to have a friend like him to learn from. And I know you will enjoy these daily devotionals. God will use them to strengthen you and bless you to live a victorious life with Christ.

Gary Franz
Vice President of International Ministry, Good News Jail & Prison Ministry

Dedication

This book is dedicated to four men who have been my role models of Christian manhood. Because of their support, guidance, and encouragement, I have been inspired to study the Bible and serve others.

I am thankful for each one of them. They took time to listen, provide candid advice, and challenge me in all the major decisions of my life. I salute each of you!

Cleo Buxton
Bill Ladd
Jerry Malone
Ted Fletcher

Preface

Several months before the COVID-19 pandemic hit in 2020, our neighborhood started meeting each week to discuss the stories of Jesus Christ in the book of Luke. Our purpose was to understand the claims of Jesus and the good news he brought to the world. Unfortunately, COVID brought an abrupt end to our meetings, but as the leader of the group, I wondered if I could do anything to continue the good sharing and encouragement we had begun with each other. Maybe I could send a Bible verse out every day to share with the group.

So I started sending out one Bible verse each day. I provided verses that would touch on who Jesus Christ is and what he did to bring salvation to the world. In doing that, I discovered that some of the folks wanted a little more detail, so I began to include short explanations about what I had learned from each passage. Not being a theologian, I gave simple and plain statements about what it means to follow Jesus.

Then, since I had plenty of time to kill, I decided to expand these brief summaries and write an interesting short story with illustrations that would supplement and clarify the Bible verse even further. I had plenty of stories from my own background as a soldier, husband, father, grandfather, and businessman. I was sure that my life experiences could bring clarity to the passages I had chosen, and I'm happy to say, they did!

Now, it is my intent to share *The Invitation* Jesus Christ offers with even more readers. I firmly believe that Jesus did not want anyone to miss out on the good news he offers or to miss being included in the family of God. This is the purpose of my book, to offer *The Invitation* of Jesus Christ to you.

Enjoy!

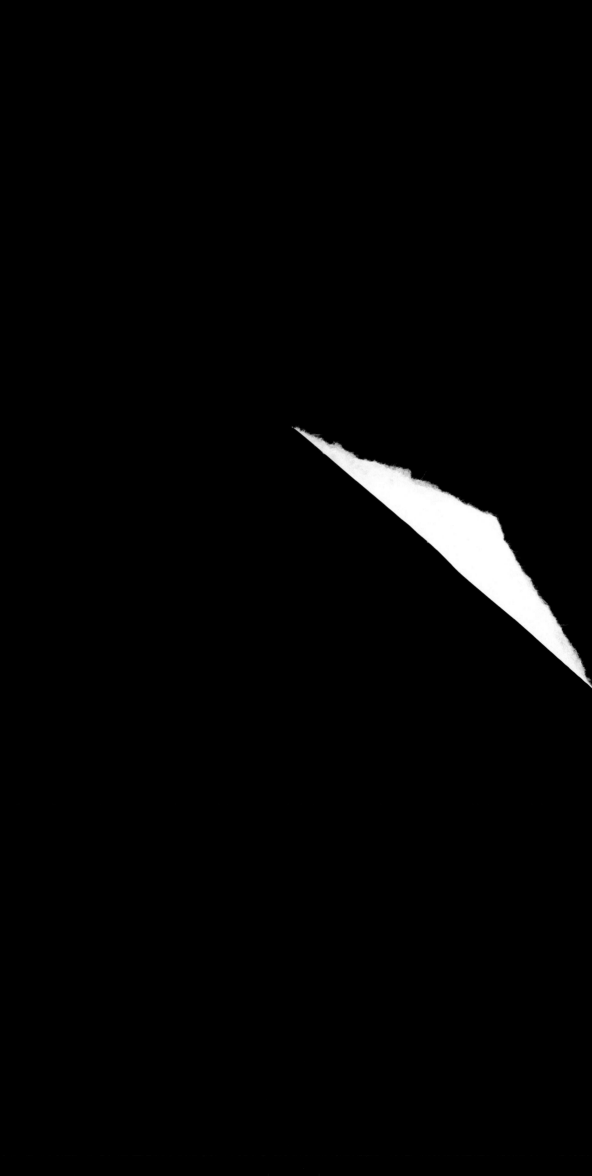

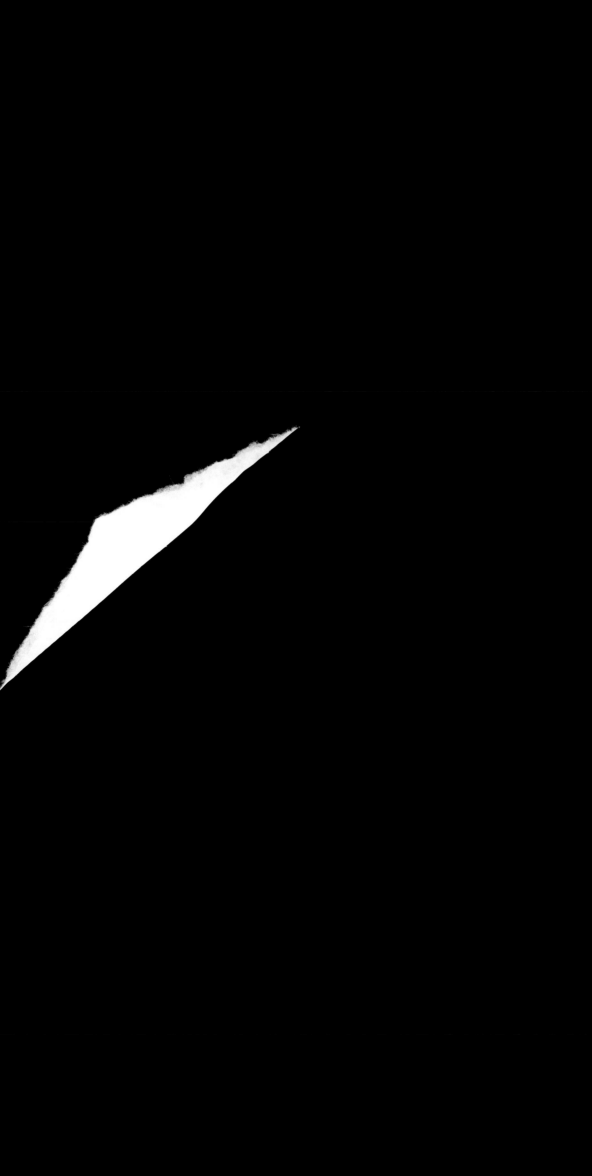

Introduction

Most people I know look forward to receiving invitations. They might be invited to a surprise birthday party, a wedding ceremony, a retirement celebration, or a baby shower. Whatever it is, special events are always meaningful and full of joy. An invitation is a gift. It is free and sends a message to the potential guest that he is welcome. And if the invitation tells you not to bring a gift or any food, it is even more delightful. But I would suggest that the absolute best kind of invitation is one that says, "Come as you are." You don't have to buy a new set of clothes or upgrade your appearance. You don't even need to do anything special with your hair. How nice it is to come to a party, free of obligations, and just spend time with people who care about you and enjoy your company!

The book you hold in your hands is an invitation. In it, you will find a catchy title, a meaningful Bible verse, a short story, a fun sketch, a simple message, and a clear truth. You don't have to be a Bible scholar to understand the points being made. As you look at this collection of stories, you will find that there is one thing that connects everything together and makes this book unique.

What is that one thing? It is God's invitation to you. It is an open-ended proposition that says that if you put your trust in Jesus Christ and follow him, you are welcome to be part of his forever family. This invitation is good news! It has been revealed in the Bible for thousands of years and was lived out perfectly by Jesus Christ when he walked on this earth. God's invitation to you is the focal point of this book.

Think of God's invitation as a tapestry. Tapestries are like life in many ways. When you look at a tapestry on the top side, you see a beautiful pattern. But when you turn it over, all you see is a messy jumble of threads tangled up with no apparent pattern at all. The individual stories in this book are like the little strings on the underside of a tapestry. But as God sews them together, they form a bigger, more beautiful picture of life. This tapestry is God's story for the human race. I call it the "Mystery of God's Tapestry." Now, be careful. You won't be able to understand God's masterpiece if you just follow your own personal story. It only makes sense when you see the broader and more complete view of God's masterpiece and your place in it. Jesus Christ is offering you an invitation to be part of his tapestry. Once you see his work, you will appreciate its beauty.

What should you expect when you read this book? I hope that these short stories and accompanying Bible verses will inspire and encourage you to examine the claims of Christ and the promises found in the Word of God. Consider reading only one devotional each day. Let its message marinate in your heart. Think and ponder what Jesus is offering you. Then come to Christ as you are. No dressing up is required! He's the one who changes you and makes you acceptable to him. You will never be disappointed when you meet Jesus and experience the beauty of the treasure he is creating.

January 1

Welcome-Home Celebrations

The Lord your God is in your midst, a victorious warrior.
He will exult over you with joy, He will be quiet in His love,
He will rejoice over you with shouts of joy.
Zephaniah 3:17 (NASB)

If you have never seen soldiers coming home from a war, you are truly missing out on a joyous celebration. The soldiers are delighted when they see their loved ones. Hugs, tears, and kissing are the norm. Those watching the celebration enjoy the party almost as much as the participants do. This type of celebration captures what is going on in these verses in Zephaniah.

King Jesus is back from the war. He is a victorious warrior who is able to save. He came to Earth to crush the devil. He won the war, and now he invites us to join the celebration. Even though there was nothing we could do to contribute to this victory, he wants us to come to the party. After all, we're the ones he fought for! Now he's rejoicing because we belong to him. He quiets our fears with his love. He blesses us with shouts of joy! And we shout for joy, too, as we welcome him to take his place and rule in our hearts. Don't just watch the celebration. Come to the party. It's a party you don't want to miss!

January 2

One of a Kind

For God so loved the world, that He gave His only begotten Son, that whoever believes in Him shall not perish, but have eternal life.
John 3:16 (NASB)

The phrase "one of a kind" refers to an item that is distinct, rare, special, or unique. It could be anything like a handcrafted piece of jewelry or an original painting. Imperfections in the product also make them one of a kind. And of course, people with unusual qualities or skills fit the description. This verse in John draws attention to the Father who willingly gave up his "one of a kind" Son.

The Father loved the world so much, that he sent his Son, Jesus, on a mission to rescue us. Jesus was his one and only Son, distinct and perfect in every way. He knew that his Son would have to die on a cruel Roman cross to accomplish this rescue. What kind of father would sacrifice his only son? What kind of son would agree to such a sacrifice? I will never fully understand my redemption, but I do appreciate the cost the Father paid for me. Who could turn down this "one of a kind" offer? All I can say is, Thank you, Father!

January 3

Mephibosheth

And David said to him, "Do not fear, for I will show you kindness for the sake of your father Jonathan, and I will restore to you all the land of Saul your father, and you shall eat at my table always." So Mephibosheth lived in Jerusalem, for he ate always at the king's table. Now he was lame in both his feet.
2 Samuel 9:7,13 (ESV)

In the Old Testament, a short story about King David and a young man named Mephibosheth highlights the incredible love God has for his children. In the account of 2 Samuel, we learn David's predecessor Saul tried unsuccessfully to kill David many times. Saul's son Jonathan, however, ended up being good friends with David. As the story continued, both King Saul and Jonathan were killed in a battle. According to God's will, David became the next king of Israel.

This is where we meet Mephibosheth. He was the son of Jonathan. It was common for a new king to kill the rest of the royal family, as any offspring of the prior king was assumed to be a threat to the new king. Not knowing what was going to happen to Mephibosheth, the servants of Saul fled with him. In the course of their escape, Mephibosheth became crippled. Now this young man in his hiding and fear would resume his new life as a weak and broken person.

Then we get a glimpse into the character of King David. David had promised Jonathan that he would take care of his family if anything ever happened to him. When King David asked his subjects if any of Saul's family were still alive, a servant by the name of Ziba acknowledged that Saul's grandson Mephibosheth was still alive. King David then ordered Ziba to bring Mephibosheth to him. I can just imagine how fearful Mephibosheth must have been. What happens next is a story of unconditional love.

David only wanted to show kindness to his best friend Jonathan and to his former enemy Saul. Do you know what David did? He restored Mephibosheth to his royal status. He gave the land of Saul to Mephibosheth as his inheritance. He even invited him to eat all of his meals at the king's table every day. He gave this broken man dignity and access to a relationship with the king.

This story of unconditional love is actually a reflection of God's love for us. Just like Mephibosheth, we, too, are weak, lame, and fearful before God Almighty. We are separated from God because of our sins. But there is hope because King Jesus has already paid for all of our sins.

Today he invites you to eat at his table. What are you going to do, my friend?

January 4

A Weaned Child

Surely I have composed and quieted my soul;
Like a weaned child rests against his mother,
My soul is like a weaned child within me.
Psalm 131:2 (NASB)

A weaned child is an interesting study in nature. A baby, who has always depended on his mother's milk for nourishment and comfort, is now being given another source of food. This can be very disturbing to the child who has completely depended on his mother and loves the taste of her milk. She is introducing new tastes and new textures, and that's hard for a baby to get used to! The child soon discovers, though, that he likes these new foods and learns, in a fresh way, that he can trust his mother and rest in her love. She is not going to abandon her baby; she is going to make life even more enjoyable with new tastes and new experiences. This illustration is used by the psalmist in Psalm 131 to teach us a very important truth about the gospel.

Our souls are often not content. We look for something better. We chase after anything we think might satisfy: a better job, a newer car, a bigger home. But none of these things brings contentment. Anything the world has to offer will never be enough. Fortunately, there is a person who offers us more. His name is Jesus. When we surrender to him and trust in his promises, we can rest and find contentment in knowing him. This is so hard to do because the world's old solutions are always being offered to us. But Jesus has new sources of happiness for us. New ways to satisfy our hunger. New ways to make our lives richer and happier than we ever thought possible. So, like a weaned child, rest against the Savior.

January 5

Siege Mentality

Blessed be the Lord,
For He has made marvelous His lovingkindness
to me in a besieged city.
Psalm 31:21 (NASB)

As I write this the COVID-19 pandemic is besieging our world. We feel helpless against an unknown virus that kills whomever it pleases. The threat alone paralyzes us and forces us into isolation. This siege mentality leads to black-and-white thinking, social conformity, and a lack of trust in others. Our fears tend to outnumber the reality of what is actually true. But the good news in Psalm 31 is that we have a God who hears and knows our fears.

He hears the little girl's prayers in a bedroom closet. He hears a young man's plea for peace in family chaos. And he knows every one of our anxious thoughts. We have a God who saves, and every time he does this, it is an act of mercy.

January 6

Geocaching

*Send forth your light and your truth, let them guide me;
let them bring me to your holy mountain,
to the place where you dwell.
Then will I go to the altar of God, to God,
my joy and my delight.*
Psalm 43:3-4 (NIV)

Several years ago, our friends from Colorado told us about "geocaching." So what is that? Geocaching is the world's largest outdoor treasure hunting game with over one million active players in the United States. Participants, armed with a Global Positioning System (GPS) or a mobile device like a cell phone, hide and seek small containers called "geocaches" at specific locations or map coordinates all over the world. There are literally millions of these sites in every conceivable location. Once the player finds the location, he or she will look for a small waterproof container that contains a logbook and sometimes a little treasure called a cache. These treasures have no monetary value. They are simply trinkets, toys, or unusual coins that can be used to trade with others. Once his treasure is found, the player logs in his identity and date, and then leaves another treasure to replace the cache he found.

I think that this popular outdoor game actually mimics our spiritual journey. Isn't life about finding the treasures of truth, love, purpose, and meaning? Aren't you looking for treasures like these? The Bible is a navigational tool much like a GPS device or cell phone. The Bible guides you to these hidden treasures. Of course, the best treasure is knowing God, the most precious treasure of all. God is our ultimate joy and delight!

God's light and truth are in the pages of the Bible. The Bible will guide you straight to God's holy mountain. Read the Bible. It is full of wisdom and guidance and the greatest stories ever told. Jesus

Christ is the one who goes before you to lead you on your journey. When you follow his lead, your life will be satisfying and filled with adventures you never dreamed of. At the end of your journey, you will find yourself at the altar of God, enjoying his presence, feeling his love, and enjoying the treasures he has prepared for you. By the way, when you treasure hunt with Jesus, your name will be officially logged into God's Book of Life forever.

January 7

Olney Hymns

*When the righteous cry for help, the Lord hears
and delivers them out of all their troubles.
The Lord is near to the brokenhearted and saves
the crushed in spirit.*
Psalm 34:17-18 (ESV)

William Cowper was an 18th-century English poet and hymn writer who has been considered one of the most popular poets of his time. Cowper's mother died when he was six years old. His father sent him away to a boarding school when he was only ten. By the time he was thirty-one years old, he had to be institutionalized for severe depression and despair. Over his lifetime he tried to commit suicide three times. Fortunately, Cowper found hope when he cried out to Christ. Meeting John Newton, who was once a prominent slave trader but later became an abolitionist, was one of the things that led to Cowper's recovery. Their friendship resulted in the writing of the *Olney Hymns*, including one of the world's most popular hymns, "Amazing Grace." Just like Cowper, the psalmist cried out to the Lord for deliverance.

You see, the Lord hears the cries of those who trust in him for salvation. They may feel there is no hope to continue on in life. Depression, anxiety, and hopelessness rule the day. But the Lord is near to the brokenhearted and to those who are crushed in their spirit. Jesus identifies with these people because he, too, was crushed on the cross for our sake. He was sent to give us life and this is what the good news is all about. Thank God we have a Savior who is near to the brokenhearted and delivers us out of all our troubles.

January 8

Who Is Your King?

*Why do the nations conspire and the peoples plot in vain?
The kings of the earth rise up and the rulers band together
against the Lord and against his Anointed, saying,
"Let us break their chains and throw off their shackles."
The One enthroned in heaven laughs; the Lord scoffs at them.
He rebukes them in his anger and terrifies them in his wrath, saying,
"I have installed my King on Zion, my holy mountain."*
Psalm 2:1-6 (NIV)

The Chronicles of Narnia is a series of seven fantasy novels written for children by the famous author, C.S. Lewis. Lewis depicts Jesus as a powerful lion named Aslan in his first book, *The Lion, the Witch and the Wardrobe*. Aslan is a king who is loving and kind to children but terrifies the hearts of his enemies. Lucy, a little girl in the story, asks Mr. Beaver about Aslan. "Is Aslan safe?" Mr. Beaver answers:

> *"Safe?" said Mr. Beaver. "...Who said anything about safe? 'Course he isn't safe. But he's good. He's the King, I tell you."*

The King in our passage today is Jesus, God's Anointed One. The nations rage against him because they believe his commands are chains that limit their freedom. But read God's response. He laughs and scoffs at them. Then he rebukes these rebels and terrifies them in his wrath. "As for me," God says, "I have decided that Jesus is the King of the universe, and I have set him on my holy mountain." In other words, "Go ahead and have your temper tantrum. I'm the one in charge, and I have already made my Son, Jesus, the King."

The conversation between Mr. Beaver and Lucy is a powerful exchange. So are these verses. They should put the fear of God in our hearts and make us ask ourselves, "Who is your King?"

January 9

Letter of Recommendation from Jesus

*Now to him who is able to keep you from stumbling
and to present you blameless before the presence
of his glory with great joy*
Jude 1:24 (ESV)

A letter of recommendation is a formal document that vouches for a person's work history, experience, skills, or academic performance. This endorsement also gives details about the person's best qualities, positive character traits, and moral values. A positive endorsement is essential to a person's success and can definitely get him somewhere!

Let me ask you something. Can you imagine receiving a recommendation from Jesus? What will he say about you when you stand in God's presence some day? All of us would have to admit that our record isn't exactly stellar. We've stumbled a lot and can be blamed for too many sins to count. Yet, it says Jesus is able to present us blameless. How does that work? Jude tells us how it works in the last two verses of the book of Jude.

These verses are about Jesus Christ. Jesus is the only one who is able to keep you from stumbling. That means he is the only one who can give you the power to say no to sin and yes to God. But how does a person access that power? Jesus gives it to us. His power is a gift! Jesus lived a perfect life. Then he sacrificed his life to pay the debt we owe for our sins. When we accept his payment, an amazing transaction occurs. His perfect righteousness is credited to us! So when God looks at us, our record is clear! It's just as though we never sinned! Jesus' sacrifice opens the door to God's transforming power. His gift keeps you from stumbling!

We don't deserve Jesus' recommendation, but he gives it to us anyway—with joy. Imagine Jesus presenting you to God and saying, "Father, I recommend (insert your name). His/her sin is paid for. I've wiped the slate clean!" You will meet God someday. Have you received Jesus' payment? Is your record clear? Will he recommend you?

January 10

Little Things Show Us

*Show us your steadfast love, O Lord,
and grant us your salvation.*
Psalm 85:7 (ESV)

I think God gives us children for many reasons. The most important one is probably to show us love. Rearing children teaches us about life, mercy, and sacrifice. All of these things are included in the total package of what we call love. The little things you do demonstrate love to your children. It is not just the words, but it is your actions and the example they set. Your children experience your love when you sacrifice your time and energy to make their lives better. They see it when you forgive an offense and do not hold it against them. Each little word and action paint the picture. Your children know it when they are truly loved. However, in spite of this fact, they want to be regularly reminded of it. They want to hear the words, "I love you." I think that Psalm 85 is this type of situation as well.

These children of God are just like us today. Even when we believe in the Lord Jesus Christ to forgive our sins, it is hard sometimes to believe it. Fortunately, the Holy Spirit reminds us and encourages us to hang in there.

You are loved! How do you know this? God showed it through all of the little things. He sent his Son Jesus to the earth as a little baby. He served the "least of these," who were the most marginalized people in society. He expressed his love when he died on the cross to pay for every one of your sins! Every single thing he did revealed just how much he really loves you.

O Lord, thank you for showing "us your steadfast love" every day. Thank you for granting "us your salvation" to guarantee we will see you in heaven one day. Your little things show us your love!

January 11

The Battle of Dunkirk

Hasten, O God, to save me; O Lord, come quickly to help me.
Psalm 70:1 (NIV)

In 1940, the Allies were losing the war against Germany on the western front. German forces outnumbered the Allies two to one. The Germans had driven the Allies all the way back to the port in Dunkirk, France. German generals decided to halt the attack on Dunkirk to make sure that no Allied soldiers escaped. During the halt in the war, the British made the decision to evacuate all of their forces from France. What happened next was the largest rescue operation of all time. Over a period of nine days, 700 private boats and 220 Allied warships rescued 331,000 British and French soldiers. The urgency in this evacuation to save the Allied soldiers from destruction is the same feeling you see in this verse.

I don't know all the details of the psalmist's situation in Psalm 70, but it is apparent that he felt like his life was seriously threatened. His broken prayer for deliverance was abrupt, short, and right to the point. I can imagine him saying, "God, I need your help right now! I am sinking!" Have you ever felt that way before? You are not unique. All of us struggle as we deal with life's problems. So what are you going to do? Where are you going to turn to for your help?

God hears every one of your pleas for help. He cares about what is happening to you right now, and he will provide for your deliverance if you call out to him. He is not some distant God at all but is right next to you. He knows your desperate situation and is in control. Since he knows all the details of your rescue plan, you can be certain that he will deliver you and help you at just the right time. What will it be for you, a private boat or a warship? I'm not sure, but I do know Jesus will be there for you!

January 12

House Hunters

For you have made the Lord, my refuge,
Even the Most High, your dwelling place.
No evil will befall you, nor will any plague come near your tent.
Psalm 91:9-10 (NASB)

House Hunters is a television show about people who are making a decision about purchasing a home. Buyers must decide between three houses or apartments to buy or rent. By the end of the episode, a decision is made. The show concludes by revisiting the buyers in their new home a few weeks later to see how things are working out. I've never seen a family who regretted their decision. This show is a little like the situation in Psalm 91.

The psalmist is choosing where he's going to dwell. His decision is whether he is going to end up trusting in the Lord or going another way. It is a decision we all make. You are choosing eternal life if you decide to follow the Lord. If you choose nothing, your indecision is actually a choice to *reject* the Lord.

Choosing your dwelling place wisely comes with a promise. When you decide to trust in Christ, no evil can destroy your secure place with God. You are in God's hands. This does not mean that you are exempt from affliction here on Earth. It means that God is your refuge whatever happens. This is a heavenly guarantee. The question of where you are going to live forever is settled. No evil trails you to your heavenly home. This is a choice you will never regret.

January 13

Final Cut

For I am confident of this very thing, that He who began a good work in you will perfect it until the day of Christ Jesus.
Philippians 1:6 (NASB)

When I go to the store to buy flowers for my wife, if she is not home when I return, I will take the flowers and put them in the refrigerator so she can attend to them later. If my wife is home, she immediately begins her routine of sorting, measuring, and cutting each flower. She creates a specific plan for a floral arrangement and places each flower in the vase, arranged by color and size. If the flower doesn't

look just right, she may cut it, shorten it, or rearrange the vase altogether. After she has made the final cut for each flower and is satisfied, she can sit back and enjoy this beautiful work of art.

Today's Bible verse reminds me of God's grace in the lives of believers. When you trust in Jesus Christ for your salvation, the Holy Spirit begins the process of conforming you into the image of Jesus. God is going to begin a good work in you with the goal of perfecting you until you arrive safely in heaven. In the meantime, the Holy Spirit starts the work of sorting, measuring, and cutting. He has a plan for your life. I don't know exactly what that looks like for you, but whatever it is, you are going to look more and more like Jesus every day.

You can be confident that you are a work in progress. God will never give up on you! He will never abandon you until his work on you is complete! When the final cut is completed, you and I will be included in this dazzling new creation with Jesus.

January 14

Living Choices

I will dwell among the sons of Israel and will be their God.
Exodus 29:45 (NASB)

When I was growing up, I didn't have a choice where I would live. My first real decision came when I graduated from high school and went away to college. Career opportunities have dictated most of my moves since then. But almost everyone goes through the process of choosing where to live at some point in his or her life. Considerations may include your job, the weather, friends, the place where you grew up, or the proximity of your children or grandchildren. What choices have you made? In the book of Exodus, God tells us his choice of where to live. It's pretty exciting.

"I will dwell among the sons of Israel and will be their God." Just so you know, during the time that the book of Exodus was being written, the "sons of Israel" was a phrase that referred to God's children. So, what God was saying in this verse is, I want to live close to my children. When we become a child of God, his Spirit comes to live in our hearts. That's right! God is a Spirit, so he can live in the heart of each of his children! He wants to live that close to us! It is God's choice where he is going to live. What an encouraging fact! Wherever I choose to live, Jesus will be there too!

January 15

Groaning

*"Because the poor are plundered, because the needy groan,
I will now arise," says the Lord;
"I will place him in the safety for which he longs."*
Psalm 12:5 (ESV)

When you hear someone groan what do you think? A groan tells us that a person is in pain or carrying a huge burden. Whatever the problem, it often appears to us like a puff of smoke. We hear a person groan one minute and then we forget all about it. We put it out of our mind as though it never happened. But it's different with God.

Our heavenly Father cares when he hears us groan. How do we know? This verse tells us so. God knows exactly what is happening to each of his children. When the poor are taken advantage of, when "the needy groan," God never forgets. Instead, he arises and takes action. Although it's not always the action we were hoping for, we can have complete confidence in God's love for us. After all, God has strategic goals in mind for his children. Difficulties cause us to draw closer to him, to turn to him in prayer, to get to know and appreciate him more. And sometimes God allows difficulties because in working through them, we become stronger in our faith, wiser, and more sympathetic towards people who need our love. Always remember, God's promises are sure. When we need him, he will arise and put us in a safe place. In time, we will all meet him in person. That is when he will wipe away every tear from our eyes and deliver each one of us from all our troubles, forever. Together with him, we will never groan again. Instead, we will live in the safety and peace for which we always longed.

January 16

Taste Test

*Oh, taste and see that the Lord is good!
Blessed is the man who takes refuge in him!*
Psalm 34:8 (ESV)

I love going to Costco around lunchtime. While my wife is shopping, I casually drift by the food sampling stations. It's great because I can try out all sorts of things I've never tasted before. Sometimes the samples are great; sometimes they're not. For the ones that are great, I go back a second and sometimes a third time. (I have no shame.) I am sure that most of you can relate to my Costco experience. Now I want to share another enjoyable experience, the pleasure of knowing God.

The verse for today is inviting us to taste and see that the Lord is good. When we taste good food, it brings a smile to our face, we want to share our experience with others, and we always want more! Likewise, when we taste the goodness of God, he puts a smile on our face and a spring in our step. We want to share the pleasure of knowing him with others, and we want to know him even better!

I can tell you about my experience with Christ, but the only way you'll really know he is good is to experience him for yourself! This will take a little stretching on your part! Seek God. Spend time with people who like to talk about him. Is he really that good? Listen to their stories of how he is changing their lives. Talk to God. Ask him to reveal himself to you as you read his words in the Bible. These might be new experiences for you, like trying out a food you've never tasted before, but if you take me up on my challenge, you will see how satisfying God is, and what a pleasure he is to know!

This is my challenge to you. Taste and see that the Lord is good. People who taste the goodness of God go back a second and third time—until they absolutely can't live without him!

January 17

Voyager 1

The heavens declare His righteousness,
And all the peoples have seen His glory.
Psalm 97:6 (NASB)

Voyager 1 is a space probe that was launched by NASA on September 5, 1977. Since that time, it has traveled over 15 billion miles from Earth. This forty-six-year-old spacecraft is still receiving commands and transmitting data to Earth. The Voyager mission has expanded our knowledge of our solar system and the universe considerably. A closer look at our planets, the discovery of new moons and new solar systems, and an expanded view of the size of the universe show us we have just scraped the surface of this phenomenon we call creation. This truth is clearly evident when we read Psalm 97.

When I look up at the nighttime sky, I get excited thinking about how incredible our universe is. Because God is the one who put every star and planet in its place, the heavens declare his righteousness and glory. The universe is vast and totally out of our control. Not to worry though, because the God of the universe is totally *in* control!

God's creation is awesome and beautiful. No honest person looking up at the sky can deny his glory. The more we see it, the more we shake our heads in amazement. That's because the same God who created the heavens is the one who came to Earth to save us from our sins. He invites you to trust in him for your salvation. So the next time you look up at the stars, remember: the same God who made all this and keeps it all going is the one who invites you into a relationship with him. Don't miss out on all he's done. Enjoy the lights! Then, bow down and worship the God who created it all!

January 18

Fickle Weather Changes

My days are like a lengthened shadow, and I wither away like grass.
But You, O Lord, abide forever,
and your name to all generations.
Psalm 102:11-12 (NASB)

Have you ever thought about how fickle the weather is? In the morning it might be windy, cold, and drizzling. By noon the wind has died down and the rain has stopped. By midafternoon the clouds are starting to clear. By 5:00 p.m., the sun is out and the sky is clear. It ends up being a great day to be outside. When I think about it, my life changes as well. Sometimes I am distressed, anxious, and worried. The days are long, and I can't sleep because of my aches and pains. I just don't feel good. Then later in the day, I see a grandchild who makes me smile and brightens my day. So, maybe *I* am as fickle as the weather! The psalmist shows his fickle emotions in Psalm 102.

He is thinking about all of his struggles. He's getting old, his bones are aching, he's losing his appetite, and his enemies are making fun of him. It's gotten so bad that he exclaims, "I'm withering away like grass!" It is so easy to get caught up with feelings like this that we forget the truths of God's word!

Look at this verse again! When you feel hopeless, it's time to start praying! It's time to look to God, instead of wallowing in your feelings. That's what the psalmist did! In spite of how he felt at the moment, he talked to the Lord. "But you, O Lord, abide forever." In other words, I might be fickle, but you are faithful. I might be "all over the place" but you are consistent and unchanging. You are just as involved in *my* life now as you were in the lives of people in past generations. They all made it through hardship, and I will too. With you beside me, I'll hang in there, and I will call you Lord! Fickle weather changes are a fact of life, but when you trust in the Lord there will be sunshine in your future.

January 19

Waiting

*O Israel, hope in the Lord; for with the Lord there is lovingkindness,
And with Him is abundant redemption.*
Psalm 130:7 (NASB)

Waiting is so hard for most of us. You see something desirable, and the world tells you that you can have it now. It could be a new car, a new ring, a new video game, or something else you might desire. You don't have to wait and save up the money before you buy it. Buy it on credit. There is always a way to acquire it, so says the world. I think we miss out on many great things because of all the lies the world tells us. They tell you that your life will be so much better when you have what you want and when you have it now! The psalmist understood this temptation and chose to hope in the Lord. He knew his only real hope was found in God's lovingkindness and redemption.

Waiting is actually a good thing for us. It refines our motives and our hearts. It requires us to look again at what we believe. Do you believe this new item, experience, or person will solve your problems? Do you believe that God will look the other way when you try to satisfy your desires without consulting him? This verse tells us where to find hope. Our hope is found in Jesus Christ! He is the only one who can offer us superabundant redemption. Nothing else in the world can do this. Jesus is our only hope, and Jesus is definitely worth waiting for!

January 20

Manna

The people of Israel called the bread manna. It was white like coriander seed and tasted like wafers made with honey. Moses said, "This is what the Lord has commanded: 'Take an omer of manna and keep it for the generations to come, so they can see the bread I gave you to eat in the desert when I brought you out of Egypt.'"
Exodus 16:31-32 (NIV)

The Old Testament account of the people of Israel being led out of Egypt is a story that will brighten your day. When the Israelites departed Egypt, approximately three million men, women, and children started on a journey across the desert that would last forty years. God commanded these former slaves to leave Egypt and to go to their promised land in Israel. I can't comprehend how difficult this must have been for the people to go to a new place to live with no idea of what to expect. The logistics of feeding these people must have been overwhelming! How do you survive the wilderness with all of these families? What do you eat and drink every day in a new land that you don't know?

Well, if you look at Exodus 16, you will find one of God's answers. God provided food for the people: manna. God's blessing, this manna, was like a bread that tasted sweet and could be prepared in many ways. Manna was what sustained all of these people every day. For forty years, God fed his people every single day! Have you ever thought about that? That means that God fed these people for 14,600 days! Do you have any idea what that would cost for a family of four people today in America? A family of four spends almost $28 each day or $196 each week or $10,192 per year on food. How about the cost for forty years? It is a whopping $407,680!

In the verses for today, God wanted Moses to take an omer of manna, which in today's terms means around two quarts, to serve as a reminder of his faithfulness to his people. If God can feed all of these people for forty years, can he not take care of you every day? Can he not take care of your family? Be encouraged, because you have a God who can. You and I have the true God who can take you across the desert and feed you every day!

January 21

Overcomer

Now behold, I have made you today as a fortified city and as a pillar of iron and as walls of bronze against the whole land, to the kings of Judah, to its princes, to its priests and to the people of the land. "They will fight against you, but they will not overcome you, for I am with you to deliver you," declares the Lord.
Jeremiah 1:18-19 (NASB)

The movie *Overcomer* is the true story of a man named John Harrison, who is a high school basketball coach in a town that has just laid off thousands of people from its largest manufacturing plant. The basketball team does not have enough players to field a team, so the school offers John a new position as coach of the cross country team. John doesn't even like the sport, but he reluctantly takes the position. The story soon includes a blind man named Thomas who is dying from diabetes and a young woman named Hannah who has asthma and a tough family background. All three of these people face physical, spiritual, and emotional obstacles. *Overcomer* reminds us of obstacles we face in our own lives, but Jeremiah reassures us with promises from God.

Jeremiah, a prophet of God, is given the task of delivering bad news to the people of Israel. The bad news is that because of their wickedness, Israel will be defeated, and the people will be exiled to Babylon. Jeremiah knows this heart-rending message will not be well-received! What will he do? Will he run and hide? Or will he rise courageously and deliver God's word? Only God can give Jeremiah the strength he needs for this task, and sure enough, God promises to give him that strength. He says he will make Jeremiah like a fortified city and like a pillar of iron. All the leaders and people will fight against Jeremiah, but they will not overcome him. God will be with him to deliver him. Jeremiah will stand strong!

This Old Testament account can be yours as well if you are walking in faith. If you trust in the Lord, he promises to deliver you from your sins. But there's more! God also promises that when you face severe difficulties, they will not overcome you. Jesus faced the greatest obstacles anyone could encounter. People scorned his message and sacrificed him on a cross. But he stood strong and conquered the greatest obstacle of all—death! I don't know what trials you are going through right now, but I do know that Jesus is there to deliver you and help you stand strong.

January 22

A Done Deal

The Lord has sworn and will not change His mind,
"You are a priest forever according to the order of Melchizedek."
Psalm 110:4 (NASB)

When you hear the phrase "it's a done deal," you know that an agreement has been finalized. Sometimes people conclude a "done deal" with a handshake or with a written document. In either case, you know that you can relax a little and start working on something else. The "done deal" we find in Psalm 110 is an announcement God makes about his Son, Jesus Christ, and his role as priest.

In days of old, the priest would raise people's sin offerings to God for his approval. Now Jesus has given himself as our sin-bearer. It's a done deal. In this verse, God is proclaiming Jesus Christ as the quintessential priest. Because he is God's one and only Son, he can speak to his Father on our behalf. Jesus is our advocate! Because he died and paid for our sins, he can grant us pardon for our sins. He is our benefactor! But there's more! God says, "You are a priest—forever!" In other words, Jesus' position of advocate and benefactor can never be revoked. His term of office is eternal!

The best news for us is that God has declared all these benefits with a solemn oath. The "deal" is done, freely given and permanent. No one can take it away because God himself has guaranteed these promises in writing in many verses in the Bible. God planned this deal perfectly and sealed it with his oath. Jesus is our Savior, a friend for sinners like you and me. Jesus is our priest—forever!

January 23

Army Physical Fitness Test

*He has told you, O man, what is good; and what does
the Lord require of you But to do justice, to love kindness,
and to walk humbly with your God?*
Micah 6:8 (NASB)

Every year in the Army, I was required to take a physical test to ensure my suitability for combat. The Army Physical Fitness Test (APFT) was designed to test muscular strength, endurance, and cardiovascular respiratory fitness for soldiers. The test included push-ups, sit-ups, and a two-mile run with combat boots. Each event was given a score from zero to one hundred points. In order to pass, a soldier was required to score sixty points on each of the three events. The Israelites were soldiers in the Lord's army and they wanted to know what the Lord required of them.

They were busy calculating their scores. How many sacrifices and offerings were needed to satisfy God? But God was looking for something more than burnt sacrifices and offerings. God was looking at their hearts. He wanted his children to love him and to love each other. And he wanted to see proof of their love. Were they just and fair with each other? Did they love kindness? Did they have a love relationship with God? Were they walking humbly with him? When people are

focused on enhancing their relationships, they forget about the minimum requirements. Relationships are always what matters most.

If you haven't entered into a relationship with Jesus, you are invited to join him for a real treat. Trust in him and he will deliver you from a life of sin and despair. He will be a friend to you. His love will enhance your life and offer you true freedom. No push-ups, sit-ups, or running in combat boots will ever be required for his friendship. Only your faith in Jesus will matter in the end!

January 24

Sold-Out!

For the eyes of the Lord range throughout the earth to strengthen those whose hearts are fully committed to him.
2 Chronicles 16:9 (NIV)

When I think of the term "sold-out," I usually think that there are no more tickets available for the concert. Or, when I try to buy something online and see that it is out of stock, I know I can't get it anymore. But in the verse for today, we find another meaning for "sold-out." Sold-out Christians are people who have committed themselves so fully to God that there isn't even one part of them they haven't given over to him. Does that mean that "sold-out" people will suddenly become perfect? No, of course not. What it means is that they are *willing* to obey God's commands, and when they fail, they admit their failure and run to God for forgiveness.

God knows exactly what's going on with you right now. He knows where you are struggling. He knows you want to do the right thing, but you desperately need his strength and support. His eyes range throughout the earth, looking for people like you, people who are fully committed to him. In this verse, God is promising to give you the support you need to do what pleases him. To those of us who trust in Christ, God's power is never "out of stock." So the next time you need support, go to Jesus. He's looking for people like you, and he will gladly strengthen you!

January 25

From Captivity to Liberation

*For the Lord hears the needy and does not despise
his own people who are prisoners.*
Psalm 69:33 (ESV)

Several years ago, one of my friends invited me to go to El Salvador to visit prisoners. I had never been in a prison before; I was a little nervous when I was told that the prison held murderers and other men who committed violent crimes. I really didn't know what to expect. But after spending several hours with these men, I discovered that many of these prisoners had something in common with me. The verse for today should get your attention.

"The Lord hears the needy and does not despise his own people who are prisoners." The oppressed and lowly are those who call out to him. They can be absolutely certain that he is not deaf to their pleas for help. If you are honest and sincere, he already knows your heart. He knows when you have turned to him and are trusting in him for your salvation. And he promises that he will not hold you in contempt for all of your past sins. That doesn't mean that you do not have to suffer the consequences for your prior misconduct: you may be incarcerated for the rest of this life, but you will be a prisoner of hope. You will be set free by God's grace. God has given you the power to break the chains which have held you in spiritual bondage. You have been given the Holy Spirit to live within you. And you have a new status: you belong to Jesus Christ. You are forgiven. Because of this, I will be able to see my friends in El Salvador again in heaven. From captivity to liberation, that is a story to tell others about!

January 26

The Great Census

The Lord will count when He registers the peoples.
Psalm 87:6 (NASB)

The Constitution of the United States mandates that a census—a counting of the entire population of a country—be conducted every ten years to determine the number of seats each state has in the US House of Representatives. It is also used to distribute funds to all of the local communities. And it gives leaders an opportunity to ask questions about your address, sex, age, and race. Censuses are not new. Ancient civilizations used them as well to do essentially the same thing. But in Psalm 87, God's great census is totally different.

He is the one responsible for counting and registering all the peoples. None of us can volunteer. Only God can do that. In this census, he counts only the chosen. These are the people who belong to him and are a part of his great family. They are the ones who have trusted in Jesus Christ to save them. They are the faithful ones who are secure. If you have acknowledged him as the Lord of your life, your name will be recorded in the Book of Life.

What an incredible event this will be when the final census is recorded. Men and women from every nation will be present to hear their name called out. Those who were faithful to the very end will be welcomed into heaven and meet Jesus Christ. Will your name be on that last census?

January 27

Welcome to the Neighborhood

*Therefore welcome one another as Christ has
welcomed you, for the glory of God.*
Romans 15:7 (ESV)

How do you welcome a new person into your neighborhood? My wife brings newcomers a gift of cookies, treats, or a cake. I would probably ask my new neighbor if he likes to play golf. A few games of golf would help us to get to know each other. Where did you go to school? Where have you lived? What do you do for a living? Questions like these get a relationship going. These kinds of gifts and invitations help people to feel welcome and comfortable. The apostle Paul welcomed the new people he met, and he wrote this verse in Romans to challenge us in our faith.

If you are a Christ follower, you are commanded to "welcome one another as Christ has welcomed you." Jesus wants you to build up your neighbors, to encourage them, and to show them love. This is exactly what Christ did when he walked on this earth. He wasn't there to please himself. He was there to serve others and to share the good news of salvation. The glory of God was his passion, the most important topic in his conversations. God's moral perfection, his power to change our lives, his protective love for his people, and his promise of eternal life are wonderful things to talk about! We who have been born into God's family have many opportunities to welcome our neighbors. Cookies and golf are just the first step. Then, keep showing your neighbors the glory of God!

January 28

Imagination

*In God I have put my trust, I shall not be afraid.
What can man do to me?*
Psalm 56:11 (NASB)

If you have ever watched little children play, you will quickly discover they have wonderful imaginations. Girls hold conversations with Peppa Pigs. Boys make loud sounds like racing cars. Both have vivid imaginations not perceived through the senses. In these play situations, children choose what to believe. Our choice to trust in a God we cannot see with our eyes is what we are talking about in Psalm 56.

We often allow the fear of man to take over our lives. We actually start believing that mere humans have some power over us. If we would just stop a moment and think about who we belong to and what that means, our fears would dwindle to nothing. Imagine this, the King of the universe has chosen you to be in his family. If you are his child, the King is protecting you and there is no one you need to fear. Jesus is watching out for you, and his power and promises are sure. Remembering that we have been chosen and that we belong to God conquers the fear of man every time. What a blessing it is to know that he is protecting us every minute of every day! This is the good news God offers. As God's child, what will you choose to believe?

January 29

Hospital Waiting Room

Our soul waits for the Lord; He is our help and our shield.
Psalm 33:20 (NASB)

Have you ever spent time in the waiting room of a hospital? It's an interesting experience. Some people are old, some are young, some are well-dressed, and some look like they have just gotten out of bed. A lady whispering a prayer, a man talking on a cell phone, or even a little girl giggling with delight might be there. The lady with the fragrant perfume, the man with coffee, or the teenager eating Fritos. There is absolutely nothing consistent in appearances, sounds, or smells in a waiting room! But there is one thing everyone has in common. Every person in a waiting room is eager for good news. The news that their friend is out of surgery. The news that the surgery went well and everything is okay. The news that the problem is fixed. We wait because we are hoping for a good outcome. We are waiting for good news.

Our life is sort of like a waiting room. When we're children, we're waiting to grow up. When we're grown, we're waiting for the person we will marry, or we're waiting for success in our career. All through life we are waiting for the good news that will solve our problems and ensure our happiness. Through all the ups and downs, a person who knows God will "wait for the Lord." Why do we wait? Because he is concerned for his children and will stand with us while we wait. Because he is powerful and will engage in our problems and help us work them through. Jesus Christ comes to us with the good news we've been waiting for. "Surely, I am with you always, to the very end of the age" (Matthew 28:20 NIV). If you are discouraged today, let me encourage you to wait on Jesus. Remember that at the end of the age, the news will be good, every problem will be fixed, and everything will be a-okay!

January 30

Cornerstone

This Jesus is the stone that was rejected by you, the builders, which has become the cornerstone. And there is salvation in no one else, for there is no other name under heaven given among men by which we must be saved.
Acts 4:11-12 (ESV)

In ancient times, a cornerstone was the foundational stone placed at the corner, or the intersecting angle, where two walls of a building came together. The cornerstone was the foundational building block aligning the entire building and therefore was its chief support. The importance of this stone cannot be understated. The total weight of a building rested on this stone, which if removed, could cause its collapse. It was also the key ingredient to keeping the walls straight. This is why the cornerstone is used in this verse as the symbol for Jesus Christ, who holds God's temple together.

What is God's temple? It's the church of Jesus Christ—all people who look to him for their salvation. He is our "cornerstone"! He was rejected and despised by the religious leaders of his time. Yet he was the only one who could unite people with God and align people with each other! He was the sure foundation for God's family of believers. The total weight of our lives together rests on him. Jesus Christ, our cornerstone, is the most important person who ever lived. If we remove Jesus from our lives, we will collapse. Without Jesus, there is no hope.

But with Jesus, there is every hope! Jesus came to build God's temple. He willingly sacrificed his life so we could live safely under God's protection. If you bow before him and ask for his forgiveness, he will save you and make you a member of his family. "There is no other name under heaven given among men by which we must be saved." In other words, there is no other option! Jesus Christ, the cornerstone, is the only one who can make you right with God. He is the only one who can support you and keep your life from collapsing. If you want to live under the protection of God's house, I suggest you consult the master builder. Jesus is the master builder, and he has already laid down himself as the chief cornerstone.

January 31

Crucibles and Furnaces

The crucible is for silver, and the furnace is for gold, and the Lord tests hearts.
Proverbs 17:3 (ESV)

Crucibles and furnaces have been used for thousands of years to produce precious metals. Solid mineral matter containing precious metals like silver or gold is placed in a crucible, and the crucible is placed in a big, hot furnace. The heat from the furnace melts the metal in the crucible, burning away the dross and other base metals like tin, lead, nickel, or aluminum, and leaving pure silver or gold. This process is very slow, but worth it. It is how precious metals are refined.

Solomon used this refining process to demonstrate what it means for us to be purified by God. God doesn't just save us and immediately transport us to heaven. He uses life here on earth to test our hearts and make us pure. This often takes some time and heat, but it's worth it. Have you noticed that Christians you know often experience severe testing? God is allowing this heat (the Bible calls it a "fiery trial") to melt our hearts, separate us from our impurities, burn up the dross, and make us even more pure than we ever thought we could be. In other words, when you submit your heart to God, he will change you, transforming you into a person who will shine like a star, reflecting his glory to the world. In time, perfection awaits you in heaven where every speck of sin has melted away and you are permanently refined as "pure gold."

February 1

Little Children

*Let the children come to me; do not hinder them,
for to such belongs the kingdom of God. Truly, I say to you,
whoever does not receive the kingdom of God like a
child shall not enter it.*
Mark 10:14-15 (ESV)

The song "Jesus Loves the Little Children," written by Clarence Herbert Woolston, is one of the most beloved Christian songs of all time. The simple message is that Jesus loves all children, regardless of their skin color or the place they call home. Every child is precious in God's sight. We can see Jesus' love for children in our verse for today. Jesus included them, took them in his arms, and blessed them. He even saw them as an example of faith and humility for us to emulate.

How are little children an example to us? They are dependent and trusting. They gladly receive all they need from their parents. And look at how they believe what their parents tell them. They trust their parents completely. They are a living metaphor for how all of us must enter into God's kingdom.

None of us can ever be good enough to enter into the kingdom of God. The only way to get in is to rely on the work of Jesus Christ. You have to believe and depend on him completely. What does this look like? Look at little children and you will see. Coming to Christ means you realize your own weakness and gladly receive his blessing. It means you realize your weakness and are completely depending on God's grace to save you.

It's good to come to Jesus as a little child. Jesus loves little children!

February 2

Come Here!

Behold, as the eyes of servants look to the hand of their master,
As the eyes of a maid to the hand of her mistress,
So our eyes look to the Lord our God, until He is gracious to us.
Psalm 123:2 (NASB)

After I started working in telecommunications, I took a job in a Japanese company. One day, an executive I didn't know very well waved to me from across the room. However, his wave looked strange. His palm pressed outward in my direction instead of inward as in an invitation. It looked like he was shooing me away. I actually was annoyed when he did this. What I did not know was that he was being friendly. This Japanese-style hand gesture was an encouragement to come and talk with him.

It's common for people to study the actions of their superiors so they will not miss any signs of their displeasure. Isn't this what we do when we work for our bosses? We study their actions or facial expressions, hoping that they are pleased with us and think we are doing a good job.

In Psalm 123, the psalmist was paying special attention to the hand of the Lord. As he studied God's hand gestures, he was encouraged. You see, the Bible is packed full of stories of God's affectionate hand on his people. God is always inviting us, not shooing us away. God is saying, "Come here!" The more our eyes focus  on the Lord our God, the more we see what pleases him. We experience his power and grace because we understand his language and are trusting his promises. God's Word is his hand gesture to us.

February 3

Wingman

Do not fear, for I am with you;
Do not anxiously look about you, for I am your God.
I will strengthen you, surely I will help you,
Surely I will uphold you with My righteous right hand.
Isaiah 41:10 (NASB)

A wingman is a pilot who flies beside or slightly behind the right wing of the lead fighter jet in an aircraft formation. His responsibility is to protect the lead plane by watching the pilot's back and remaining close enough to the leader to warn of any immediate threats. The wingman needs to be constantly reacting to his surroundings to prevent attacks. A similar figure is found in the book of Isaiah.

Jesus is our wingman. He is always watching our back. According to the Bible, Jesus sits at his Father's right hand, a special place of honor. Jesus is all-powerful. When he tells us not to fear, it's because he is with us and will surely help us. He is in combat with us as the bullets fly. Three times this verse says, "I will strengthen you" and "I will help you." And then it says, "I will uphold you with My righteous right hand." When I think about the fact that God loves me and is constantly upholding me, it encourages me to continue in the fight. What a blessing to know that Jesus is always watching our back.

February 4

You Can Bank on It!

*Behold, as for the proud one, His soul is not right within him;
But the righteous will live by his faith.
Habakkuk 2:4 (NASB)*

When someone says, "You can bank on it," he is saying, "Believe me! This is really going to happen!" When God told the prophet Habakkuk that "the righteous will live by his faith," he was, in effect, saying, "Believe me! No matter what happens, you will be eternally safe and secure. You can bank on it!"

In this particular verse in Habakkuk, God speaks about two groups of people: the proud and the righteous. Proud people are lovers of themselves. They believe their looks, their brains, their strength, or their ingenuity will save them. They taunt God's people and mock what we believe. They're sure they will never be judged in the end. But they get it all wrong. They are only fooling themselves to think God will not hold them accountable for their life and their record. The righteous, on the other hand, are those who live by their faith. They trust in God for their salvation. They realize they are sinners and know they are guilty before a holy God. The righteous person believes that it is only God's mercy and grace that can save him.

Although most people do not want to believe that judgment is coming, the truth is that the only way you can be eternally safe and secure is to trust your life to Jesus Christ. If you trust in Christ, you will be saved. You can bank on it!

February 5

General Tso's Chicken

*The Lord does not let the righteous go hungry,
but he thwarts the craving of the wicked.*
Proverbs 10:3 (ESV)

Have you ever had a hankering for Chinese food—a good egg roll or General Tso's chicken? My wife and I usually get this craving once a week. When my immediate hunger is satisfied, my long-term hunger clock starts ticking again. I start planning what I am going to order next week. Will it be hot crispy beef or scallion pancake rolls with string beans? Hunger is a need that is never satisfied, so it demands our constant attention. Today's word picture from Proverbs shines a bright light on our spiritual hunger, something we see all the time in our world today.

God has given us a wonderful promise: "The Lord does not let the righteous go hungry." If you know the Lord as your Savior, he will satisfy your soul. This means he will fill your heart, mind, and even your body with everything you need to live for him. After that, he will take you to heaven, where you will never feel hungry again. God knows that you need him, and he assures us in this verse that he will satisfy our hunger over and above anything we could ever dream.

On the other side are the wicked. These people have determined to disregard God and satisfy their cravings some other way. These might be people who commit atrocious crimes, or they might be people we consider to be model citizens. In any case, people who reject God's gift of redemption in Jesus Christ will be excluded from God's spiritual nourishment, so their souls will continue to be hungry. If you notice, it says "he thwarts the craving of the wicked." This means that he will prevent the wicked from having their hunger satisfied any other way than the way he has provided. This is a fearful thought and has terrifying ramifications. If you have never considered Jesus, I would strongly recommend you do so before you die of hunger, and it is too late!

February 6

Holy Joe

Exalt the Lord our God and worship at His footstool; Holy is He.
Psalm 99:5 (NASB)

If someone called you a "Holy Joe," what would you think? Is that label a compliment or an insult? The first known use of this phrase was in 1874. It signified a priest, parson, or chaplain who was serious about his faith. The title "Holy Joe" is mostly obsolete now, but it is still used at times to refer to a person who has a strict moral code or is an aggressive proselytizer. In other words, people use this title as a label to insult a person who is serious about his faith. So why would anyone want to be called a Holy Joe? Hmm? Good question. The verse today focuses on God and says that his holiness is a positive thing. As a matter of fact, it is God's holiness that makes us praise and worship him.

What does holiness mean exactly? Holy means "set apart." God's holiness sets him apart from all creation. Holiness is God's core attribute. He is above everything, in every way! Holiness is the only attribute in the Bible that is mentioned in triplicate, so it must be pretty important! "Holy, holy, holy is the Lord God Almighty! The whole earth is full of his glory!" A holy God is pure and completely set apart from sin. He cannot sin himself, and he can't tolerate sin in anyone else. Holiness and sin cannot live together.

But what about us? We sin and he still loves us and puts up with us! This is where Jesus steps in. Because Jesus paid the price for our sins, when God looks at us, we look perfect, forgiven, and worthy of his love. If you are a child of God, you are "holy" in Jesus Christ. The Holy Spirit lives within you and makes you a "Holy Joe" (in the best sense of the phrase, of course)! When we praise and worship Jesus Christ, when we live for him, we are being holy. So the next time someone calls you a "Holy Joe," smile, and take it as a compliment!

February 7

Hide and Seek

*You will seek Me and find Me when you search
for Me with all your heart.*
Jeremiah 29:13 (NASB)

Hide and seek is a game I played with all of my children and now my grandchildren. The game starts out with the game of peek-a-boo when they are infants. Once they can run and hide, the game gets even better. My favorite place to hide was always in the dark bathroom behind the shower curtain. All of the children, including my wife, always have the same reaction. When the curtain is pulled back, I scream and then they scream. Why do they all like this game? Psy-

chologists will tell you that it is good for their developmental skills. But from a child's perspective, it is just a lot of fun. This game has been around a long time, as we find in the book of Jeremiah.

If you seek for God with your whole heart, he promises that you will find him. This promise is good news to anyone who wants to know God. Seeking God requires an open heart. This means that you are receptive to him. He has done the work; we merely accept or reject his offer. God already knows where we are, so hiding from him is useless. When we finally pull back the curtain, we will find Jesus who loves us.

February 8

Gatorade Thirst Quencher

Jesus said to her, "Everyone who drinks of this water will be thirsty again, but whoever drinks of the water that I will give him will never be thirsty again. The water that I will give him will become in him a spring of water welling up to eternal life."
John 4:13-14 (ESV)

Over fifty years ago, a new energy drink was developed claiming it could satisfy all your cravings of thirst. "Gatorade Thirst Quencher" was scientifically researched to replace the electrolytes you lose in sweating. Producers even started comparing Gatorade to water! The debate still continues today. What is the best quencher for thirst? This question was answered a couple of thousand years ago. Go look in the book of John, Chapter 4, and you will discover the best thirst quencher ever.

Jesus encountered a Samaritan woman who was coming to draw water. In his exchange with the woman, Jesus took the opportunity to distinguish his water from the water she was going for in the well. Jesus told her that the water she was drawing would only satisfy her thirst for one day. It was only a temporary fix. Then Jesus offered the woman living water that would quench her thirst forever. He knew her heart, and he was addressing her need for a Savior who could fill the emptiness and ache in her soul. She was looking for someone who would take her guilt away and give her life meaning and purpose.

What do you do to quench your thirst? Do you chase after material things, enjoyable activities, and people who can satisfy your yearning for love? Jesus Christ is offering you living water that will satisfy your thirst forever. When you believe in Jesus, his Holy Spirit comes to live in you and becomes "a spring of water welling up to eternal life." So, how will you quench your thirst today?

February 9

Till Death Do Us Part

Put me like a seal over your heart, like a seal on your arm.
Song of Solomon 8:6 (NASB)

There is a part of the traditional wedding vows that I am sure you have heard. It is the sacred promise the couple makes to spend the rest of their lives together—until death parts them. Unfortunately, as human beings we sometimes fail in the promises we make. But the commitment of the lovers in this verse offers a picture of the Lord's unfailing love for his people.

In the ancient world, an engraved stone or metal seal was a mark of ownership, a lot like our wedding rings today. Possession of this seal meant a woman belonged to her husband, and they were committed for life. So when a young lady said to a young man, "put me like a seal over your heart," the meaning was clear. They belonged to each other.

This is how God feels about you if you love him. The Lord is staking a claim on your life. He has chosen you and you belong to him. Nothing can tear you away from God. He will never give you up. You are his, and *he* is the lover of your soul. Praise God that nothing can separate you from the love of Christ. Even death will never part Jesus from the people he loves!

February 10

Shattered Dreams

Why are you downcast, O my soul? Why so disturbed within me?
Put your hope in God, for I will yet praise
him, my Savior and my God.
Psalm 42:11 (NIV)

If you have lived long enough, you will understand what "shattered dreams" are all about. It could be a break-up, a divorce, a job loss, or something else that destroys everything you were hoping for. It's broken promises, unfulfilled plans, and a future that doesn't seem so bright anymore. Everything seemed to be okay when, out of the blue, everything fell to pieces. Your plans are completely ruined now. Suddenly your thoughts turn to grief, despair, and depression. "My life wasn't supposed to be like this." "Why would you allow this to happen to me, God?" "Where are you anyway?" "I thought you were looking out for me." These thoughts are no different from King David's thoughts thousands of years ago.

David wrestled with depression, doubts, and feelings of grief just like you and me. "Why are you downcast?" David asked himself. He knew he had a choice to make between hope and despair. Yes, he was feeling depressed, but instead of giving in to his feelings, he chose to praise God. He remembered God's promises to him. He remembered who was in charge. So, David chose hope.

Isn't this really about whom you are going to trust? At some point in your life, you are going to face a situation you will not be able to overcome. Your dreams will be shattered. But Jesus Christ has offered hope if we put our trust in him. When we truly put our hope in God, our grief and despair, our depression and doubt, will disappear. After all, we have the ruler of the universe on our side! But is this attitude adjustment automatic? No! We have to do what David did. Challenge our feelings. Question our thoughts. Take command of our attitude.

What are you going to do? Fall prey to depression and fear, or put your hope in Jesus, your Savior and your God?

February 11

Armor-bearer

*O God the Lord, the strength of my salvation,
You have covered my head in the day of battle.*
Psalm 140:7 (NASB)

In Biblical times, an armor-bearer had many responsibilities to his superior. He was completely loyal, devoted to protecting his master, and sensitive to all of his needs. In battle, an armor-bearer carried a large shield and other weapons to defend his master. His main duty was to ward off blows to his master's head. In the heat of battle he stayed close and was prepared to lay down his life for him.

In modern times, an armor-bearer could be compared to a Secret Service agent to the President. On March 30, 1981, Timothy McCarthy spread his body out to protect Ronald Reagan as six bullets were fired by a would-be assassin. McCarthy took a bullet to the chest but was able to prevent the death of President Reagan. Fortunately, McCarthy made a full recovery and was hailed as a hero for his courage and valor. This verse in Psalm 140 identifies God as our armor-bearer.

We are in battles every day of our lives. Some of those battles are physical: like losing weight, fighting depression, conquering addiction, building friendships, or saving our marriage. Some of those battles are spiritual: loving God, obeying his commands, or loving our neighbors. Our enemy, the devil, attacks our minds, making us think that God doesn't care about us, that we have to fight our battles ourselves, that we are just going to lose anyway, so why fight? We often forget we have an armor-bearer who is willing to protect us in these battles. We wander away from his protection. We forget that Jesus is there to protect our heart and our head in battle, that he has laid down his life to save us from death. Tomorrow when you get up and sense the enemy's bullets flying around you, remember that Jesus is covering you with his armor and he is prepared to save your life!

February 12

Honeycombs

*Gracious words are like a honeycomb,
sweetness to the soul and health to the body.*
Proverbs 16:24 (ESV)

Honeycombs are some of God's most incredible creations. They are clusters of repeating hexagonal beeswax cells made by honey bees to hold honey and eggs. A colony of honey bees, which number between 20,000 and 60,000 bees, is needed to make a honeycomb. Each worker bee visits at least fifty flowers each day to collect nectar and pollen. This nectar is used as food and as an energy source to travel home. The pollen is also used to feed larvae. All of these worker bees in their colony will call upon approximately two million flowers to produce just one pound of honey.

The honeycomb is basically beeswax and raw honey. The honey and its comb are a sweet and healthy food source that offers multiple health benefits. I think that God must have known that these little bees would provide an excellent example for us to use when comparing gracious words in this proverb. Why are gracious words like a honeycomb? These words are "sweet to the soul and health to the body."

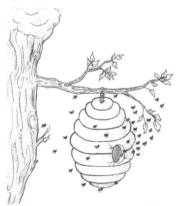

They are encouraging, uplifting, supporting, and reassuring. They are words that build up people and offer real hope. They comfort and inspire others who are struggling in life.

Do you have any idea who did this every day of his life? Jesus Christ did it during his three years of ministry. He offered words of grace that encouraged mankind to trust in him for their salvation. He now invites you to join him in his colony and to become children of light. Why not be a part of his army and take the opportunity to build up one another? It will bless your life!

February 13

The Sun Comes Up

*The Lord is righteous within her; He will do no injustice.
Every morning He brings His justice to light; He does not fail.*
Zephaniah 3:5 (NASB)

The sun comes up every day. What a blessing this is! It is a new day, a fresh start, and a new opportunity to live your life with purpose and meaning. No matter how bad your life is right now, tomorrow is a new day! The rising sun is a gift from God. It tells us he is faithful, and it speaks to us of endless possibilities. This verse in Zephaniah can be a great encouragement to all of us who trust in the Lord.

The Lord is the standard for everything that is right and just in the world. Every morning without fail he brings his justice to light. Some people resist the light and commit acts of injustice. But God uses the rising sun and good people to fight the darkness and work for what is true and right.

Just like the sun that rises, God is faithful and true. He is never late for work; he is the one we can always depend on. Why does God make the sun rise? To show us his impeccable glory, his majesty, and his incredible love. He does this to encourage us to accept his offer of forgiveness and mercy. I think God has given us the example of the sun coming up every day because he wants everyone, everywhere in the world, to know he is faithful and he is true!

February 14

Drumbeat Marketing

*Give thanks to the Lord, for he is good,
for his steadfast love endures forever.*
Psalm 136:1 (ESV)

A repeating drumbeat adds structure and impact to a song. This term is used in marketing too. Drumbeat marketing is the term for a sales campaign with a clear message that is repeated over and over again for impact. When you beat your drum with the same message every day, people start to believe it. "Maybe it's true," they say. "Maybe I should buy this product after all!"

As we read Psalm 136, we notice another repeating drumbeat. All twenty-six verses in this psalm end with a clear message from God: "His steadfast love endures forever." God repeats this message over and over again, so we start to believe it is true. Look at the sun. It rises faithfully every morning, giving the world life and warmth and beauty! Think about your heart, beating eighty times per minute, 4,800 times each hour, or 115,200 times per day—keeping you alive! God's goodness, his steadfast love, impacts you every day in many ways. This never-ending drumbeat is his invitation for you to trust him with your life—forever!

February 15

Driving Alligator Alley

Your way was through the sea, your path through the great waters; yet your footprints were unseen. You led your people like a flock by the hand of Moses and Aaron.
Psalm 77:19-20 (ESV)

If you have never driven across the Everglades, the quickest route is Route I-75 between Naples and Fort Lauderdale. It is about eighty miles long and is affectionately known as Alligator Alley because of all of the surrounding swamps that Florida's alligators call home. The only time that my wife and I ever drove that road we encountered a horrendous thunderstorm. The sky turned black and then a pounding rain pelted us with the biggest raindrops we have ever seen. Within minutes, we could not even see the road. I can't begin to tell you the fear and panic you feel when you are driving seventy miles an hour on a major interstate road not knowing whether another car is going to hit you. What a relief it was when the storm finally passed and we could once again see the sun on this beautiful highway.

This road trip is a good example of the picture painted in Psalm 77: a man is clearly overwhelmed by an impossibly dreadful situation. He is going through a severe trial. For most of us, it is only a matter of time before we, too, will go through some trouble that will rock our world. Where are we going to turn for help?

The psalmist sought the Lord because he believed that he would protect and care for him every step of the way. He knew God's record of accomplishment, so he understood that God was on his side. What did he conclude? God's "way was through the sea." God wanted him to go through an incredible storm and to face an overwhelming flood. Why do you think that God does this? Why would he want us to go through a trial and not around it? Why would he lead us into a situation in which we cannot even see his footprints?

God wants you to turn to Jesus Christ for your help. He wants you to trust in him for your deliverance from the storm. He has promised that he will lead you to safety. He will take your hand and guide you through every situation in your life. This is a pretty good deal when I think about it. Maybe it is time to plan on another driving trip to Florida!

February 16

Olive Trees

But I am like an olive tree flourishing in the house of God;
I trust in God's unfailing love for ever and ever.
Psalm 52:8 (NIV)

Olive trees start bearing fruit at about five years of age. After that they can live for thousands of years. Some olive trees have been carbon-dated to be 1,600 years old and are still producing abundant fruit today. Large olive trees produce an average of 400 pounds of fruit annually. The root system of the olive tree is so vibrant that it is capable of regenerating itself even when the tree above ground has been destroyed by fire, frost, or disease. David, in our verse for today, likened himself to an olive tree.

David realized there were two different kinds of people in the world. One kind of person is the "mighty man." This person brags all the time and finds ways to destroy others by practicing deceit instead of speaking the truth, by loving evil rather than good. David knew that a man like that was trusting in his wealth and that he was growing strong by destroying others. He knew that God would bring that "mighty man" down to everlasting ruin.

But David wanted to be a different kind of person. He wanted to be like an olive tree, flourishing in the house of God, bearing tons of good fruit, blessing others instead of destroying them, trusting in God's unfailing love forever and ever.

No one has 1,600 years to decide what kind of person he will be. Life goes by pretty fast. Do you want to be a mighty man or an olive tree flourishing in the house of God?

February 17

Blind Auditions

For God shows no partiality.
Romans 2:11 (ESV)

The Boston Symphony Orchestra was the first to try blind auditions in 1952. Like other major orchestras in America, nepotism was rampant. Friends and family of existing orchestra members were usually guaranteed winning auditions and cushy jobs. Other competent musicians opposed this discrimination as unfair, and a new kind of audition took its place. "Blind auditions" leveled the playing field and made selections fair for everyone.

In blind auditions, a screen is placed between the judges and the performers, making it impossible to see their forms or faces. To further ensure fair competition, no performer is allowed to speak, and each has to play the same musical selection. The Boston Symphony Orchestra made these changes, concealing the identity of each musician. But even with these precautions, gender identity remained an issue. Male selections outnumbered females two to one. A clever observation overcame this one last problem: if candidates removed their shoes, the male to female ratio changed immediately. This requirement resulted in a near-fifty fifty split between males and females. We see here that impartiality makes selections fair. In our verse for today we see the impartial God, guaranteeing a fair selection for eternal life.

"God shows no partiality" when he awards people eternal life. He doesn't look at the color of our skin, our titles, our family, friends, or past history to determine our final destiny. God sees through these external appearances and looks strictly at our hearts. He knows exactly what's going on in there, and let's face it, it's not lookin' good. In fact, our performance looks like a bunch of dirty rags next to God, who is perfectly holy. The fact is, we're in big trouble! We need help! Thankfully, God saw our need and, in his love, he sent us help. God the Father sent his Son, Jesus, to "audition" on our behalf. From head to toe, he never sinned! His performance was perfect! The beautiful thing is that God credits Jesus' performance to us. When this happens, we win the audition and eternal life in heaven. How God can be perfectly holy, perfectly impartial, and perfectly kind is a mystery to me. But I'll trust him for that mystery. Will you?

February 18

Corrie ten Boom

*Above all, keep fervent in your love for one another,
because love covers a multitude of sins.*
1 Peter 4:8 (NASB)

Corrie ten Boom's father was a well-known Dutch watchmaker. Her family lived during the German occupation of Holland in World War II. During that time, they hid many Jews in their family home, helping them to escape the Nazi death camps. The Ten Boom family believed that the Jews were precious to God and that all people were created equal in God's image. On February 28, 1944, a Dutch informant told the Nazis what the Ten Booms were doing, and the entire family was arrested. Corrie and her sister, Betsie, were later sent to Ravensbruck, a Nazi concentration camp. This was a time of great suffering for both of them, but they spent that time sharing their hope in God, encouraging fellow inmates, and introducing many of them to Jesus Christ. Betsie finally succumbed to the terrible living conditions at Ravensbruck. Her death broke Corrie's heart. After she was released, Corrie wrote *The Hiding Place,* a book detailing her life's experiences. Her story exemplifies the great love God has commanded us to have for our fellow man.

In *The Hiding Place,* Corrie tells an inspiring, personal story. Several years after World War II, she was asked to speak at a church in Munich, Germany. Corrie's message to the German people, many of them plagued with guilt, was that God forgives. After the service, a man came up to her and revealed that he had been a Nazi guard at Ravensbruck. This man welcomed Corrie's message and was thankful that God had forgiven him for the cruel things he did in that place. He smiled, held out his hand, and asked Corrie, "Will you forgive me?" This request made Corrie's message personal. Could she forgive this man? Corrie knew that forgiveness is not an emotion. She understood that forgiveness is a choice. So, Corrie chose forgiveness and shook the man's hand. Jesus set this high standard for us when he died on the cross, choosing to forgive all our sins and give us new life. If Corrie could forgive a Nazi, there is hope for all of us too.

February 19

Point of View

*Until I came into the sanctuary of God;
then I perceived their end.*
Psalm 73:17 (NASB)

My parents bought our first television set in the late 1950s. Watching *The Ed Sullivan Show* on a black and white 16-inch television set versus watching the Super Bowl football game on a 4K UHD 75-inch color monitor in 2024 makes a world of difference. When you can identify football teams by the colors of their jerseys, your point of view changes quickly. Color expands your thinking. Your viewpoint changes. Your vision broadens. I think this verse clearly illustrates what happened when the psalmist entered God's sanctuary. He had a different point of view, and that changed everything he had been thinking about.

When you think like a natural person, you tend to see a world filled with hatred, greed, and despair. It is a world of chaos where there is no hope. This type of thinking is centered on self. It is based on your circumstances, your feelings, your moods, and your emotions. It is all about your troubles in life. This is what governs your thinking completely. The black-and-white viewpoint of life limits your ability to see color in every aspect of your life.

When the psalmist "came into the sanctuary of God," he started thinking like a spiritual person. His point of view changed from himself to God. Whenever you start to realize that it is not all about you and that your story is not the most important one, then you will start to understand that only God's story matters. His story is about redemption. It is a story of how God rescued lost sinners. It is the story of Jesus Christ.

When you come to Jesus, your point of view is going to change. You are going to see life in an entirely different way. You are going to see just how dark and serious your sins really are, and you will perceive your end. Exposing yourself to God's truth in the Bible gives you a broader view of Christ's forgiveness for you. If you have never looked into Jesus' claims, let me challenge you to do so. Your viewpoint may change when you see the vibrant colors in heaven!

February 20

What Time Is It?

*The years of our life are seventy, or even by reason of strength eighty.
So teach us to number our days that
we may get a heart of wisdom.*
Psalm 90:10, 12 (ESV)

I recently saw a book entitled *Time for God* written by a Christian theologian Dr. Leslie Weatherhead that gives an illustration about the importance of time. He calculated that if your age is fifteen, the time is 10:25 a.m. If your age is twenty, the time is 11:34. If your age is twenty-five, the time is 12:42 p.m. If you're thirty, the time is 1:51. If you're thirty-five, the time is 3:00. If you're forty, the time is 4:08. At age forty-five, the time is 5:15. If you're fifty, the time is 6:25. By age fifty-five, the time is 7:24. If you're sixty, the time is 8:42. If you're sixty-five, the time is 9:51. And if you're seventy, the time is 11:00 p.m.

The Bible tells us, "The years of our life are seventy, or even by reason of strength eighty." The bottom line is that our life is very short. Every one of us only has a set number of days to live. Psalm 90 is a good reminder of this truth.

I would like you to consider the fact that our lives are fragile and temporary. God has given you a bottle of time for each day. In this bottle there are twenty-four hours or 1,440 minutes. This precious gift that God has blessed you with is limited and expires at midnight. This gift is your opportunity to pursue what you deem important, those things you value. The question is, "What are you going to do with this?" How are you going to invest your time each day? If you take out the time you spend working at your job, sleeping, and eating, you only have about six hours (or 360 minutes) left each day to use this wonderful blessing we call time.

So the ball is in your court. What are you going to do with this time? This verse tells us that we need to "get a heart of wisdom." What does that mean? If you want a heart of wisdom, you need to have a relationship with Jesus Christ. You need to know him personally. He will give you the Holy Spirit to live with you when you call out to him. He will give you a new heart and help you to use this gift of time for eternal things that will impact your destiny. So the only question I have for you is, "What time is it?"

February 21

The Vine That Ate the South

I am the true vine.
John 15:1 (NASB)

If you grew up in the South, I bet you know all about kudzu. This ground root from China and Japan has been a common ingredient in foods and medications for centuries. It was first introduced in the US in 1876 and used in gardens. In the 1920s, nurseries in Florida discovered that animals could use it for forage. Then in the 1930s, kudzu was used for erosion control during the Great Depression. It was actually called "the miracle vine." The problem with this vine is that it grows too well in the southeastern United States. During the summer months, vines can grow a foot per day and grow sixty feet each year. By 1972 however, it was declared a weed. Each year attempts are made to eliminate it without success. In the book of John, Jesus is compared to a vine.

Why a vine? Vines are plants with thin stems that use neighboring plants, rocks, and trees for physical support. The plants can climb, creep, and spread out horizontally as well as vertically. Despite their inability to support their own weight, vines have remarkable tensile strength. It is very difficult to pull or break them apart. Most of all they are very vigorous and healthy.

Jesus calls himself the only true vine, and we are the branches. This picture is intended to teach about the relationship between the vine and its branches. Our lives as the branches are completely dependent on the vine, Jesus, our source and sustenance. All nourishment, support, and vitality depend on Christ. This is the picture of those who trust in Christ for their salvation. By faith, we are connected to the true vine.

February 22

The Works

How many are your works, O Lord!
In wisdom you made them all; the earth is full of your creatures.
Psalm 104:24 (NIV)

"I'll take a burger with the works." When I say this, I mean, "Give me everything! All the toppings: the lettuce, tomatoes, pickles, onions, relish, mustard, ketchup, and mayonnaise." Getting "the works" guarantees the best hamburger in the world, a true delight. God's world is full of delightful things. He made them all for us to enjoy! I can just hear the psalmist exclaiming, "Lord, the world is full of your wonderful works! I want to experience them all!"

It seems that the psalmist is especially delighted with God's creatures: the sweet puppy, the soft kitten, the regal lion, the funny-looking hippopotamus, the irritating mosquito, and us totally awesome human beings! Do we really understand just how great our God is? He made every wonderful creature and gave them an

environment where they could flourish. We're not sure how many creatures there are; we just know the earth is full of them. God has blessed us so much. In fact, I like to think that when God was putting the world together, he said, "Give my people the works so they can see my limitless forgiveness and abounding love!"

February 23

Deep Doo-Doo

*If You, Lord, should mark iniquities, O Lord, who could stand?
But there is forgiveness with you, that you may be feared.*
Psalm 130:3-4 (NASB)

The funny phrase "in deep doo-doo" is actually quite serious. "Deep doo-doo" is another way to say I am in serious trouble. In business matters, I might have charged too much or broken my promise to a customer. In personal matters, I might have betrayed a confidence or lied to a friend. However you say it, "deep doo-doo" is a grave situation. It is where the psalmist found himself in Psalm 130.

When he realized the depth of his sins, the psalmist felt fear. When we face the fact that God sees everything we do, we realize our record is a long list of shame and guilt. We have little for which to feel proud. We realize we can never stand before God in this condition. This is why the psalmist seeks God's mercy. He consoles himself with this truth. "There is forgiveness with you, that you may be feared." Fear and hope aren't mutually exclusive! We fear God because we are in deep doo-doo, but we have hope because he is willing to forgive our sin! Where does this hope and comfort come from? Jesus, the Savior who paid the price for our salvation! Putting our trust in him clears our record of shame and guilt and pays our debt. No more doo-doo for us! We are cleansed by the blood of Christ!

February 24

Do-Over

*Therefore if anyone is in Christ, he is a new creature;
the old things passed away; behold, new things have come.*
2 Corinthians 5:17 (NASB)

Sometimes I have heard my wife say, "I need a do-over as a parent." This is a new attempt or opportunity to do something after the previous attempt was unsatisfactory. Isn't this our thinking so often? If I could only do it again, I would be a better parent. The Bible addresses this painful situation. It zeroes right in on the heart of the matter.

When you trust in the Lord for your salvation, you are "in Christ." This means that you are reconciled to God through Christ's death on the cross. Old things have passed away, and now new things have come. Jesus gives us the opportunity to start over and be "new creatures." Our broken relationship with God is restored, and now we have the hope of restoring other relationships as well. We can pray, trusting God to do miracles in this process. What an encouragement to know that even though I might have messed up in the past, God can give me a do-over. With all the power he has, that do-over can be miraculous!

February 25

Whom Are You Following?

*May the Lord direct your hearts into the love of God
and into the steadfastness of Christ.*
2 Thessalonians 3:5 (NASB)

"Follow your heart" is a popular phrase today. It tells you that the way you feel is the right way you should go. It promises that if you follow your heart, you will find true happiness. This phrase sounds good, but it is filled with difficulties. If you depend on your feelings, they could point you in the wrong direction; even your intuition might not be fully informed. This is the time for you to reconsider where you are heading. Paul's second letter to the Thessalonians gives us valuable advice.

Instead of following the desires of your heart, ask the Lord to direct you. God is all-wise and all-good. He knows the future and everything about you. He keeps careful watch over your life. If you ask the Lord to direct your life, he will lead you right into the love of God. He will also make you steadfast. No more confusion and anxiety. You will become a stable person, like Christ. When the Lord directs your heart into the love of God and the steadfastness of Christ, you will become wise, and you will be able to share your wisdom with others. So leave behind this notion of following your heart and accept the direction of the Lord, Jesus Christ.

February 26

Confession

*Then I acknowledged my sin to you and did not cover up my iniquity. I said, 'I will confess my transgressions to the Lord'—
and you forgave the guilt of my sin.*
Psalm 32:5 (NIV)

One of the most difficult things to do is confess a sin to your wife and ask for forgiveness. "Honey, I sinned against you and I was wrong. I take full responsibility for my actions, and I will try not to do it again. Will you forgive me?" Why is that so hard to do with someone you love? I think it's because of pride. We realize we are the ones who were wrong. But what do we do? We make excuses. "It's actually not my fault," we argue, but we know the truth and are miserable until we own up to it. The verse for today is David's account of how he dealt with his guilt and pride.

When you try to cover up your transgressions and keep silent, God's hand will be heavy upon you. David, the psalmist, said that when he was silent, even his bones wasted away and his strength dried up. That's one way to put it! But no matter how silent you are, it's impossible to cover up your sin. God knows exactly what you did. Yes, I know how hard it is to admit that you have failed. It is the most unnatural thing for any of us to do. But if you want to find peace in your relationships with other people and with God, you are going to have to admit when you are wrong and ask for forgiveness.

Forgiveness was bought by Jesus when he shed his blood on the cross. Jesus offers you a complete pardon for all of your sins when you acknowledge them and ask him to forgive you. There's no sense in covering up your sins. God wants each of us to be honest with him. With this act of obedience, he will restore your relationship and forgive you. He will remove your guilt and give you peace. Isn't this what we are all looking for?

February 27

Ten Lepers

*When he saw them, he said, "Go, show yourselves to the priests."
And as they went, they were cleansed. One of them, when he saw he
was healed, came back, praising God in a loud voice. He threw himself
at Jesus' feet and thanked him—and he was a Samaritan. Jesus asked,
"Were not all ten cleansed? Where are the other nine? Was no one found
to return and give praise to God except this foreigner?"
Luke 17:14-18 (NIV)*

In the Bible, there is a story in the book of Luke about Jesus and ten lepers. These men were outcasts since they suffered from the dreaded disease of leprosy. They lived outside their communities with nearly no human interaction and virtually no hope. On the way to Jerusalem, these lepers saw Jesus from a distance and shouted to him. They asked Jesus if he would have mercy on them. In other words, they were asking to be healed. When Jesus saw them, he told them to go and show themselves to the priests. These lepers faithfully obeyed Jesus' command to go, and when they departed, all of them were healed of their leprosy.

All ten of these lepers saw that their leprosy was gone as they were traveling. Can you imagine the joy and gladness they must have felt when they knew they were healed? They were given a new life and a new future. What do you think these men did when they realized this miracle? Believe it or not, only one leper turned back to thank Jesus. The other nine men went on their way back to their past lives. What would you do if you were one of the ten? I would like to think that I would turn back to thank him.

This story in the Gospel of Luke is one of these accounts that should challenge you to consider what God has done for you. Take a moment and think about it.

    Most of us are so caught up in our own lives with families and jobs that we forget about God. Yes, we know that God has blessed us, but have we taken the time to thank him for what he has really done for us? Do we fully grasp it? We have a God who has created us, knows everything about us, and who loves us without any constraints. We have a God who sent his Son to Earth to sacrifice his life just so that you and I could have forgiveness, a new life, and a new future. These are the reasons to be thankful every day when we get up.

February 28

Never Give In

*I pray that the sharing of your faith may become effective
for the full knowledge of every good thing
that is in us for the sake of Christ.*
Philemon 1:6 (ESV)

It was October 29, 1941, and Winston Churchill was visiting his alma mater, Harrow School. He had gone there to hear the traditional songs of the school and to give a short speech. Britain was engaged in a terrible war with Germany at that time, and since Churchill was the leader of the British nation, people were looking to him for words of encouragement. His comments did not disappoint as he spoke these famous words, "Never give in." Churchill was challenging his nation to remain steadfast in the war effort against Nazi Germany and to continue England's strong relationship with America to stop the spread of communism. He was successful in both of these goals, giving strong encouragement to a world filled with fear. The apostle Paul gave a man named Philemon a similar admonition in our verse for today.

Philemon was a wealthy man from Asia Minor. Paul was writing to him about his runaway slave, a man named Onesimus. We don't know the reasons Onesimus ran away, but Paul didn't shy away from admonishing Philemon. Philemon was a practicing Christian, but his testimony for Christ wasn't effective. Philemon had "given in" to the cruelty of slavery, and Paul was writing to challenge him to come to a "full knowledge of every good thing." Don't give in to temptation, Paul was saying. Take Onesimus back and treat him as a brother, not as a slave. We can assume that Philemon accepted Paul's advice, and that's when the sharing of his faith became effective. Philemon was useful to Christ because he was obedient to Christ. As a result of Paul's exhortation, Philemon stopped "giving in" to sin, and both Philemon and Onesimus were able to live their lives for the sake of Christ. With the strength that comes from God's Spirit, "never give in" applies to resisting temptation!

February 29

Origins

In the beginning God created the heavens and the earth.
Genesis 1:1 (NASB)

Last year over three billion dollars were spent on genealogy products and services. People want to know the ancestries of famous personalities and to link them to their own careers and lives. DNA and genetic testing are also gaining traction in the field of forensics, with technology that enables investigators to solve crimes. We are curious people when it comes to origins.

In the very first verse of the Bible, God claims his place as the originator of the heavens, the earth, and everything that exists. He knew exactly what he was doing, and everything was just perfect! God was the one who gave us our specific genetic code, the DNA that makes us unique. The Bible says that God formed our inward parts and knitted them together in our mother's womb and that we are fearfully and wonderfully made. What is even more amazing is that he did it so we could point people to him! He loves each one of us so much that even though we have rebelled against him, Jesus makes it possible for us to be reconciled to him. The DNA in our body is amazing, but the one who created it is infinitely better. Search for him and you will discover your origin.

March 1

Ain't No Mountain High Enough

Thus says the Lord, "Heaven is My throne and the earth is My footstool. Where then is a house you could build for Me? And where is a place that I may rest? For My hand made all these things, Thus all these things came into being," declares the Lord.
Isaiah 66:1-2 (NASB)

"Ain't No Mountain High Enough" is a soul song written by Nickolas Ashford and Valerie Simpson in 1966. It became a big hit in 1967 when Marvin Gaye and Tammi Terrell recorded it. Here is the chorus:

"Ain't no mountain high enough
Ain't no valley low enough
Ain't no river wide enough
To keep me from getting to you, babe"

The message speaks about the extreme love between two people. Nothing can come between them. No obstacle can stand in their way. This love song actually captures the message of the gospel. It is a story of extreme love told by the prophet Isaiah.

When I think about God's throne being in heaven and his footstool on the earth, it is all about extremes. I can't fathom this. How could anyone build a house that contains a God this big? It is impossible. His realm extends higher than the highest heaven and reaches all the way down to Earth. If this isn't extreme, what is? To think that God sent his Son down to this earth to save us and show us his love is astonishing! Jesus has never let any mountain, valley, or river keep him away from getting to the ones he loves. This is good news for all of us.

March 2

Follow Me

For even the Son of Man did not come to be served, but to serve, and to give His life a ransom for many.
Mark 10:45 (NASB)

Follow Me is a sculpture located at Fort Moore (formerly Fort Benning), Georgia. It was created by two soldiers depicting a 1950s-era infantry soldier charging forward and gesturing for others to follow. The statue sits in front of Infantry Hall where all US Army infantry leaders are trained. The large bronze statue of the soldier is holding a rifle in one hand. The other arm is raised as if signaling to others behind him. His head looks back over his shoulder, and the plaque on the base of the statue commands, "FOLLOW ME!" This simple but powerful message conveys the leadership style needed to inspire others in battle. Over two thousand years ago, Jesus set the standard for leaders. He is our best example.

Jesus Christ came to Earth to save sinners and lead us to God. "I am the way, the truth, and the life," he said. "Follow me!" But saving sinners wasn't easy. It took some serious conflict, and it took Jesus, the greatest leader of all time. Jesus was fighting for light over darkness, right over wrong, belief over unbelief, and love over hate. When we decide to follow Jesus, we join the fight too. He didn't expect to be served. He served instead, healing the sick, raising the dead, and speaking the truth, even when it offended others. In the end, he suffered the consequences, giving his life so his people could live forever. "Follow me!" is the charge Jesus gives each of us. He is inspiring us to fight the darkness and give our lives for others. By accepting this charge, we are joining a band of brothers and sisters who follow their leader, wherever he leads, whatever the consequences.

March 3

The Elephant in the Room

Judge not, and you will not be judged; condemn not, and you will not be condemned; forgive, and you will be forgiven; give, and it will be given to you.
Luke 6:37-38 (ESV)

In 1814, a writer named Ivan Krylov wrote a Russian fable entitled "The Inquisitive Man." In this story, a man goes to a museum and notices all sorts of tiny animals but fails to see the elephant in the room. This little story eventually led to a familiar English expression. "The elephant in the room" refers to a topic that is glaringly obvious but willfully ignored. It is a huge issue and very controversial. Everyone knows about it, but no one wants to talk about it. It's just too uncomfortable. When I studied these verses in the book of Luke, it became obvious to me that the elephant in the room for all of us is pride and sin.

Jesus taught us to love our neighbors, even our enemies. Unfortunately, this does not come naturally to us. We love ourselves and are careful to guard ourselves, hoping no one will discover our own imperfections. We often judge our neighbors, find fault with them, and condemn them. But Jesus is firm in his commands. As his followers, we are called to show mercy to one another. Jesus does not want us to be judgmental; he isn't calling us to be critics. Instead, he is calling us to be forgiving, generous, and tenderhearted.

There are a lot of benefits that come with obeying the Lord. When we love others, they are more apt to love us back, to be tenderhearted, generous, and forgiving of our own imperfections. Give grace, and grace will be given back to you. Are you having a hard time forgiving? Remember, God has been tenderhearted with you;

he has forgiven your sins. You don't have to pretend that you are perfect. The elephant in the room is gone, and you are set free to admit your own faults and to love your neighbor. Now this is good news!

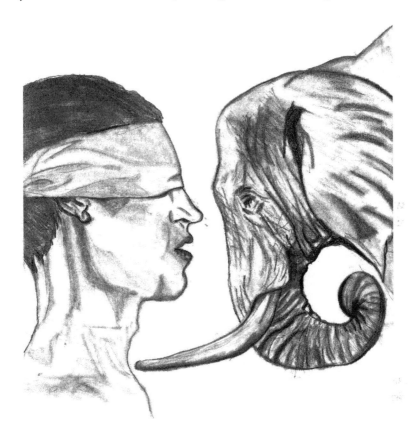

March 4

Staking a Claim

*"The Lord is my portion," says my soul,
"Therefore I will have hope in Him."*
Lamentations 3:24 (NASB)

Did you know that for a mere $155 a year you can own a twenty-acre mining claim? The General Mining Act of 1872 set a price of $2.50 to $5 per acre, and it hasn't been changed since. The claim does not give you ownership, but it does give you mineral rights to that land. People staking a claim like this are hoping to strike gold, silver, or some other mineral. There is always the possibility their claim will yield a profit. A claim can only be made with public domain land that is owned by the federal government. Unfortunately, there are only a few parcels left in the eastern half of the US. But in the western half of the country, many are still available. The prophet Jeremiah knew all about staking a claim, which is exactly what he did in the book of Lamentations.

"The Lord is my portion," he said. "Therefore, I will stake everything on him." The question for all of us to consider is, "What am I going to stake as my claim?" What will be my portion? Will it be riches, a good reputation, a title, or a memory? Jeremiah made a decision to stake his claim on the life-changing power of God. He decided he would put all his eggs in one basket. He would claim forgiveness from sin, a brand-new start in life, and the hope of living in heaven forever. At the end of your life, what will your portion be?

March 5

Sunsets at Little Round Top

Its rising is from one end of the heavens, and its circuit to the other end of them; And there is nothing hidden from its heat.
Psalm 19:6 (NASB)

Little Round Top is one of my favorite places to watch sunsets. It is in Gettysburg, Pennsylvania, where the last day of that great battle took place. Today the portrait statue of General Warren stands atop the boulder where he noticed the Confederate advance on July 2nd. Standing on Little Round Top, you can see the most incredible sunsets. The colors and view are spectacular. When I look at it, I am always reminded of the God who created it all.

The verse in Psalm 19:6 compares Jesus with the sun. Just as we see the bright light of the sun warming the earth every day, so we see the grace and truth of God's love in Jesus. Every sunrise and sunset speaks to us about his faithfulness and all he has done for us. You cannot miss it. He loved us so much, and he went to the cross to prove it. No more words ever need to be spoken. Drive to Gettysburg and see a sunset. There you will see the greatness of God.

March 6

Triple Play

*For the Lord is good; His lovingkindness is everlasting
And His faithfulness to all generations.*
Psalm 100:5 (NASB)

In baseball, a triple play is made when there are two base runners on with no outs. The batter at the plate hits a ball in play resulting in both base runners being called out as well as the batter, resulting in three outs in one play. This is a very rare event. Since 1876, there have only been 735 triple plays in Major League Baseball. The rarest type of triple play is for a single fielder to complete all three outs. There have only been fifteen unassisted triple plays in MLB history, which means this feat is rarer than a perfect game. In Psalm 100, we see God making triple plays every day as he demonstrates his perfect character.

First, the Lord is good. He is completely holy and righteous. He never makes mistakes. He never does anything wrong. Second, his lovingkindness is inexhaustible. It never ends. He never calls it quits. He will never let you down. Third, God's faithfulness is offered to every generation. So you can stop worrying about your kids! They will have an opportunity to know God too! You see, God is the star player in the game of life, and this is the only game that really matters. He is making triple, unassisted plays all the time. Sinner—forgiven! Life—changed! Home run—complete! The devil—OUT! OUT! OUT! These triple plays happen every time a person admits his sin, looks to the cross, and receives Christ's forgiveness. By trusting in Christ, you, too, can be saved by God's triple play.

March 7

I Own It!

If we confess our sins, he is faithful and just to forgive us our sins and to cleanse us from all unrighteousness.
1 John 1:9 (ESV)

When a person sees he has failed and says, "I own it," he is taking responsibility for his mistake or failure. He is saying, "I acknowledge" or "I admit I was wrong." Confessing is agreeing with another person that you messed up. When you confess your sins to God, you are admitting to God that you have broken his law. When you break God's law, you come under the condemnation and wrath of a holy God. Sin is rebellion against God and the penalty is eternal death. This is a terrifying situation. What can a person do? There are only three options available:

I can plead my case before God. I can give all the reasons I should not be convicted. "I'm not really that bad." "My sins were just little white lies."

I can tell God that it wasn't my fault. I can blame everyone else. "The devil made me do it."

I can own it. I am a sinner and deserve condemnation for my rebellion against God. I am desperate and I need help! I need someone to save me.

If you select the third option, God has come to your rescue. He sent Jesus Christ to be your Savior, to pay for all of your sins. Jesus agreed to die in your place and to give you life instead of death. He makes this offer to you when you confess your sins. If you choose this option, God has promised to be faithful and just. He will forgive your sins when you confess them, and he will cleanse you of your unrighteousness. Forgiveness means that your debts have been canceled and the charges dismissed. No more excuses are needed. Jesus owns you now!

March 8

Happily Ever After

But the Lord was with Joseph and showed him steadfast love and gave him favor in the sight of the keeper of the prison.
Genesis 39:21 (ESV)

Happily Ever After is a Walt Disney show that debuted at the Magic Kingdom on May 12, 2017. The show consisted of projection mapping across Cinderella Castle, laser lights, pyrotechnics, and music clips from a wide array of Disney films. The opening of the show included the following words: "And they all lived happily ever after. Each of us has a dream, a heart's desire. It calls to us. And when we're brave enough to listen, and bold enough to pursue it, that dream will lead us on a journey to discover who we're meant to be." This introduction sounds wonderful. Isn't this what we all want—to live happily ever after? But what if things don't turn out that way? If you read the story of Joseph in Genesis, you'll see a heart-rending example of everything going wrong, and you'll discover an important truth about God's steadfast love.

"The Lord was with Joseph." This was the promise Joseph relied upon, and this is the promise God gives us today. When we read the story about Joseph, we are amazed at the many disappointments he experienced. Betrayed by his brothers, sold into slavery, falsely accused, and put into prison, his life was filled with disappointments galore. But in spite of his difficulties, he maintained his hope that the Lord was with him. He realized that his story mattered to God. The most important story has always been God's story and his faithfulness to us. In time, Joseph was released from prison, promoted by Pharaoh, and reunited with his family. The best part is that he saved the people of Egypt from a deadly famine. It's an exciting story you can read in Genesis 39-45.

Joseph's story is true and can be your story too—not the details, of course, but the reality that Jesus Christ goes with his children through the ups and downs of life. None of us knows what life will bring. But we can be sure of God's steadfast love. We can also feel privileged to be part of his amazing story. Have you experienced his steadfast love? Will you live happily ever after?

March 9

Dreams

It is He who reveals the profound and hidden things;
He knows what is in the darkness,
and the light dwells with Him.
Daniel 2:22 (NASB)

A dream is a series of images, ideas, and emotions that occur in the mind during certain stages of sleep. The content and meaning of dreams are rarely understood. Most dreams happen in the rapid eye movement (REM) stage of sleep when brain activity is very high and resembles that of being awake. The length of the dream varies from a few seconds to thirty minutes, with the average person having three to five dreams per night. Babies typically spend at least fifty percent of their sleep time dreaming. In the elderly, it is less than twenty percent. The interpretation of dreams has always been a topic of interest for people around the world. If you read the book of Daniel, you will find a Babylonian king named Nebuchadnezzar who wanted to know more about the dreams he was having.

Nebuchadnezzar had a recurring dream that was troubling him. So he summoned his magicians, enchanters, sorcerers, and astrologers to tell him about his dream and its interpretation. Because the king did not trust the group of soothsayers, he commanded them to reveal both the dream and its interpretation. When the prophet Daniel heard about this difficult situation, he prayed, asking God to reveal both the dream and its interpretation. God revealed the dream to Daniel, and he successfully unraveled the mystery. All the wise men in Babylon were helpless to assist Nebuchadnezzar. Only God knew the deep and hidden things in the king's heart. I believe God sent Daniel to Nebuchadnezzar to show his wisdom and mighty power. Daniel proved to Nebuchadnezzar that there was a God in heaven, and that God was the only one who could reveal mysteries.

Do you realize that God knows the mysteries of every person's heart? And he sent Jesus to show God's wisdom and mighty power. He wants to reveal the meaning, the mystery, and the power of the gospel to you and me. Jesus came to Earth to shine light on mysteries, to live, to die, to rise again, to reveal his power, and to transform lives. This is the most profound message ever given to mankind. What a blessing it is to know that the one who knows all our dreams is the one who reveals to us the light of the gospel! Unlike Nebuchadnezzar's bewildered spiritual advisors, we can trust Jesus Christ.

March 10

Where Is Your Treasure?

*Do not store up for yourselves treasures on earth,
where moth and rust destroy, and where thieves break in and steal.
But store up for yourselves treasures in heaven,
where neither moth nor rust destroys, and where thieves
do not break in or steal; for where your treasure is,
there your heart will be also.*
Matthew 6:19-21 (NASB)

When we moved last time, I quickly discovered that my oak television wall unit was completely obsolete. I wanted to sell it, but nobody wanted it. I thought it was worth something, but it ended up being worthless. What we think of as treasure today ends up as trash tomorrow. Jesus warns us about this truth in Matthew's Gospel.

All of our treasures on Earth will pass away. If you let that sink in for a while, you will have a much different perspective on life. Jesus uses the example of the moth because moths destroy clothing. Rust destroys metal as well. And sometimes thieves break in and steal all those precious things we are so worried about. So, if all of these treasures are going to pass away, what do we have to look forward to when we die?

Just living forever in paradise—with Jesus! The Bible tells us that no eye has seen and no ear has heard the things God has prepared for those who trust in him. Moths, rust, or thieves will never rob you of your relationship with Christ and what he has prepared for you. Let me suggest to you that the next time you need to sell anything on eBay, especially oak furniture, take any offer they give you. But right now, seek after Jesus and you will never regret it. Jesus is our treasure!

March 11

Radical Loyalty

But Ruth said, "Do not urge me to leave you or turn back from following you; for where you go, I will go, and where you lodge, I will lodge. Your people shall be my people, and your God, my God."
Ruth 1:16 (NASB)

This story begins when a man from Bethlehem named Elimelech travels with his wife, Naomi, and their two sons to the land of Moab. There is a famine in Israel, and they are hoping to find food in this foreign country. On their journey, tragedy strikes and Elimelech dies. Over the next ten years, the two sons marry Moabite women. However, both of the sons die as well, leaving all three women as widows. When the famine ends, Naomi decides to return to Bethlehem. Loving her daughters-in-law, she urges both of them to stay in Moab, where they can find new husbands from their own people. One of the daughters-in-law agrees to stay. But the other, Ruth, decides to accompany Naomi back to her home in Judah.

Why would this young Moabite woman want to move to Israel? Why would Ruth leave all of her family and friends behind? Why would she abandon her religion, customs, and language to go to an unknown land and an unknown future? Why was she willing to give up everything to go with Naomi and take care of her? It seems that Ruth knew exactly what she was doing. She was impressed with Naomi's character and with Naomi's God. She had been watching Naomi, and her God seemed far better than anything she had ever seen in the gods of her own religion. Ruth went with Naomi because she had come to trust in Naomi's God.

This story can be our story as well. When we watch others and see what God has done for them, we want to experience him too. Jesus is amazing. Could he care about me? Would he provide for all of my needs? Does he keep his promises? Does he forgive my sins? Can I trust him with my life? I think Ruth watched Naomi and decided that Naomi's God was the real deal. With an example like Naomi, Ruth was sure she wanted to stay close and experience the brand-new life God was offering to her. It was easy to be loyal to Naomi because Naomi was loyal to God!

March 12

Won't You Be My Neighbor?

*I will walk among you and be your God,
and you will be my people.*
Leviticus 26:12 (NIV)

From 1968 to 2001, Fred Rogers hosted a preschool television series called *Mister Rogers' Neighborhood*. This show focused on little children's emotional and physical concerns. Fred was known for his creativity and kindness. He was the best example of a good neighbor. He modeled what it means to stay close, to be willing to help, to be a true friend, and to live in relationship with others. The question Fred posed to his viewers every day was, "Won't you be my neighbor?" He wasn't inviting all the children to live next door to him. He was inviting them to follow his example, to be kind, to be connected, and to show love for each other.

In the Bible, God frequently mentions the neighborly relationship he enjoys with his people. He calls this relationship a covenant. In this covenant relationship, God always takes the first step. He also makes substantial promises. He will always stay true to us, love us, and be there to help us. In the end, he will take us to heaven where we will live in his neighborhood forever. Most people feel far away from God, but he wants to change all that. He is close and he wants you to know that. He wants to be our neighbor!

We see this fact in the verses for today. God promises to walk among us and be our God. He wants a warm and personal relationship with us, not a distant connection. How does he make this happen? When people put their trust in Christ, the Holy Spirit comes to live in their bodies, their hearts, and their minds. So very close, God's Spirit begins to empower and change you to be more and more like Christ. In this new and wonderful relationship, you and God will be more than neighbors. You will be a member of God's family.

March 13

The Mask

Thus says the Lord, "Let not a wise man boast of his wisdom, and let not the mighty man boast of his might, let not a rich man boast of his riches; but let him who boasts boast of this, that he understands and knows Me, that I am the Lord who exercises lovingkindness, justice and righteousness on earth; for I delight in these things," declares the Lord.
Jeremiah 9:23-24 (NASB)

The Mask is a Jim Carrey movie produced in 1994. Stanley Ipkiss, the main character, is a timid, insignificant bank teller who wants to be a courageous, fun-loving person. Stanley contemplates suicide after he is denied entrance to a nightclub. As he ponders his fate, he finds a green mask in the water. When he gets home, he tries on the mask and is transformed into a comic book character like Batman. When Stanley wears the mask, he instantly possesses all the characteristics he has desired. Although this fictional movie is funny, it touches on a very important question.

The question is, "Why does a man boast who is wise, mighty, or rich?" Boasting is self-glorification. We think of a man who boasts as a person with a sense of self-respect and personal worth. He is satisfied with his achievements. But this verse cautions us not to boast. When you boast, you are actually putting on a mask of insecurity. We like to think that we have it all together and are independent. However, this is a lie. The truth is that we have nothing to boast about at all. Our wisdom, might, and riches can never be compared to that of God.

If we want to boast, we should boast in our relationship with God. We should drop *his* name on others to impress them. The Lord is the one who exercises lovingkindness, justice, and righteousness on the earth. If you want to know what brings delight to the Savior, it is forgiving sinners just the way they are. This is good news. No longer do we need a mask!

March 14

How Long?

How long, O Lord? Will you forget me forever?
How long will you hide your face from me?
But I have trusted in your steadfast love; my heart shall rejoice in your salvation. I will sing to the Lord,
because he has dealt bountifully with me.
Psalm 13:1, 5-6 (ESV)

How long? Have you ever heard this question? This is the number one question children ask their parents on a trip. "How long will it take before we get there?" This is the same question the psalmist asked the Lord in Psalm 13. It is the same question we all ask when hardship makes life seem long and dreary.

When we face a severe test, we feel like it will never end, like God has forgotten us, like he doesn't really care, like he has more important things to do. But is this really true? What does God's Word say? The Bible is where we find what is really true.

What I know from God's Word is that God is faithful, and I can trust in his steadfast love. I can trust that he will never abandon me. I can "rejoice in his salvation" and "sing to the Lord," even when the way is long and dark and I have trouble seeing him.

How does the presence of God help? He comforts me. I am not alone. He gives me strength to endure. I can tolerate the pain. He gives me wisdom to overcome. I can find solutions to my problems. He deals bountifully with me. Why? Because I belong to him, and he only wants what is best for me.

So the next time you feel that God has left you, remember this: no matter how long your trip lasts, your heavenly Father will be with you. And when it is the right time, he will bring you home to heaven where he will wipe away every tear from your eyes and you will never again have to ask, "How long?"

March 15

Walking with Bare Feet

*But as many as received Him,
to them He gave the right to become children of God,
even to those who believe in His name.*
John 1:12 (NASB)

Have you ever walked with your shoes off? Believe it or not, this is a gift. It allows you to feel the ground. You get to feel the cold soft mud between your toes when the ground is wet. You get to sense the sharp edges of the rocks as you uncomfortably walk over them. This little gift is something fun, enjoyable, and quite a delight. It is a gift of life that reminds you that you are alive and not dead. This verse from the apostle John is a special promise from the heart of God.

The promise is that if you believe or trust in Jesus for your salvation, you are in God's family. You are a beloved child, a daughter or son of King Jesus. When you believe in Jesus, you are accepting a close and vital relationship with him. This gift belongs to you, and it cannot be taken away. God loves us so much that he gives us a clear choice. Reject or receive it. What will you choose to do? I hear that walking with bare feet is actually quite enjoyable!

March 16

Traveling the Roads

Your word is a lamp to my feet and a light to my path.
Psalm 119:105 (ESV)

The Bible verse we are considering today is wonderfully illustrated by the famous preacher and author Charles Spurgeon. He describes what it was like to travel on small-town roads over a century ago. "Having no fixed lamps in eastern towns, in old time each passenger carried a lantern with him, that he might not fall into the open sewer, or stumble over the heaps of ordure [manure] which defiled the road."

With this picture in mind, we can imagine how necessary a lamp was for people at that time! Thank God for the wonderful roads we all enjoy today. But right now, I would like for you to think about a different road all of us still travel, the road of life.

The road we travel today is dark and riddled with difficulties. Fear and evil are all around us; confusion and chaos seem to be the new norm. But following God's Word changes everything. God's word is "a lamp to our feet and a light to our path." It is like a flaming torch revealing the way we should go. It gives us practical guidance, principles we can build our lives on, and the wisdom we need to avoid getting tripped up or falling into the "open sewers" of sin and despair. If you have trusted in Jesus Christ for your salvation and are spending time reading and thinking about God's Word, you have a lamp for your feet and light to illumine your way. You will not "stumble over the heaps of ordure" that are there to ruin your journey and defile your soul.

March 17

Lightning Bolts

The voice of the Lord is over the waters;
the God of glory thunders, the Lord thunders over the mighty waters.
The voice of the Lord is powerful;
the voice of the Lord is majestic.
Psalm 29:3-4 (NIV)

Approximately one hundred lightning bolts strike the Earth's surface every second. That adds up to eight million lightning bolts per day. The size of a lightning bolt when it hits is only about one inch in diameter, but it can be seen up to ninety miles away, and the claps can be heard as far as ten miles away. Lightning bolts can be five times hotter than the sun. One lightning bolt can produce up to a billion volts of electricity, which equates to powering eighty million car batteries.

These facts about lightning are pretty impressive, but the verses we have from the Bible today tell us even more. The power of thunder and lightning can be compared to the voice of God! He speaks to us through the things he has made and in the case of thunder and lightning, he is telling us that he is unbelievably powerful! Think about God that way, and it will blow your mind! Do you think that God, who created thunder and lightning, can't handle any problem you may face today? Is there any obstacle or crisis he cannot overcome? If you have a relationship with Jesus, God promises to give you the wisdom and the power to deal with your most difficult situations. Lightning bolts are nothing compared to the majestic voice of the Lord. He is the powerful one I want for my friend!

March 18

Coffee Creamer

*Let me hear Your lovingkindness in the morning;
for I trust in You.*
Psalm 143:8 (NASB)

The first thing I do in the morning is ask my wife which creamer she would like. Will it be sweet cream, caramel macchiato, or Snickers? Then I go about my business boiling water for five minutes to prepare my French press coffee maker. I select the Starbucks brand, either Yukon or Express Roast, and pour the boiling water over the coffee grounds. I let it settle for four minutes, then I press it down. After a few more minutes, I pour coffee for my lovely wife to enjoy. Why do I do this every day? The short answer is that I love her. In Psalm 143, the psalmist wanted God to give him that same assurance.

The psalmist's request to God was, "Let me hear your lovingkindness in the morning." He needed tangible assurance of God's love every morning as soon as he got up. He wanted to experience God's saving love every single day. He wanted to trust God again and digest that delicious truth, so he could ponder it all day long. God's lovingkindness is one of those things you can never get enough of. So after getting your coffee, go ahead and read your Bible, and you will hear Jesus whispering, "I love you!"

March 19

The Old Hammer

He who offers a sacrifice of thanksgiving honors Me.
Psalm 50:23 (NASB)

I have a very old hammer, well over a hundred years old, that belonged to my Dad. It was the hammer he used as a carpenter. I display this on my bookcase as a memento. Why do you think I keep it? I keep it to honor my Dad. Even though he is not here, it is a reminder of his love and care for me all those years. How do you honor someone you love? Maybe you give him a plaque or picture to hang on the wall. Or maybe you give him a gift certificate for a Caribbean cruise. God gives us a hint about what honors him the most, the thing that he appreciates above all else. It is a sacrifice of thanksgiving. It is acknowledging his goodness. It is being grateful! Look at the verse for today. "He who offers a sacrifice of thanksgiving honors me."

Do you want to know how to honor the Lord? Stop taking credit for the good things that happen to you! Give the credit to Christ. He gives you so many good gifts every day. He even gives you the grace to do the right thing when you don't feel like it! Most of us feel like *we* deserve the credit for something like that! Nope! Not true!

God isn't impressed with all kinds of religious ceremonies or the amount of money you put in the offering plate or give to charity. These things might make you feel good, but what he's looking for is a grateful heart. When you tell him from your heart that you are thankful he is your Savior, that you love him because he died for you, and that you appreciate his blessings, that's what honors him! And that's what changes you! The next thing to do is give him the credit when people compliment you. Tell them how good God is and what he has done for you. That is what honors him and what will change people's lives.

I think my Dad would smile if he saw me using his old hammer. It would make him feel appreciated and loved. Thank God every chance you get. It will put a smile on his face too.

March 20

Doolittle Raid

Moses said to the Lord, "O Lord, I have never been eloquent, neither in the past nor since you have spoken to your servant. I am slow of speech and tongue."
The Lord said to him, "Who gave man his mouth? Who makes him deaf or mute? Who gives him sight or makes him blind? Is it not I, the Lord? Now go; I will help you speak and will teach you what to say."
Exodus 4:10-12 (NIV)

Two weeks after Pearl Harbor was attacked by the Japanese, President Franklin Roosevelt ordered an attack on the Japanese capital of Tokyo. LTC James Doolittle was invited to lead the raid. Although he was forty-five years old and retired, he recruited one hundred and forty flyers to be part of this "extremely hazardous" mission. B-25 planes had to be modified so they could fly all the way to Japan and drop bombs on the Japanese homeland. On April 18, 1942, eighty volunteer airmen flew sixteen B-25 bombers 2250 miles to Japan and successfully accomplished their mission. The attack caused minor damage, but it sent a message to the Japanese that their mainland was vulnerable to American air attacks. It also boosted American morale. But the Doolittle Raid was a sacrifice. All sixteen planes were lost, and there were many casualties. Those courageous volunteers willingly took on an impossible mission for the greater good of our nation. This story reminds me of Moses in the Bible when God recruited him to take on a mission just as dangerous for his people, the Israelites.

God saw the sufferings of the Israelites who were enslaved and cruelly mistreated by the Egyptians. God's plan to rescue them included Moses, but Moses wasn't on board.

Go to Pharaoh? Demand that Pharaoh let God's people go? Nice opportunity, but, um, I'm pretty sure I'm not your man. I'm eighty years old, I've never been a good speaker, I've been living in the desert for forty years, and I've lost my self-confidence. I really need to start thinking about my retirement. You need a younger man!

And what did God say about that? Well, he had some good questions for Moses. "Who gave man his mouth? Who makes him deaf or mute? Who gives him sight or makes him blind? Is it not I, the Lord?" Moses' skills were inconsequential. His obedience to God was what mattered. Moses took on the mission, and God freed the Israelites from Egyptian slavery. The God who created Moses is the same God who collaborated with Jesus to come to earth on a very dangerous mission. He did so willingly, and it cost him his life. But his sacrifice has freed countless people from slavery to sin and brought them into a whole new life. Now it's our turn. Are you up for the challenge? God made you just right for the mission he has for you. Your skills are inconsequential. Your obedience to God is what matters. His Spirit will fill you with his power. Trust him!

March 21

Family Reunion

*Steadfast love and faithfulness meet;
righteousness and peace kiss each other.*
Psalm 85:10 (ESV)

What are reunions all about? Meeting friends, sharing common stories about growing up, and gathering around the table with your favorite foods. And don't forget about the endless string of picture taking. Joy, sadness, victories, and loss all unite to form the story of a loving family. This gathering of unique people is what I see when we compare these four divine attributes of God in this verse with a family reunion.

I would like you to think about the place where all of these characteristics of God come together. When do "steadfast love and faithfulness meet"? When do "righteousness and peace kiss each other"? The only time this happens is at the cross of Jesus Christ. This is a reunion between God and humanity. This is when mercy and truth hold hands to fulfill God's promise to save lost sinners. This only became possible at the cross when Christ bore our sins—God's righteousness made peace between a holy God and a sinful world, and they kissed each other. This is the only time I know that holiness, justice, faithfulness, and righteousness interact with mercy, grace, and forgiveness to initiate a family reunion for mankind.

Because of Jesus Christ's willingness to come to Earth and his submission to a cruel cross, you are invited to a family reunion. This invitation is extended to all people. It does not matter who you are or what you have done in life: it is an open invitation. All you have to do is follow Jesus to the cross and meet him there.

All of Jesus' family will be going to a better place in a new heavenly home. When we get there, there will be a reunion that will last for all of eternity. Now that is a family reunion I do not want to miss!

March 22

Life Without the Sun

There was the true Light which, coming into the world, enlightens every man.
John 1:9 (NASB)

Can you imagine what life would be like without the sun? If the sun suddenly vanished, we would not know it immediately because it takes light eight and a half minutes to travel the ninety-three million miles to Earth. If it happened at night, the moon would disappear. It would no longer reflect the sun's light. All the planets in the sky as well would disappear, one by one, as the darkness reached them. Within days, Earth would cool to one hundred or so degrees below freezing. The atmosphere would also freeze and fall to Earth, exposing everything to the harsh radiation from space. All vegetation on Earth would die. Our days would be numbered.

But just think about what it would be like without Jesus Christ, the Son of God, the true Light. He came into the world to enlighten every man. We all live in spiritual darkness until the true Light comes. Our hearts grow cold and life is harsh. Jesus Christ is the true Light that warms our hearts, exposes our sin, and offers us forgiveness and hope if we trust in Him. It is hard to imagine a world without hope. Hope in God. He has sent us a true Light who is even better than the sun.

March 23

Our Scapegoat

*As far as the east is from the west,
So far has He removed our transgressions from us.*
Psalm 103:12 (NASB)

A scapegoat is a person who is blamed for the wrongdoings of others. Scapegoats are first mentioned in the book of Leviticus. They were essential to the Day of Atonement. On that day, the priest would confess the sins of God's people, lay them symbolically on the head of a sacrificial goat, and send it into the wilderness. That heavy load of guilt would depart with the scapegoat, never to return. This is the picture we see in Psalm 103.

This is every person's dream—exactly what we wish could happen. Someone would take away the sins we've committed, all the terrible things we've done. Wouldn't it be great if we could take our guilt and give it to someone else—if we could "wipe our slate clean"? Well, here's the good news! That wish can come true! This is exactly the point of the gospel. Jesus is our scapegoat. He takes our sin upon himself and removes it as far as the east is from the west. Here's how it works: First, you confess that you are guilty. You have sinned against God and deserve his condemnation. Then, you lay your sins on Jesus. He's given you permission to do this because he loves you and died for you on the cross. Those sins you committed—those terrible things you've done—are paid for! When you truly believe that Jesus died for you, he takes your sins far away. Forever! His mercy is so great that it extends higher than the heavens. He has removed our sins so far that the distance could never be calculated.

March 24

Hands-on Person

He heals the brokenhearted and binds up their wounds.
He counts the number of the stars; He gives names to all of them.
Psalm 147:3-4 (NASB)

A hands-on person has first-hand experience with the task at hand. This person is actively involved in his work and knows the pitfalls and tricks of the trade. A person who can only talk about the problem is disadvantaged because he doesn't have that first-hand experience. He is "handicapped." Psalm 147 tells us that God is the ultimate hands-on person and is actively involved in the tasks at hand.

Is there anything at all that God's hands have not touched? He has created everything in this universe, so he has first-hand experience with everything. He knows every detail. When I think about this, I am filled with awe. God created every star and knows the exact number of stars in the universe. Do you realize that scientists have now admitted that the stars in heaven are so numerous that they cannot be counted? But God is so hands-on that he has given each star a name!

Our Creator is awesome! Not only did he create each star, he created each *person* who has ever lived—and he has a name for them! Consequently, every baby in the womb and every person born is important to him. It doesn't matter if you are healthy or diseased, rich or poor, black or white; every single person is priceless in God's eyes. Each person has a heart and God knows the condition of his heart, whether it is broken or healed. The good news is that the Creator is hands-on to heal and restore broken hearts. Whatever the wound, he can heal it. This is the gospel of Jesus!

March 25

Virginia Hall and Cuthbert

The Lord is near to the brokenhearted and saves the crushed in spirit.
Psalm 34:18 (ESV)

A Woman of No Importance is a true story about an American woman, Virginia Hall, who became one of the most feared spies in France during World War II. In 1933 at the age of twenty-seven, she accidentally shot herself in her left foot while hunting birds. Her leg had to be amputated below the knee to save her life. Her leg was replaced with a wooden appendage which she named "Cuthbert." Surprisingly, in spite of this disability, she lived and excelled as a spy during the war. The Nazis considered her the "most dangerous of all Allied spies." They nicknamed her the "Limping Lady." Why they didn't catch her, I don't know, but she served as a spy for the entire war. She was later recognized for her accomplishments in World War II and was the only civilian woman awarded the Distinguished Service Cross by the United States government.

The book about Hall's life not only describes her heroic deeds, but also includes her struggles, especially with her handicap. She and her "best friend Cuthbert" never disclosed it to anyone. She went to great lengths to keep it all a secret. Most people who saw her limp didn't know she was missing a leg. All she wanted was to be a part of the team, to be equal and treated that way. She wanted to be whole and complete in spite of her handicap. Isn't this our desire as well? We want to be seen as whole in spite of our mistakes, our disabilities, and our imperfections.

And so we come to our verse of the day. God is near to the brokenhearted, disabled, needy—to anyone who calls upon him. If you are part of God's family, the Holy Spirit lives within you. You can't get closer to God than that! He hears all of our prayers because Jesus died to bring you close. Being in his family means that you are safe, and his promises are true for you. In heaven, you won't have any disabilities. You will be perfect in every way. Right now, you are on the team and he is with you—even closer than Cuthbert!

March 26

"Just Do It"

*But let justice roll down like waters
And righteousness like an ever-flowing stream.*
Amos 5:24 (NASB)

Nike's "Just Do It" campaign was coined by an advertising agency in 1988. The owner of the company credited Gary Gilmore with saying, "Let's do it," his last words just before he was executed in Utah in 1977. The Nike company decided to use his words to launch their highly successful advertising campaign, and Nike became a trendsetting sports apparel merchandiser. Before 1988, Nike only sold sneakers to fitness gurus. After 1988, the company became a multi-billion-dollar fashion icon. Today the words "Just Do It" usually appear alongside the Nike logo known as the "Swoosh." This popular phrase "Just Do It!" is the message God gave to his people, Israel, through his prophet Amos. It is exactly the message he is giving us today.

Amos' message was challenging. First, he told them to return to God and stop worshiping idols. Second, he told them to stop living like hypocrites. People in Israel were pretending to be religious, but their hearts were selfish and cold. I can just imagine Amos, a rough-looking outdoorsman, shouting to the people, "Love justice! Live righteous lives! Stop mistreating people, exploiting the poor, and denying them justice. Let your actions reflect the goodness you say you have in your heart. JUST DO IT! And don't just "do it" sometimes. Do it all the time!" Let justice and righteousness roll down like water in an ever-flowing stream. This is what God expects from his children: kindness, goodness, generosity, justice. JUST DO IT!

March 27

Money Tree in the OK Cafe

*For you, O Lord, are good and forgiving,
abounding in steadfast love to all who call upon you.*
Psalm 86:5 (ESV)

When my children were young, they sometimes asked for something we could not afford, like a toy. So being a good father, I would tell them to go outside to the money tree and pick off any money that they need to buy it. Fast forward ten years later to when I took my youngest daughter on a trip to Atlanta. We went out for breakfast at the OK Cafe, and we were shocked to find a fake tree in the middle of the restaurant. On the leaves of this big tree were pinned dollar bills! My daughter was simply amazed: there is a money tree after all! Isn't that something we all would like to have? To have all of our needs and wants satisfied. Well, the truth is that we actually do have someone who can do that. Look to Psalm 86, and you will find the one you can call upon.

The only person I know who is good and forgiving is the Messiah who is called Jesus Christ. He is the only one who was sinless and could pay for all of my sins. He is the only one I know that can fulfill not just all of my needs and wants, but can provide freedom from my past. He is "abounding in steadfast love." That means that he has an overwhelming supply of mercy that never runs out. This mercy and forgiveness is found only in Jesus. Who else could do that? Who else would willingly die on a cross so that you and I could spend eternity with him?

Friend, if you do not know who Jesus Christ is, call out to him. He will deliver you from your burden of sins. He will hear your call and he will respond to you. When you accept his gift of salvation, he will send the Holy Spirit to dwell within you. He promises that he will never abandon you and will be by your side until you join him in heaven. This is simply amazing! We never have to go to the money tree again, because we have Jesus!

March 28

Tattoos

Behold, I have inscribed you on the palms of My hands.
Isaiah 49:16 (NASB)

Tattoos have been around for thousands of years. People get them for many reasons. For some, it is a memorial of an experience that has deep personal meaning. For others, it is artistic freedom, rebellion, or a religious/cultural tradition. Whatever the reason, tattoos are a visual reminder of a meaningful experience. Did you know that God has a tattoo as well?

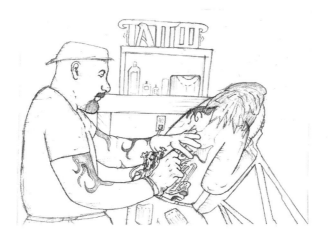

In the book of Isaiah, God says, "I have inscribed you on the palms of My hands." That sounds like a tattoo to me! Why would God inscribe you on his hands? To memorialize his personal and meaningful connection with you! This "tattoo" reminds him that *you are his!* I can't tell you exactly what this looks like, but I can tell you that it also makes me think about what Jesus did for us on the cross. He was nailed to the cross and I am sure that those nails left holes in his hands! This is another clear reminder of how much we mean to God. Here is a story you can tell other people. You are etched on the palms of God's hands so he will never forget you!

March 29

Good Housekeeping Seal

The Lord is good, a stronghold in the day of trouble,
And He knows those who take refuge in Him.
Nahum 1:7 (NASB)

The first Good Housekeeping Seal was issued in 1909. Nobody could have imagined how many products this seal would cover over the next hundred plus years. Companies making everything from cordless vacuum cleaners to blue-light filtering lenses to high-tech dishwashers can apply for the Good Housekeeping Seal of Approval. This seal has become a signal to consumers that the product they are considering has passed rigorous testing and can be trusted for reliability. Currently, there are around 1,800 products that are Good Housekeeping seal-holders. Nahum, the prophet, was issued *God's* seal of approval, which is the most trusted guarantee ever!

We are all going to have a "day of trouble." It's a day when everything seems to go wrong. We make mistakes, our plans break down, and we feel like we're falling apart. We need to remember this truth, "The Lord is good; he is our stronghold in the day of trouble." When rigorous testing comes, he can be fully trusted for his reliability. He knows those who take refuge in him. In fact, he has issued them his seal of approval, identifying them as a member of his royal family. The best thing about God's seal is that it has a lifetime guarantee. It actually lasts forever!

March 30

The Rock of Gibraltar

Forever, O Lord, your word is firmly fixed in the heavens.
Your faithfulness endures to all generations;
you have established the earth, and it stands fast.
Psalm 119:89-90 (ESV)

The Rock of Gibraltar is a limestone cliff that stands at the entrance to the Mediterranean Sea. It is located near the southwestern tip of Europe on the Iberian Peninsula. It has a height of 1,398 feet, and its Great Siege Tunnels attract visitors from around the world every year. Officially Gibraltar is a British Overseas Territory of the United Kingdom. The area of this land is only two and a half square miles, but over 30,000 people live there. Why is this rock so famous?

First of all, since The Rock keeps watch over the Mediterranean Sea, it is a choke point on the route to India, making it strategically valuable and worth fighting for. Secondly, it has great historical significance. Gibraltar has never been conquered by any enemy. Under British control, it has endured fifteen sieges with the most famous siege lasting over three years. These factors make the Rock of Gibraltar a symbol of stability, strength, and security. They also make Gibraltar a good example of the Word of God.

God's Word is "firmly fixed in the heavens." No person can replace the Bible, and no enemy can destroy it. God's Word is too high for that! Because of this fact, God's faithful promises are here to stay. God never says, "I know I created the earth and promised to keep you strong and secure, but I'm sorry to say, things are changing. The last siege was just too strong. The enemy has won. I can't help you anymore." No, no, no! This will never happen. God established the earth, and he isn't going anywhere. His purposes, his promises, and his precepts will endure to all generations. His Word is sure, immovable, and eternal. His work on Earth for you and for humanity will never end.

Maybe the Rock of Gibraltar is a bit overrated. Jesus is my Rock, and he will never be moved!

March 31

Daily Reminders of Hope

*The Spirit of the Lord GOD is upon me,
Because the Lord has anointed me to bring good news to the afflicted;
He has sent me to bind up the brokenhearted, to proclaim liberty to
captives And freedom to prisoners.*
Isaiah 61:1 (NASB)

Every new year seems to bring a unique set of circumstances that each of us navigates. Take 2020 for example. At the beginning of 2020, we started hearing about COVID-19 and how devastating it could be. That year, many people died, and even today the long-term effects have yet to be seen. It was a year of loneliness, anxiety, and fear. Many people lost their jobs, and some are still struggling financially. It was a long year, one we will never forget. What about next year? What challenges will you face? The one thing I know for sure is that they will definitely include change. But in that change, we can be filled with hope and encouragement as we see in this verse in Isaiah.

In Isaiah's prophecy, Jesus the Messiah reveals his mission to mankind. It is to bring good news to the afflicted. It is to bind up the brokenhearted who need a bandage for their wounds. It is for those who are seeking hope and deliverance. It is for those who need their hearts revived. Jesus came to proclaim liberty and freedom for those who are oppressed and to give spiritual sight to those who are blind. Jesus is the only one who can do this. His message of forgiveness and healing offers us real encouragement. What a blessing it is to know that we have a Savior who loves us 365 days of the year and gives us reminders of his tender care for each person, whatever his circumstances.

April 1

Finding Hope

How blessed is he whose help is the God of Jacob,
Whose hope is in the Lord his God.
Psalm 146:5 (NASB)

Where do you find hope? If you look to world news, it is bleak. If you look to political leaders, you feel pessimistic. And if you look at the worldwide pandemic, nobody knows for sure when it will end. What do you trust in? Better plans and policies? Positive thoughts and feelings? The psalmist struggled as well. His life wasn't perfect! But in Psalm 146 he found the hope he was looking for.

The psalmist concluded that we should not put our trust in political leaders or mortal men. Even if their policies seem good, they won't save the world. There's always something or someone who will come along and mess everything up. Besides that, mere mortals won't live forever, and when they die, their plans will die with them. The psalmist got it right. God's plans and policies are always perfect. We can count on him for that. He is the ruler of this world! Another thing is this: God never dies, so we can trust his plans forever, for ourselves, our country, and the world. The bottom line is that God is our only hope, and God is our best hope! People who "hope in the Lord" are blessed. Does that mean we will never be stressed or disappointed? No, it means we trust him in the ups and downs. It means we share his hope with the oppressed, the hungry, the disabled, the addicted, orphans, widows, and prisoners! Our hope is found in the grace of God. God fulfills our needs. He also gives us the love and the means to help people who are in distress. If you are looking for hope, open the Bible and meet God, who has all situations under control and who will give you the blessings you need to give hope to the world. The hope of the world is found in Jesus Christ!

April 2

What Are You Looking For?

Do not be amazed; you are looking for Jesus the Nazarene, who has been crucified. He has risen; He is not here; behold, here is the place where they laid Him.
Mark 16:6 (NASB)

If someone asked you what you are looking for, how would you respond? Maybe a new job, a relationship, retirement, or even meaning in life. But whatever it is, you may be surprised when you get the answer. This was true with the three ladies who went to the tomb of Jesus in Mark 16.

These women were alarmed when they saw a young man they didn't recognize sitting inside Jesus' tomb. They were looking for Jesus' body, assuming he was dead. But his body wasn't there. He was alive! Isn't this our story as well? We think we know what we are seeking in life, but in the end, we find something quite different. These women were looking for a dead Jesus, but instead they got a living Savior. This was the best news ever! Nothing in life is as good as finding Jesus as our living Savior!

April 3

"My Way"

> *Why does the wicked man revile God?*
> *Why does he say to himself, "He won't call me to account"?*
> *But you, O God, do see trouble and grief;*
> *you consider it to take it in hand.*
> Psalm 10:13-14 (NIV)

Frank Sinatra's song "My Way" carries a clear message. The last verse sums it up:

> "For what is a man, what has he got?
> If not himself, then he has naught
> To say the things he truly feels
> and not the words of one who kneels
> The record shows I took the blows and did it my way
> Yes, it was my way"

Wow, this song smacks you right in the face, doesn't it? It sums up the theme of every person who dares to stand in rebellion against God. People say, "I am in charge of my life, and I will do whatever I please. It's all about me and how I feel. I will not bow before anyone, not even God. In the end, no matter what happens, the record's going to show—I did it my way!" This kind of thinking has been around since the fall of man. It demonstrates the pride of man and his utter disregard for God's authority. The wicked man actually believes he's going to get away with his rebellion, and that God won't hold him to account. But if he reads Psalm 10:13-14, he will discover that this is only wishful thinking.

God sees everything you do. And if you think he just overlooks your sins, you are sadly mistaken. He knows just how selfish you are, how many times you have taken advantage of others, how thoughtless you've been to the feelings and well-being of others. We can't live our lives under the radar. And if we think that God just forgets what we've done, we better think again. God is all-knowing and all-righteous. We will stand before him one day, and we will all be judged!

This is not the end of the story though. God sent his Son, Jesus, who offered his life to pay for our sins. He offers to take away our flawed record and to give us a new life and a new way—His way.

So, if you turn from your rebellion, bow before God's authority, receive God's forgiveness, and go God's way, *your* song will change forever.

April 4

Let's Finish Well

Let everything that has breath praise the Lord. Praise the Lord!
Psalm 150:6 (NASB)

One of my very dear friends, who was a special inspiration to me, passed away years ago. His last words were, "Let's finish well." I think of his exhortation often. It is a good challenge for me to serve the Lord wholeheartedly until my very last breath. We read the same parting words in the last chapter of the book of Psalms.

In just six verses, the psalmist encourages us a whopping thirteen times to "praise the Lord." This shows how important praising God really is! When we praise the Lord we are revering him. We are loving, honoring, and worshiping him. We do this because he is worthy of all our praise.

At the beginning of our lives, God gives us our first breath. Every minute of every day we breathe without even thinking about it. Breath is life, and life is a gift from God. So, all creatures owe their Creator gratitude—because they are alive! This gift of life was what Jesus gave up willingly, when he took his last breath. When I recognize this, what Jesus gave up for me, it calls me to make a decision. Will I accept his gift of eternal life, or will I reject it? How about you? Will you finish well? Every breath gives you an opportunity to make this decision. Will you be praising God when your time comes? My friend finished well, and Jesus was there to welcome him home.

April 5

911 Call

God is our refuge and strength, a very present help in trouble.
Psalm 46:1 (NASB)

911 is an emergency telephone number. This number is to be used only in emergency circumstances. Dialing 911 will link the caller to an emergency dispatch office in over ninety-nine percent of US locations. In most cases it automatically pairs the caller number with a physical address. Believe it or not, the first 911 call was made in Haleyville, Alabama in 1968. But implementation of this service took many years. By 1987, the service extended to fifty percent of the country. Finally, in 2017, 98.9 percent of the US population had access.

How did we survive without 911? Moreover, how did we survive without cell phones? These technologies have made it easy to report emergencies or just to stay in touch. We now expect 100% coverage anytime and anyplace. This whole thinking has spread now to our health, finances, recreation, entertainment, and even to our spiritual needs. We want guarantees and protection plans that cover everything. No disruptions to our life and no emergencies. We want to plan for every contingency. But "little things" like a pandemic throw a monkey wrench into our plans. Psalm 46 provides another viewpoint for our consideration.

God is our refuge right now. He is here to help immediately. We don't have to dial and wait for a response. As a matter of fact, he is "abundantly available." He is more capable and more near. All of our coverage plans are unable to do this 100% of the time. God gives the only 100% guarantee. Many of us have not considered spiritual emergencies. God offers a protection plan that covers everything when we trust in him for our salvation. We don't even need to dial 911 to connect to him.

April 6

The Sons of Korah

*For a day in Your courts is better than a thousand outside.
I would rather stand at the threshold of the house of my God
Than dwell in the tents of wickedness.*
Psalm 84:10 (NASB)

The story in the Old Testament of the sons of Korah is about two different destinies. When Moses led the Israelites out of Egypt and through the wilderness, a situation developed that would determine the fate of both families. God had set aside the tribe of Levi for full-time service to the Lord. This included setting up the tabernacle, curtains, hauling ropes, sacred objects, and other items that were needed as they traveled to the promised land.

The family of Kohath was assigned to carry the sacred items on their shoulders. This was a very difficult burden and a lowly task. One of Kohath's grandsons by the name Korah began to plot with a few other men because they were not happy with their assignments. Korah and 250 men led a revolt challenging the authority of Moses and Aaron. They wanted to lead Israel instead of God's appointed men. If you read Numbers 16 in the Bible, you can see all the details of the outcome of this rebellion. The bottom line is that Korah and the other 250 rebels and their families were swallowed up by the earth and destroyed.

Now comes the second story. When Korah and his family perished, there were some little children in his family that God spared because they did not understand what was happening. If you fast forward seven generations, the prophet Samuel assigns the sons of Korah to become doorkeepers and custodians for the tabernacle of God. They would also be involved in the music program for all of their celebrations. In the book of Psalms, many of the songs are attributed to the sons of Korah.

The sons of Korah are just like every other family. One son rebels against God and the other trusts in God for his salvation. Both are given choices. In Psalm 84, we see a son who is completely in love with God. He would rather be a doorkeeper in God's house for only one day than spend 1,000 days outside. Whom will you trust for your salvation? Which son of Korah will you follow?

April 7

Winking at Grandkids

*For the eyes of the Lord are toward the righteous,
And His ears attend to their prayer.*
1 Peter 3:12 (NASB)

When I wink at my grandkids, I am sending them a non-verbal message. I am letting them know that I love them and they are a joy to me. This communication assures them of a truth not spoken in words. God does this so often, but we fail to see it. However, in Scripture we see his wink.

When we call out to the Lord for help, we are trusting him to answer our prayers. Our requests are heard loud and clear. When he answers our prayers, he is winking at us. This non-verbal communication tells us that he loves us and we are a joy to him. God speaks to us with words when we read the Bible. He winks at us when he answers our prayers.

April 8

The Choice

How blessed is the one whom You choose and bring near to You
To dwell in Your courts.
Psalm 65:4 (NASB)

The line between rejection and acceptance is very fine. From the youngest child all the way to the oldest senior, we feel the pain of rejection and the pleasure of acceptance. We experience rejection when no one picks us to be included. Or we feel good when someone chooses to spend time with us. So when the psalmist understood that God had chosen him to be in his kingdom, it must have been an awesome blessing.

David knew that it is always God's choice to allow us to come to him. It is his decision alone. There is nothing we can do to influence him. No good deed nor any amount of money will suffice. Salvation is strictly a matter of God's grace, and it is free to you if you accept Christ. Quite frankly, I will probably never understand why he would choose me. To be included in his royal family and to dwell with him in eternity goes beyond my wildest imagination. I am so glad that it was God's choice to bring me close to himself. I am blessed.

April 9

Wonders of the World

*Many, O Lord my God, are the wonders which You have done,
And Your thoughts toward us; there is none to compare with You.
If I would declare and speak of them,
they would be too numerous to count.*
Psalm 40:5 (NASB)

If you were to compile a list of the seven top wonders of the world, you would have a difficult time finding a consensus. Contenders might be the Great Pyramid of Giza, the Hanging Gardens of Babylon, or maybe the Great Wall of China. There are so many incredible wonders to behold that you would never be able to count them. I think the psalmist felt the same way when he started thinking about God's wonders in the world.

When I first looked at this verse, my focus went to the phrase, "Your thoughts toward us." God thinks about us! Another passage tells us that God's thoughts about us are so numerous, they would outnumber the grains of sand! God is always thinking of ways he can bless us! Unfortunately, it doesn't work the other way. Our thoughts aren't usually about God. Our thoughts are usually focused on ourselves, what pleases us, and what we want to accomplish. Jesus, on the other hand, was always speaking about the wonders of his Father, and how he has blessed the world. Can you imagine how things would change if we were more like Jesus, directing our thoughts and actions towards the wonders of God and how he wants to bless the world? Circling back to the list of the top wonders of the world, there is no dispute about which one takes the lead. The love of God is the wonder that gets my vote!

April 10

Tubing in Pigeon Forge

*But you are to cling to the Lord your God,
as you have done to this day.*
Joshua 23:8 (NASB)

My wife and I spent a few days in Pigeon Forge, Tennessee. Since it was early July, I thought it would be fun to go tubing on a nearby river. So we rented tubes, intending to enjoy a leisurely afternoon. Everything was fine until we noticed that the lazy river seemed to be moving a little faster. After a short distance, my wife and I started to drift farther apart. Within minutes my tube hit a rock and I flipped upside down and started gulping water. Thinking that I would hit bottom, I was surprised to learn that it was far deeper than I expected. I couldn't even climb to the top of the tube, and by now I was exhausted. The last time my wife saw me was when I flipped over, so she didn't know where I was and was getting frantic. I am not a good swimmer, so all I could do was hope that I would see a hanging branch and grab onto it. Thank goodness I found such a branch, and thank goodness I found my wife. This little story is a good reminder I found in Joshua about clinging to the Lord.

In one of Joshua's last talks to the Israelites, he reminded the nation that it was God who was responsible for all of their victories and the peace they were enjoying at that time. He then charged the nation to cling to the Lord. When you cling to something, you are holding on tight. When I found that hanging branch, I grabbed it and held on real tight! This is what we do in an emergency, like when we learn we have cancer, or when we lose a loved one, or some other disaster befalls us. We grab onto God and hang on tight. Emergency prayers are important, but the command Joshua was giving Israel was even more vital. He was commanding them to cling to God every day. When you grab onto God, you are trusting in his promises and cultivating a deep affection for him. Relationships take time and effort. They don't happen overnight. If you want to know the Lord, it will be in your little prayers, verses of Scripture, and songs of thanksgiving. It will be taking one step of faith at a time, believing God will deliver you. This is what it means to cling to the Lord. It's nice to go tubing on a lazy river, but clinging to the Lord is even more important.

April 11

Plagiarism

*Help me, O Lord my God; save me according to
Your lovingkindness. And let them know that this is
Your hand; You, Lord, have done it.*
Psalm 109:26-27 (NASB)

Plagiarism is a problem for students, politicians, writers, and everyday people. It is as old as creation itself. Students want good grades, so they copy words from a book or article. Politicians steal other people's words or phrases to make an eloquent speech. We might retell someone else's story or joke as though it were our own. We want to be admired by others, and we are willing to cheat to gain people's respect. We want credit for what others have done. King David was careful to give God credit when he wrote Psalm 109.

David needed lots of help during his lifetime. He was plagued by enemies both before and after he became king. Many times he cried out to God for help. He realized he could never make it alone. He needed God to rescue him. But he never cheated by taking the credit. "Let them know," he prayed, "that this is *your* hand; You, Lord, have done it." Everything Jesus did—coming to Earth, going to the cross, dying, rising from the dead, sending his Spirit to fill our hearts—makes it possible for us to join his family and experience God's lovingkindness. Because of Jesus, we can give credit to God. It is the Lord's hand that rescues us. He has done it!

April 12

3rd US Infantry Regiment

Behold, bless the Lord, all servants of the Lord,
Who serve by night in the house of the Lord!
Psalm 134:1 (NASB)

The 3rd US Infantry Regiment was nicknamed "The Old Guard" after its victory in the Mexican War. It is the oldest active-duty infantry unit in the Army, serving our nation since 1784. The Old Guard is the escort to the President and is the official ceremonial unit in Washington, DC. One of its primary duties is to guard the Tomb of the Unknown Soldier at Arlington National Cemetery. Soldiers in The Old Guard have been posted at the tomb twenty-four hours a day, 365 days a year, regardless of the weather, since 1937. They guard the tomb alone in two-hour shifts. To be selected, you must volunteer and pass a series of mental and physical tests. As you can imagine, this duty is one of the highest honors any soldier could have. This was also true of the priests who guarded the temple of the Lord in Psalm 134.

The priests were guarding the temple because it was a holy place, the dwelling place of God. They were serving God by making sure that no one would be able to raid or defile God's house. The priests served God twenty-four hours a day, 365 days a year. They guarded the temple even in the middle of the night, in the dark, when no one was watching. It was in the darkness that the temple was especially vulnerable. The priests had to stay awake and be alert, doing their job without complaining. It was a privilege and an incredible honor to serve God this way.

    I am never going to receive an Old Guard badge; nor will I ever see the inside of the Old Testament temple, but I can serve the Lord wholeheartedly by protecting his church. There are many people who would like to do away with the church of God. They would like to raid it of its place in our society. They would like to rob it of its moral beauty. They would like believers to renounce biblical principles and trust in faulty human thinking. Sometimes, when times are dark, we get sleepy and fail at our duty. Sometimes we look to others for praise for our service. What I try to remember is that my service to God is an opportunity, a privilege, and an incredible blessing. Because of the gospel, we have hope that God, even when we fail in our duties, never gives up on us. He knows our hearts, and he sees every prayer and every act of service—even in the dark, in the middle of the night! Why do I serve him? Because I love him, because I want to protect his church, and because I want to honor Christ.

April 13

The Incredible Hand

For the Lord is a great God and a great King above all gods,
In whose hand are the depths of the earth,
The peaks of the mountains are His also.
The sea is His, for it was He who made it,
and His hands formed the dry land.
Psalm 95:3-5 (NASB)

The human hand is an incredible engineering phenomenon. It is powerful and yet it is able to manipulate small objects with great precision. A small motion of the hand can signal approval, generosity, and hospitality. A firm handshake indicates strength, friendship, and blessing. A skilled hand can work with great precision to perform surgeries that remove abnormal or diseased tissue. The versatility of the human hand sets us apart from every other creature on Earth. In Psalm 95, we get a glimpse of the hand of God.

God's hand is powerful. He created the depths of the earth and the peaks of the mountains. God's hand is also able to manipulate small objects with great precision. His hand created incredibly intricate microscopic organisms and even the innermost systems of our human bodies.

But there's more! God's skillful hand can perform spiritual surgery to replace our hard, sinful hearts with new hearts that trust and obey him. Jesus Christ, God as a human being, is both our Creator and our Savior! Next time you look at your hands, remember the hand of God, powerful and precise, the Life-Giver and the Life-Savior!

April 14

Hacksaw Ridge

For the grace of God has appeared, bringing salvation to all men.
Titus 2:11 (NASB)

On April 1, 1945, American forces began landing on Okinawa, Japan. This was the beginning of one of the last battles of World War II. One of the sites on this island was Hacksaw Ridge. As the name implies, Hacksaw Ridge was one of the bloodiest battles in the war with Japan. Unfortunately, nearly 500 of the 800 men who fought became casualties atop Hacksaw Ridge. However, the hero of the story was a young American soldier, PFC Desmond Doss. Doss was a conscientious objector, who refused to carry a weapon in combat or kill an enemy soldier. But in this bloody battle, he became a wartime hero, courageously living out his mission to save lives, not end them. As the battle progressed, Doss crawled amongst the rocks, identifying seventy-five wounded soldiers and rescuing them by lowering each one on a rope-supported litter down a 400-foot cliff to the friendly hands of his comrades. For his actions under fire, Doss received the Medal of Honor. Desmond Doss is a good example of what Jesus did for us.

This verse in Titus is the core of the gospel message. Jesus Christ came to earth to save sinners. His mission was completely focused on rescuing lives—not ending them. He was all about taking the wounded out of the battle and saving them. As sinners we are wounded because of our sins. There is nothing we can do to save ourselves. What Jesus did was seek wounded sinners and offer God's kindness. God's grace is the rope that brings us to safety. Jesus displayed remarkable courage when he died for us sinners. Because of his courage, he deserves to be the recipient of all our faith, worship, and praise!

April 15

Plastic Beauty

For the Lord takes pleasure in His people;
He will beautify the afflicted ones with salvation.
Psalm 149:4 (NASB)

According to the "Plastic Surgery Statistics Report" by the American Society of Plastic Surgeons, Americans spent over $17 billion on cosmetic plastic surgery in 2019. Over 18 million people had these procedures. Spending on cosmetics topped $49 billion in 2019. Beauty products currently average over $250 a month with an estimated spending between $200,000 and $300,000 in a lifetime. This data surprised me. However, it's not hard to believe. We like to look and feel good about ourselves. Everyone wants to be beautiful. This was actually a topic in Psalm 149.

The first part of this verse must have blown the psalmist away. The Lord takes pleasure (or delights) in his people. Let this truth sink into your heart. It will amaze and encourage you. Are you one of God's people? Do you trust in Jesus Christ for your salvation? If you do, God is pleased with you and delights in his relationship with you. Is this because you are such a good person? No, it's because Jesus was a perfect person, so he was able to pay the debt for your sin. As a result, you are God's delightful child!

The second part of this promise is that "He will beautify the afflicted ones with salvation." Who are the afflicted ones? Everybody really! We are all afflicted by sin. It makes us unclean and reveals the ugliness in our hearts. Rich or poor, humble or proud, successful or defeated, we are all broken and in need of repair. We all need a makeover! Now look at this promise again: the Lord can make the ugly, beautiful! He can transform us with salvation, beautify us with new hearts, and crown us with victory. When we have a relationship with Jesus, he makes us more beautiful, inside and out. The good news is that this makeover is real and totally free. I think God's spiritual surgery is better than the world's plastic surgery. What do you think?

April 16

Choosing to Run in a Marathon

*I shall run the way of Your commandments,
for You will enlarge my heart.*
Psalm 119:32 (NASB)

I have never run a marathon, but I admire anyone who has. This grueling 26.2-mile foot race is an intense physical and mental experience that requires total commitment. If you choose to do it, you had better be prepared. The cost in terms of training, running time, and expenditures is great. On the flip side, the benefit of regular cardio workouts is that they make your heart more efficient at pumping blood to your body. Your heart actually gets bigger over time, growing larger and stronger with increased capacity. The other benefit of running a marathon is the incredible feeling of satisfaction you get when you complete this difficult race. I think the psalmist experienced these feelings of satisfaction as he chose to run his life God's way.

King David, the writer of this psalm, trusted in the Lord for his salvation. He chose to accept the offer of forgiveness, follow the Lord, and run God's marathon. His decision was well thought out. Even though he didn't know where the course would lead him, he knew it would take longer than 26.2 miles to complete. He also knew his Counselor, the Holy Spirit, would be with him every step of the way. What an awesome God we have! He invites you to run in his race, gives you a new heart, and then grows it, giving you a greater and greater capacity to love him and to love the people who come your way. The Christian life gets more and more satisfying as a person runs his race. Hopefully, you are headed for the finish line. Your Counselor is waiting for you. Don't give up!

April 17

Gender Reveal Party

*The Lord has made known His salvation;
He has revealed His righteousness in the sight of the nations.*
Psalm 98:2 (NASB)

*For this reason also, God highly exalted Him,
and bestowed on Him the name which is above every name,
so that at the name of Jesus EVERY KNEE WILL BOW, of those who
are in heaven and on earth and under the earth, and that every tongue
will confess that Jesus Christ is Lord,
to the glory of God the Father.*
Philippians 2:9-11 (NASB)

A gender reveal party is an event or celebration given during pregnancy. The goal of the party is to reveal the baby's gender to the family and friends of the expecting parents. Activities might include a smoke bomb, powder and confetti cannons, a party piñata, or even an extravagant fireworks show. All these activities celebrate the identity of the baby's gender. Psalm 98 is also a reveal party—the greatest reveal of all time.

It is the reveal of the King of Kings, Jesus Christ. After his coronation ceremony, he will take his throne, and every knee will bow to

him. Every person who has ever lived will acknowledge that Jesus Christ is Lord. God's children will be revealed too, from every nation, tribe, people, and language. There will be shouts of joy, songs of praise, trumpets, an orchestra, and best of all, the final obliteration of every evil thing. None of us has ever seen a party like this! Our King has conquered sin and death, and he will share his gifts of salvation and eternal life with his children: the most extraordinary party favors, ever!

April 18

Hidden Gems

*We will not hide them from their children,
but tell to the coming generation the glorious deeds of the Lord,
and his might, and the wonders that he has done.*
Psalm 78:4 (ESV)

Years ago, I discovered the AAA TourBook guides. These handy travel books provide detailed information about states, cities, hotels, restaurants, attractions, and even travel routes. But out of all of these helpful notes, I uncovered something called "hidden gems." This feature is a little icon in the book that looks like a gemstone. It is those places of interest that you should not miss. It is one of those special items on your trip that you may not know about or that is simply hidden away. These hidden gems became one of my favorite things to seek out on our road trips. Many of them are part of our favorite memories. I think that gems like these are easily forgotten unless we make a point to talk about them.

This verse in Psalm 78 instructs us to embrace our responsibility to not hide scriptural gems from the coming generation. These life-changing Biblical truths are for our children and our grandchildren! They need to know who God is (his might), and "the wonders that he has done."

If you are a grandparent, please consider telling your salvation experience to your grandchildren. Let them hear your story of how you became a Christ-follower. Your story of God's grace will be precious and memorable. Why not take the opportunity and begin planting little seeds of the gospel into the next generation? Isn't this one of the best things you could ever do? Remember, hidden gems are only valuable if you tell others about them. This is what love looks like!

April 19

The Legacy of George Washington Carver

This is the message we have heard from Him and announce to you, that God is Light, and in Him there is no darkness at all.
1 John 1:5 (NASB)

George Washington Carver lived over one hundred years ago. He was born into slavery, but he grew up to become one of the greatest scientists of all time. After the Civil War, farmers in the South suffered financially. They had been growing cotton for years, but cotton plants depleted the soil. The only crop that continued to grow was peanuts, and farmers' yards were piled high with them. Sure, they made a good snack, but what else were they good for? It was a dark day for southern farmers.

Carver was an agricultural scientist. He also was a committed Christian. He had a habit of getting up at 4:00 every morning and going to the woods to talk with God. He was deeply concerned with the plight of these farmers, and one morning he asked God to give him fresh ideas on the use of peanuts. And God answered his prayer with more ideas than he ever dreamed. Within the next ten days, Carver's research led him to develop 300 derivative products from peanuts and another 118 products from sweet potatoes! These included things like soap, face creams, axle grease, insecticides, glue, medicines, and charcoal—products that improved the financial circumstances of southern farmers and revitalized the economy of the South. Carver's dependence on God, his work ethic, intelligence, and creative mind are a challenge to us all. His many discoveries opened the door to financial success and healthy living for Americans and people around the world.

Carver's life and discoveries remind us of the verse for today. God is light. When Carver asked God to enlighten his mind with fresh ideas, God gave him 300 of them! God is not stingy! He is all-knowing and willing to help! He sent his Son, Jesus, to be the Light of the World. Without Jesus, we are in the dark. With Jesus, the eyes of our hearts are opened. We see him clearly and all of life comes into focus. Darkness conceals, but light reveals. Jesus says to us, "Come into the light. Come to me."

April 20

Plans

"For I know the plans that I have for you," declares the Lord,
"plans for welfare and not for calamity
to give you a future and a hope."
Jeremiah 29:11 (NASB)

When I got married, I had an idea of what my detailed plans would include. I would have two children with my wonderful wife. My children would be completely well-behaved. I would have a good job and then retire when I was sixty-two years old. I would be healthy and able to play golf several times a week. Isn't this what we do when we start planning our lives out in detail? So how did this work out for you? Nobody I know plans for disaster. This was true for Jeremiah the prophet as well. He never planned that he would suffer through captivity, but he did.

None of us knows what the future holds. But the Lord definitely does. He knows everything about us. He knows our heart better than we do, and he knows when we are trusting him for our salvation. He knew all about my stroke, so it was never a surprise to him. He had a plan for my life that was never intended to harm me but to bless me. God's plans are for our welfare, and that gives us real hope. My plans for the future have changed many times over the years, but I thank God I have a Savior whose plans give me an even brighter future.

April 21

Bell Curve Thinking

*For by grace you have been saved through faith;
and that not of yourselves, it is the gift of God;
not as a result of works, so that no one may boast.*
Ephesians 2:8-9 (NASB)

Many teachers follow the practice of grading on the bell curve. This means that students' grades are based not on what they have learned as individuals, but on the combined performance of all the students in their class. If a student's scores are in range or better than most of his classmates, he will get a passing grade. This way of evaluating learning is seriously flawed. It encourages students to settle for doing "pretty good" instead of shooting for perfection. I think many of us like the bell curve model because it allows us to measure our performance with respect to other people. "I know I'm not perfect," we might say, "but look at the people around me. They are a *lot* worse than I am!" This kind of attitude hampers our potential in every area of life. It especially contradicts what the Bible tells us about our relationship with God.

Ephesians 2:8-9 tells us that God doesn't grade on the curve. God is perfectly righteous, and he requires us to be righteous too. He doesn't accept us because we are better than most people. In fact, a person may have done more good deeds than most people, but those good deeds would never be able to make up for the sins he has also committed. Why? Because a truly holy God requires perfection. If you have sinned even once, you fail, and just for the record, every one of us has sinned thousands of times during our lifetime!

The good news is that God is righteous, but he is also a loving Savior. His Son, Jesus, was the only one who ever lived life perfectly. He wasn't guilty of any sin himself, so he was able to take the penalty for all of my sins and yours. Jesus' perfection met God's perfect standard. Jesus passed the test in our place; Jesus made the grade for all of those who put their trust in him. Salvation from eternal punishment is a gift of God. No one can say, "I'm going to heaven because I've been *such* a good person." We are *considered* by God to be good and worthy of heaven because *Jesus* is good and has *gifted* us with a place in heaven. No bell curve for me! I'm putting my faith in Jesus, 100%!

April 22

A Stick of Dynamite

For I am not ashamed of the gospel, for it is the power of God for salvation to everyone who believes, to the Jew first and also to the Greek.
Romans 1:16 (NASB)

What would you think if one of your friends offered you a stick of dynamite? That he wants to get rid of you? Or that he wants to help you get rid of that tree stump you've been wanting to remove? Dynamite is powerful, and in the right circumstances it can be used to solve big problems. *Dynamis* is the Greek word for "power." It is used in the first chapter of Romans to describe the work of salvation to anyone who believes. Why would the apostle Paul use this particular word? Because the gospel is powerful and can be used to solve big problems!

God's power blows up our self-righteousness and sin. It changes our hard, unbelieving hearts. It rescues us from the kingdom of darkness and transfers us to the kingdom of his dear Son. And it frees us to live for God! In other words, the power of the gospel transforms people's lives! Jesus showed his power on the cross. When he shed his blood, the very ground shook and everything changed. Why would anyone be ashamed of power like this? No one else has these capabilities. Politics, money, climate change, human rights, social justice, entertainment—none of these things can bring the change we are looking for! Only Jesus can solve big problems. He is the only one who can use the dynamite of the gospel to transform your life.

April 23

Sunshine

But for you who fear My name,
the sun of righteousness will rise with healing in its wings;
and you will go forth and skip about like calves from the stall.
Malachi 4:2 (NASB)

Sunshine is one of the best gifts given to mankind. As soon as the first rays of the morning sun light upon your face, your body starts producing serotonin and cortisol. This is credited for improving immune systems, repairing your skin, and reducing stress, depression, and fatigue. It even regulates your appetite. In ancient Egypt, sunlight was used to heal wounds, treat bone diseases like rickets, and heal lung infections such as tuberculosis. Sunlight is our primary source of vitamin D, so vitamin D is called the "sunshine vitamin." Sunshine is a free gift. It's simply amazing what a little bit of sunshine can do!

The Bible verse today is from the book of Malachi. This book was written as a stern warning to evil-doers and those who reject God's gift of salvation. But, as the book concludes, we see hope and encouragement for those who fear God's name. This world is dark and cold, and we often feel tired and sick. But for those who fear God's name, the "sun of righteousness will rise with healing in its wings." With these words, God was predicting his "Son of Righteousness" would rise up to illuminate our hearts and heal us from our sins and infirmities. If you trust in Jesus Christ, if you fear God's name, he will rise up and shine upon your life, just like the sun shines on the earth every day. His power will flood you with light, improving you, repairing you, and reducing the effects of stress, depression, and fatigue. Just like God's gift of sunshine, God's gift of salvation is free. When it rises upon you, you will "go forth and skip" in freedom and joy!

April 24

Meeting a High School Friend

My God in his steadfast love will meet me.
Psalm 59:10 (ESV)

Meeting a special high school friend after fifty years apart can be both awkward and exciting at the same time. I wonder what he looks like now? Has his personality changed? Is he the same person I spent so much time with so long ago? How do you prepare for a meeting like this? Well, I would like to report to you that meeting my old friend was pure joy and delight. It only took us a few minutes before we were laughing and remembering other friends. The memories we shared were still fresh and alive. It was just like we had never been apart after all these years. Meetings like this are a true blessing. I wonder if the psalmist had thoughts like this when he wrote Psalm 59?

I am not exactly sure what situation King David was facing when he wrote this verse, but I do know that he went to meet a friend. His friend was God. He wanted to be in God's presence because he knew his enemy could not reach him there. This verse is a blessing because it is a promise for everyone who is feeling a little lonely today.

"My God in his steadfast love will meet me." We can count on our God because he is steadfast. He always shows up! His mercy and grace were present before you even realized you needed him. He prepared for your salvation before you were even born. Jesus Christ has prepared a meeting just like this for anyone who calls him his friend. It doesn't matter how you look or if your personality has changed. Jesus accepts you just like you are, and he is willing to meet with you anytime.

April 25

"I Shall Not Want"

The Lord is my shepherd; I shall not want.
Surely goodness and mercy shall follow me all the days of my life,
and I shall dwell in the house of the Lord forever.
Psalm 23:1,6 (ESV)

I always wondered about the phrase, "I shall not want." What does that mean anyway? Most Bible experts say it means, "I shall lack nothing." This goes along with a song I heard a while ago by Audrey Assad entitled "I Shall Not Want." The lyrics include this prayer to God: "Deliver me, O God, from the love of my own comfort, from the fear of having nothing, from a life of worldly passions, from the need to be understood, from the need to be accepted and from the fear of being lonely." These words hit pretty close to home for most of us. King David, who wrote the verse for today, experienced all these needs and saw God as the answer for all of them. The Lord was David's shepherd.

When you accept God's call to follow the Lord Jesus Christ, you become his sheep and he becomes your shepherd. As his sheep, you lack nothing. He provides everything for you. The rest of Psalm 23 says that God leads you to green pastures and still waters. He restores your soul and leads you in paths of righteousness. He is the one who loves you and cares for you. He is always looking out for you in every situation.

But what if you have decided to follow Christ, and you still feel anxious, fearful, and lonely? Don't worry. God hasn't abandoned you. Don't run off, chasing relief from the world. Instead, draw close to God. Read his words in the Bible, talk to him about everything that is troubling you. Ask him for help and receive the comfort and strength, the peace and joy that he offers. Get to know your Shepherd, and your trust in him will grow. It might take some time. Habits don't disappear overnight. But take God up on his promises, and remember that his spirit walks beside you, lives within you, and is looking out for you in every situation. You don't lack anything. After all, if God is for you, who can be against you? Surely goodness and mercy shall follow you all the days of *your* life, and *you* will dwell in the house of the Lord forever.

April 26

Clouds

Who covers the heavens with clouds, who provides rain for the earth,
Who makes grass to grow on the mountains.
He gives to the beast its food, and to the young ravens which cry.
Psalm 147:8-9 (NASB)

Nephology is the science of clouds. We see clouds every day. Sometimes they are white and puffy. Sometimes they are dark and cover the entire sky. Meteorologists study the clouds to understand their function in regard to Earth's environment. Clouds are the key regulator of the planet's average temperature. Cloud systems also help to spread the sun's energy evenly over the surface of Earth. Depending on their type, clouds consist of dry air mixed with liquid water drops or dry air mixed with ice particles. Droplets fall down to the ground as rain or ice. This scientific study of Earth's water systems is based on observation. The more we learn about clouds, the more we discover the wonder of our Creator. In Psalm 147, the psalmist studied nature, and this is what he learned.

God makes clouds to produce raindrops, and he determines when and where the rain will fall. He produces vegetation to feed people and animals. He waters the grass to feed cattle. He provides for the care of young ravens crying for food. The entire sequence from the formation of the clouds to the feeding of these little birds is God's doing. Earth's water system is a magnificent demonstration of the goodness of God and his gracious acts of love toward his creation. So the next time you hear "Singin' in the Rain" remember the one who created clouds, raindrops, and Earth's wonderful water system.

April 27

Under His Wings

Be merciful to me, O God, be merciful to me, for in you my soul takes refuge; in the shadow of your wings I will take refuge, till the storms of destruction pass by.
Psalm 57:1 (ESV)

Have you ever watched a hen with her chicks? If not, you are about to learn some interesting facts. Before the chicks are even hatched, a hen will turn the eggs in her nest as much as thirty times a day, using her feet, beak, and body to move each one. She does this to ensure that all conditions in the three-week incubation period are carefully maintained, including temperature, ventilation, and humidity. Two to three days before the chicks are hatched, they begin to peep. This notifies the hen that the time is nearing for the chicks to be born. It also draws attention to any distress the chicks might be experiencing, signaling her to turn the eggs appropriately. The mother's devotion to her chicks does not end when the shells come off. She continues her duties. Now it's time to collect food for her chicks. She will make sure that each chick eats its fill even before she satisfies her own hunger. The mother hen also protects her little chicks. She will droop her wings at the first sign of a predator and will stand her ground defensively while the chicks flee under her wings for protection. They will stay under her wings until they are safe from harm. I believe that hens can teach us a lot about God's devotion to his children, his protection, and the place where we can hide when we are in danger.

The psalmist knew that God was the very best place to hide. He understood that the place to go was under the protective wings of God. As much as you would like to believe that you can ward off all your worries and struggles, you need a Savior like Jesus to turn to. He is the one who can give you a hiding place and shield to protect you. So run to Jesus. Security is always found under his wings.

April 28

Take a Bow

For this reason also, God highly exalted Him,
and bestowed on Him the name which is above every name,
so that at the name of Jesus EVERY KNEE WILL BOW,
of those who are in heaven and on earth and under the earth,
and that every tongue will confess that Jesus Christ is Lord,
to the glory of God the Father.
Philippians 2:9-11 (NASB)

When a play has finished, the actors line up to take a bow. This gives the audience an opportunity to applaud the actors' performance and acknowledge their remarkable success. In the book of Philippians, Jesus is mentioned for his performance as well.

What did Jesus do to receive his acclaim? Jesus willingly died as our substitute to pay for our sins. To recognize this remarkable act of sacrifice, God has exalted Jesus to the highest place. The word "exalted" in the Greek language is actually "super-exalted." There is no one in the universe who will ever receive a higher commendation than Jesus. We can never praise him enough for what he has done. These verses say that every knee will bow and every tongue will acknowledge that Jesus Christ is Lord. That means that every person who has ever lived will applaud him for what he has done. Trusting in Jesus now is our way of praising him for his performance.

April 29

The Investment

The Lord will accomplish what concerns me;
Your lovingkindness, O Lord, is everlasting;
do not forsake the works of Your hands.
Psalm 138:8 (NASB)

When we raise our children, we make a big investment in each one of them in time, in energy, in hopes and dreams. Why do we do this? We love them, so we sacrifice for them to help them become successful. We never give up on our children. They are part of our family. David understood this truth but celebrated it in a new way in Psalm 138.

In this verse, David was reassuring himself of his *heavenly Father's* lovingkindness. He wrote, "The Lord will accomplish what concerns me." Another rendition of this verse says, "The Lord will fulfill his purpose for me." There was no doubt about it! David's life was precious to his heavenly Father. David was his child, and God loved him. So as David's Father, God was willing to sacrifice for him, even to make the ultimate sacrifice, to bring David into his family. The Lord had a plan for David and was deeply invested in his life. He was never going to give up on him. He was never going to abandon him—no matter what! In fact, the Lord Jesus Christ's genealogical line comes from this very David.

The amazing thing is that this promise to David is available to all of us today in what we call the "gospel." The gospel is that Jesus died to pay for our sins, and if we turn to him and surrender our lives to him, God adopts us into his family. God is concerned about us and all of our children and future grandchildren. We become sons and daughters of the King of the universe. We become his treasure. He invests in us, and he promises he will never abandon us. When we start to recognize these truths, God gives us a sense of confidence and freedom. We are part of his royal family, and no one can ever take our title away!

April 30

The Rock

Blessed be the Lord, my rock.
Psalm 144:1 (NASB)

In 1775 a Spanish naval officer and explorer named a small piece of land in the San Francisco Bay "de los Alcatrazes" or, when translated, "Island of the Pelicans." Pelican was the archaic Spanish name of "Alcatraz." By 1827, it was widely known as Alcatraz Island. It first served as a lighthouse and then became a military fortification in the Mexican War and the Civil War. During the Civil War, it served as a military prison housing prisoners of war. In 1933, Alcatraz Island was turned over to the Department of Justice to serve as a new kind of prison. The new name was "Alcatraz Federal Penitentiary." This federal prison housed the most notorious criminals in the United States until it was finally closed in 1963. You probably know its popular name, "The Rock." This name is not new since the psalmist had already given the name to a person in Psalm 144.

David's rock was Jesus. The Hebrew word for *rock* expresses strength and power. If you call someone your "rock," you are referring to a person you can rely on for help and support. In this verse in Psalms, David is referring to Jesus, who rescued him from physical and spiritual disaster again and again. The Bible refers to Jesus (and he also refers to himself) as a rock many times. Jesus would visit Earth in human form later on in history, but during David's time he was just as real, working from heaven as David's refuge, shield, stronghold, and salvation. Jesus is the only one anybody can trust for forgiveness and pardon for his sins. I'm thankful Jesus isn't a rock who imprisons us, like Alcatraz Penitentiary. Instead, he is a rock who protects us and sets us free!

May 1

The Real McCoy

*I ask that we love one another. And this is love;
that we walk in obedience to his commands.*
2 John 1:5-6 (NIV)

Have you ever heard someone say, "It's the real McCoy"? Or how about, "It's the real deal"? Both of these phrases mean that something is genuine, not an imitation or fake. Some people have associated this expression with Elijah McCoy's 1872 invention of the oil-drip cup. This invention was so popular with railroad engineers that they wouldn't buy a locomotive unless it was fitted with what people referred to as "the real McCoy."

I think we want our relationships to be "real" as well. Today's passage was written by the apostle John to a special friend. He was warning his friend about a problem in their community and encouraging everyone there to "love one another."

But how do we obey God's command to "love one another" in a world filled with conflict, hatred, selfishness, and pride? Jesus showed us. He obeyed every one of God's commands perfectly. He did this by daily renewing his relationship with his Father and then plugging into people's everyday lives. He walked with people, ate meals with people, worked, encouraged, and healed people. He shared in all the things that concerned people, and in doing these things, he showed what it means to be authentic and genuine. He willingly served others because he loved them. "Love one another" is one of God's top two commands. By loving people, you point them to the love of God and eternal life. You will also experience the joy of being "the real deal."

May 2

Carry Me, Daddy!

*Save Your people and bless Your inheritance;
Be their shepherd also, and carry them forever.*
Psalm 28:9 (NASB)

"Carry me, Daddy!" I heard this plea many times when I was rearing my children. It was usually on a hot day when we were taking a walk and they were getting thirsty and tired. What do parents do when they see their little one, with his hands lifted up, pleading to be carried? We all know the answer. We look down, smile, and pick up our forty-pound bundle of joy. Why? Because our children mean the world to us!

Don't you suppose that when we lift up our hearts to God, he feels the same way? He sees when we are exhausted or sick or hurt or confused. He hears us pleading to him, "Carry me, Daddy!" When we look at the verse for today, we see four powerful appeals we can make to God. Save us. Bless us. Be our shepherd. Carry us forever. What do you suppose God is going to do when he sees us pleading for his help? He's going to pick us up and carry us through our time of need. Why? Because his children mean the world to him!

This kind of thinking is contrary to our culture today. Aren't we supposed to be independent, strong, and able to carry our own weight? Let's be honest. Life is difficult and full of struggles. We live in a world with family members, neighbors, and co-workers who aren't necessarily looking out for our best interests. The truth is that most of us are tired of fighting the battles we face. We need help.

Jesus sees our suffering and hears our pleas for help. When we say, "Carry me, Daddy!" What does he do? He smiles and picks us up. Why? Because his children mean the world to him!

May 3

How to Catch a Bird

Our soul has escaped as a bird out of the snare of the trapper;
The snare is broken and we have escaped.
Our help is in the name of the Lord,
Who made heaven and earth.
Psalm 124:7-8 (NASB)

Hunters catch birds with a snare. There are many types of snares that will work. The hunter uses food, water, or decoys to lure the bird into the trap. His intentions are good. The bird will make a tasty meal for the hunter and his family. Most people don't blame hunters for their sport. It takes skill and provides food, a necessity of life. But this verse tells about another kind of hunter. It is Satan, the trapper and destroyer of our souls.

Our soul is like a bird. We are weak and enticed by many things. Satan is the trapper, and his intentions are not good. He is always looking for ways to catch an unsuspecting soul. What is the trap in your case? Procrastination? Addiction? The love of money? An unforgiving heart? The good news is that Jesus has broken the snare that traps you. You can escape. You can be free! Your escape will come when you put your trust in Christ. It's time to feel your wings! Will you go free?

May 4

Facing Your Giant

*You will not have to fight this battle. Take up your positions;
stand firm and see the deliverance the Lord will give you,
O Judah and Jerusalem. Do not be afraid; do not be discouraged.
Go out to face them tomorrow, and the Lord will be with you.*
2 Chronicles 20:17 (NIV)

During the reign of King Jehoshaphat, several nations formed an alliance intent on invading Judah. Completely outmanned, Jehoshaphat had few options since his enemies surprised him with an unconventional attack plan. Facing overwhelming odds, he was powerless against this great horde. He did not know what to do, so he looked to God. He proclaimed a national time of fasting, and the king prayed for his people instead of preparing battle plans.

God heard the king's humble prayer, and the Spirit of the Lord came upon Jahaziel, who was a worship leader. God used his lone voice to speak to all of the people who had gathered. In his dramatic speech, he said, "You will not have to fight this battle. Take up your positions; stand firm and see the deliverance the Lord will give you." God told them to not be afraid or discouraged because this battle belongs to the Lord. Then he charged them to go out and face the impossible situation. He wanted them to trust in the Lord for their deliverance. This is faith in action. Do you know what happened when these people obeyed? God completely destroyed their enemies. God did it all without the help of any of King Jehoshaphat's soldiers.

When I think about this story, I am reminded of the personal battles that I face every day. How many times do I try to win this fight by myself? What do I do when I am faced with a giant that is threatening to destroy me? How many times do I flee before I humble myself and pray?

What is it going to take before you realize that God can handle it all? Jesus Christ is your only hope. When you trust in him, you will be able to face your giant and stand firm because "the Lord will be with you."

May 5

Great Is Thy Faithfulness

*Every good thing given and every perfect gift is from above,
coming down from the Father of lights,
with whom there is no variation or shifting shadow.*
James 1:17 (NASB)

The song "Great is Thy Faithfulness" was written by Thomas Chisholm in 1923. He wanted to give personal testimony to the fact that God had been faithful to him throughout his life. In the first verse of the song, he writes, "There is no shadow of turning with Thee." This means that God is consistently faithful. We never have to worry about him loving us one day and then turning against us later on. There is no shadow, no darkness, in him at all! In fact, Chisholm declared, "*All* I have needed his hand has provided. Great is thy faithfulness, Lord unto me!" James reiterates this truth in this New Testament verse.

"Every good thing, every perfect gift, comes down from the Father of lights." That's good! But to make things even better, James tells us that God is never "shifty," playing games at our expense. Even when things seem "oh, so wrong!" our loving God is working his flawless plan. This plan might involve an important learning experience. It might be a wake-up call to warn us about some slavery to sin. It might be a test to give us an opportunity to take a stand for him or an opportunity to gain a deeper sense of his spiritual presence. If so, he will reward us in the end. Whatever it is, God's plan is just and merciful and is working for our benefit. He never makes a mistake. He has no flaws. Sometimes we might think he's being shifty. This is a lie. There is never a variation in his perfect character. Of course, God's best gift is his Son, Jesus Christ, who is also always faithful and true. Our God is the Father of lights. Our God is good!

May 6

Jesus, Take the Wheel

Trust in the Lord with all your heart and lean not on your own understanding; in all your ways acknowledge him, and he will make your paths straight.
Proverbs 3:5-6 (NIV)

"Jesus, Take the Wheel," by Carrie Underwood, is a country song about a young, single mother driving home to visit her parents at Christmas. As she travels, her mind turns to the hardships of her life, the difficulties of taking care of her child, and the myriad other difficulties she is facing that completely overwhelm her. Not paying attention to the hazardous driving conditions, she loses control of her car and starts spinning on a sheet of black ice. Her life and the life of her child are now in danger. Knowing she is completely powerless in this situation, she throws her hands up in the air and prays to Jesus to save her life. "Jesus," she cries out, "take the wheel!" Miraculously, the car ends up resting on the shoulder of the road. She is safe and her baby is still asleep. As a result of this life-altering event, she vows to change her life and let God take control. This familiar story has applications for us all. Whatever our story, we are constantly confronted with important questions. How can I stop worrying all the time? Whom can I trust? Whom can I rely on for security when life gets chaotic? Who is going to take control of my life? This passage in Proverbs gives us excellent answers.

Most people's lives are filled with problems that need to be solved. "Trust in the Lord with all your heart." Sometimes everything seems to be going just fine and the next minute your life is spinning out of control. "Lean not on your own understanding." Unexpected events challenge our beliefs. They test our innermost being. If I am honest with myself, I discover that I am a broken sinner. "In all your ways, acknowledge him." I don't have all the answers and need someone who can help me in my distress. "He will make your paths straight."

The good news is that Jesus Christ is willing and ready to take the wheel of your life. If you "trust in the Lord with all your heart," "he *will* make your paths straight." This doesn't mean that all the problems in your life will disappear. There will be potholes to avoid, black ice that slows you down, and circumstances over which you have no control. But when Jesus is your friend, you have a traveling partner who will guide you on your way. What a relief it is to know that when Jesus takes the wheel, you are surrounded by his care and protection. You can be at peace because he is in control, and you can trust him completely.

May 7

Musical Chairs

And the Lord will be king over all the earth;
in that day the Lord will be the only one,
and His name the only one.
Zechariah 14:9 (NASB)

If you have ever been to a birthday party for children, one of the most popular games is "musical chairs." The children walk around a circle of chairs as the music is playing. There is tension in the air because there is one fewer chair than the number of children. When the music stops, each child has to find a chair and sit down. The child who is left standing is automatically eliminated from the game. The game continues by eliminating one chair at a time until only one chair remains. The child sitting on that chair is the winner. This children's game is a standard for birthday parties around the world.

When I first started thinking about this game, I asked myself, "Why do kids like this game so much?" Children love it because it is competitive and exciting. Their parents love it because it burns off energy. It also teaches many practical lessons such as fair play, good sportsmanship, and coping with disappointment. However, there is an underlying reason I believe we all like a game like this. We like to be number one. We like to win! This Bible verse in Zechariah points to the fact that, in the end, there will only be one winner, one King over all the earth.

This verse is found in the Old Testament, written hundreds of years before Christ was born. It is a prophecy about Jesus. Jesus is the Lord in this verse, the only one sitting on the throne and ruling as King of the whole earth. On that day, he will be the winner, and that will be all that matters. In truth, Jesus is already Number One, but on that day, everyone will acknowledge his sovereignty. Every knee will bow and every tongue will swear allegiance to the King of Kings,

Jesus Christ. This fact brings us to a critical question. Who is number one in your life? Is it you or is it King Jesus? Who will be the winner? Who will be sitting on the last chair when the music ends?

May 8

Peeling an Onion

*He does not deal with us according to our sins,
nor repay us according to our iniquities.*
Psalm 103:10 (ESV)

How do you peel an onion? I would first cut the top off. Then I would peel off the papery layers of the skin that look a little wrinkled. After that, I would take off the next two layers just to make sure the onion isn't dirty or damaged. The next part depends on the onion itself. How does it look? Is it damaged too? This judgment call could mean taking off one more layer before you get to the good part, the part you want to eat. This description of peeling an onion is a good metaphor for self-examination.

Let me explain. If you want a true evaluation of yourself, you have to start by peeling off your top layer. That layer is your facade, the part of you it's okay for people to see. We create our facades very carefully. It's a kind of game we play to protect ourselves from being criticized and getting hurt. But when we peel off this first layer, we get a look at who we really are. This is hard stuff. You may discover that the facade you've created is a lie, that you are actually a sinner and quite a selfish person. It's no fun to face the truth. Our "self" is often more damaged than we thought!

"Peeling our onion" is often such a shock that we want to throw in the towel and forget the whole thing. When King David examined himself, he discovered he had sinned quite grievously. He didn't throw in the towel though. He confessed his sin and asked God to forgive him, and God did forgive him! Thank goodness that "He does not deal with us according to our sins, nor repay us according to our iniquities." He will do the same for you and me. He is calling all of us to examine ourselves, to peel off the layers that stop us from being totally honest. It's a difficult thing to do, but God has given us this promise: "If we confess our sins, he is faithful and just to forgive us our sins and to cleanse us from all unrighteousness" (1 John 1:9). We don't have to back away from the truth about ourselves. Instead, we can embrace God's love and his wonderful gift of forgiveness.

May 9

Anxious Thoughts

Search me, O God, and know my heart; try me and know my anxious thoughts; And see if there be any hurtful way in me, and lead me in the everlasting way.
Psalm 139:23-24 (NASB)

In 2002, I was awakened by a dream that I was having a heart attack. My nightmare was true. Over the next year, I had a hard time going to sleep at night because of all my anxious thoughts. I even started having panic attacks. During one of these stressful times, I met a doctor friend who talked to me about what was happening. It wasn't until I confronted these thoughts that I was able to sort out the truth. King David was just like us and wrestled the way we do with our anxious thoughts.

Feelings of anxiety force us to examine our beliefs in God's character. Do I really believe that God knows everything about me? Is God present with me in every circumstance? Did he really form me in my mother's womb, and does he have a plan for my life? Does God really love me? Can he calm my anxious thoughts and bring peace into my heart? I want to believe he can, but I continue to doubt his character and capabilities. When you are in this situation, you can do two things: 1. Recount his faithful deeds to you in the past. 2. Remember his gift to you—his only Son. Does God really love you? The answer is Yes! Yes! Yes!

May 10

Importance of Clothing

I will rejoice greatly in the Lord, my soul will exult in my God;
For He has clothed me with garments of salvation,
He has wrapped me with a robe of righteousness.
As a bridegroom decks himself with a garland,
And as a bride adorns herself with her jewels.
Isaiah 61:10 (NASB)

One purpose of clothing is to protect our bodies from the elements. Clothing keeps us safe from cold, heat, wind, rain, and even insect bites. But clothes also tell the world who we are. Personal taste, social status, standards of modesty, and even style are revealed by what we wear. Our outward choices reveal what is going on inside. This was the case for Isaiah, who rejoiced greatly in the Lord.

Why was he so joyful? Because God had given him new spiritual clothes. Our old clothes are like filthy rags in the presence of God, who is perfect, pure, and holy. There's no way to cover up how filthy we are. Our guilt is revealed by the spiritual clothes we wear. But God wants to change all that. When we trust in the Lord for our salvation, we are given a new wardrobe. We are given protection from the judgment we deserve. We are given a new identity and a new life. We are given new spiritual tastes and a new status: child of the King of the universe! We are wrapped in the righteousness of Christ! We are actually brand-new people! God clothes his people in righteousness!

May 11

Invasion of the Cicadas

Alas for that day!
For the day of the Lord is near;
it will come like destruction from the Almighty.
Has not the food been cut off before our very eyes?
Joel 1:15-16 (NIV)

And everyone who calls on the name of the Lord will be saved.
Joel 2:32 (NIV)

This year we witnessed the invasion of the seventeen-year cicadas. The life cycle of the cicada is very interesting. First, it lays its eggs on plants or in trees. When the eggs hatch, the nymphs burrow underground where they will live for most of their lives. After seventeen years, they emerge, shed their outer shell, and lay eggs to produce the next generation of cicadas. Adult cicadas die about six weeks after that. Although these insects can be annoying, loud, and damaging to trees, the destruction they cause is minimal.

I always thought that cicadas were a kind of locust, but this is not true. Cicadas belong to the same family as locusts, but locusts are far more dangerous. In the year 2021, there was an invasion of locusts that did major damage in five countries in Africa. Because locusts can live three to five months after they lay their first batch of eggs, they have plenty of time to lay more. One locust can lay as many as 1000 eggs before it dies. Swarms of locusts can't be compared to cicadas since the damage and economic impact they do is so much greater.

In the book of Joel, we read about a historic locust invasion in the country of Judah. Crops were ruined. The economy was disrupted. Every level of society suffered. God used this natural disaster to warn the people of Judah, who had turned away from him and were living lives of sin. God was sounding the alarm, warning people of his judgment, and calling them to repent. He was also assuring them of his mercy, with this wonderful promise: "…everyone who calls on the name of the Lord will be saved." When disaster strikes, repent of your sins, call on the name of the Lord, and he will save you.

May 12

Objects of Compassion

Nevertheless He looked upon their distress when He heard their cry;
And He remembered His covenant for their sake,
And relented according to the greatness of His lovingkindness.
He also made them objects of compassion in the
presence of all their captors.
Psalm 106:44-46 (NASB)

During the 1700s and 1800s, there was a serious crime problem in England. Lawmakers decided to solve the problem by placing harsh punishments on people who broke the law. Many of these offenders were poor children under eighteen years old. Thank goodness compassionate lawmakers came up with an innovative program to spare the children from harsher punishments. Young offenders would be transported to Australia where they would have an opportunity to break free from a life of crime, learn a trade, and live productive lives. On New Year's Day in 1837, the convict ship *Frances Charlotte* sailed from Portsmouth, England, bound for Tasmania, Australia. On board this British ship were 140 male "juvenile offenders." Over the next five years, a total of eight ships would sail, taking over 1,200 "boy convicts" to Australia. These children were called "objects of compassion."

In Psalm 106, we see that God had a similar problem with his people, the Israelites. They were breaking God's laws, worshiping idols, and even sacrificing their children to demons. So God punished them by allowing foreign nations to conquer and oppress them. When they cried out to God, he always delivered them, but then they went right back to sinning. Finally, he implemented his own innovative program. He made them "objects of compassion" by those who held them captive. Compassion was unthinkable to ancient conquerors, but God saw to it that his people were treated kindly.

    How many chances does God give us to repent? We don't know. But these verses say that God sees us and hears our cries for help. He is so merciful that he will forgive all of our sins. Just when I think that God cannot love me anymore, I find that he still has more love for me. God's love never runs out; it is infinite. Just like those British "boy convicts," we are God's "objects of compassion." Thank God for second chances!

May 13

The North Star

But You, O God, the Lord, deal kindly with me for Your name's sake;
Because Your lovingkindness is good, deliver me;
For I am afflicted and needy,
and my heart is wounded within me.
Psalm 109:21-22 (NASB)

Polaris is the North Star. It sits almost directly above the North Pole. This makes it a reliable gauge of north. Because of its brightness, navigators can use it to determine their position at night. This star is the anchor of the northern sky, and as such it is a trustworthy guide. It has also been used as a symbol of inspiration and hope. Just like the North Star, the psalmist turned to God for inspiration, comfort, and hope.

This prayer in Psalm 109 describes a man who is afflicted and needy. His heart is wounded, and he needs someone to deliver him from his own personal storm. This is the situation we find ourselves in when we begin to realize just how desperate our spiritual condition really is. We are drowning in our sin and need someone to throw us a life preserver. We need someone to deliver us from our raging guilt. Just when we believe there is no hope for ourselves, along comes Jesus Christ to the rescue. He deals kindly with us, forgives our sins, and declares us "not guilty." He is the one who encourages us to hang in there. When we trust in Jesus, we are leaving all our afflictions in his hands. The Lord can handle all of our problems. Because of his steadfast love, we can find peace even though the storms of life are crashing upon us. The next time you feel lost and need hope, let me suggest that you look in the Bible where you will see Jesus who is our North Star!

May 14

Parade Rest Guest Ranch

*You have filled my heart with greater joy
than when their grain and new wine abound.*
Psalm 4:7 (NIV)

Many years ago, my wife and I took a trip to Yellowstone National Park. One night on the trip, we got to our hotel and discovered they had no room. After many frantic calls, a helpful lady at the Parade Rest Guest Ranch agreed to take us in. She let us know that our room was one of the last rooms available. Since it was dark and the hotel was a distance away, she gave us specific directions. We were so relieved to finally find a room for the night.

When we checked into our new hotel, however, we discovered there was no way to lock the door to our room. "It will be okay," the lady said. "You are safe here." Since my wife and I were not used to this type of situation, our minds automatically became concerned. Will we be murdered tonight? Are we really safe here? But it was so late, and we were so sleepy, we agreed to trust the nice lady. And when we woke up the next morning, our hearts were filled with surprise. We were still alive! And we had enjoyed a great night's rest. Actually, this ranch in West Yellowstone turned out to be one of the most delightful places of our trip because of its friendly staff and hearty breakfast. Our hearts were filled with joy as we said goodbye to our new friends.

This story makes me chuckle. It's a great story for those contemplating God's kingdom. Is it getting late? Are you tired? When you trust Christ and follow him, he will fill your heart with greater peace and joy than anything the world has to offer. Good food, delicious wine, a nice hotel? These things are nothing compared to what God has in store for those who put their trust in him. The Holy Spirit will come to take up residence in your heart and will start a new work in you. It might seem a little dangerous at first. Everything is changing and there's no lock on the door of your heart. But his work is far more precious than anything you could ever experience. Nothing can compare to the surprise and joy you will sense as you surrender to the lordship of Jesus Christ. This is a story I'm going to tell my kids!

May 15

How Many Stars?

*The heavens declare the glory of God,
and the sky above proclaims his handiwork.*
Psalm 19:1 (ESV)

Do you have any idea how many stars there are in the heavens? On a clear night, about 3,000 stars are visible to our eyes. But if you have a small telescope, the number of stars you can see grows to about 100,000. Scientists with powerful telescopes tell us there are around 100 billion stars in the Milky Way alone. Beyond this galaxy there are more than 100 billion known galaxies! If you take the average number of stars in the Milky Way and multiply it by 100 billion you have an estimated ten billion trillion stars in the universe!

When I go outside and look at the moon and the 3,000 stars that are visible to me, I am simply amazed. They are breathtaking! Who did this? Psalm 19 tells us it was God, the Creator of the universe. In fact, everything we see in nature declares his glory, his power, his intelligence, and his creativity. When I think about this, I am humbled and amazed that he would care about me, a mere speck in the universe.

Think about this! God is so big he can create ten billion trillion stars (probably more) and place them in the heavens. And yet, he is so personal and so loving that he sacrificed his only Son on the cross to save his people from their sins. God loves people; humanity is his treasure! How can people refuse him? How can people not fall down before him in worship and in praise? God is using the vastness of his universe to capture our attention and to call us to turn to him in repentance and faith. He is inviting us to be part of his family and to serve him as Lord of our lives. He is preparing a place for us in heaven where we will view all of his handiwork firsthand! This offer from God is just too good to pass up!

May 16

Greasing the Skids

Jesus said to him, "I am the way, and the truth, and the life; no one comes to the Father but through Me."
John 14:6 (NASB)

To "grease the skids" means to facilitate the way to success. In shipbuilding, skids were used to make it easier to move huge ships into the water from the shipyards. Today this idiom means to help pave the way to success. This is something you do to "make things happen." There are many good examples of this, especially when it comes to business deals. But according to Jesus, when it comes to life's problems and eternal matters, "greasing the skids" isn't the answer at all.

In one conversation between Jesus and his disciple Thomas, Thomas revealed just how confused he was with life and its difficulties. Jesus gave a simple response: "I am the way, and the truth, and the life." The answer is Jesus. He is the answer to all the questions of life and death. If you want to solve your problems for now and eternity, you need to have a relationship with Jesus Christ.

There is only one way to facilitate your salvation. There is no back door to get in. There is no other VIP that can give you access. And there is no other good deed to pay your way. There is only one way to find salvation, and that way is Jesus Christ. He is the only one who can make it happen. Greasing the skids will never work when it comes to finding heaven. If you want to find heaven, look for Jesus.

May 17

Water Jars in Africa

Then, leaving her water jar, the woman went back to the town and said to the people, "Come, see a man who told me everything I ever did. Could this be the Christ?"
John 4:28-29 (NIV)

There are three things I saw on my first trip to Africa that I will never forget: wild zebras, herds of goats, and women carrying water jars on their heads. One of the projects I participated in involved the digging of water wells. One day, I got to meet one of the Kenyan women who carried water for her family. What an eye-opening experience! This lady would take her water jar to a local water hole first thing every morning. She needed the water to drink, to cook her food, to bathe herself and her family, and to keep her house clean. When I asked her how long it took to walk to the water hole, I was blown away. It took over three hours just to get to the water hole, and then another three hours to get back home. She spent seven hours every day just providing water for her family! Can you imagine? The water jar she balanced on her head carried three to four gallons of water and weighed around twenty-five to thirty pounds. This was her task—every day!

The verse for today is part of a bigger story in the book of John. Jesus was on a trip through the countryside of Samaria. There, at a well, he met a Samaritan woman who had walked a good distance to get water for her family. Jesus asked her to draw a drink of water for him, and that started a life-changing conversation.

This woman had a checkered past, but she didn't want to reveal that to Jesus. She started talking about religious things to avoid getting too personal. But Jesus led her right to the truth of the matter. What she needed was living water, the kind that would cleanse her sinful heart and satisfy her soul. He let her know that he was the Savior of the world and could give her a spring of *living* water that would never run dry and would well up in her to eternal life. She knew that kind of water was exactly what she needed. It sounds like she put her trust in Jesus right then and there! But there's more!

She was so excited about finding Jesus that she ran back to her town (she didn't even think to take her water jar with her) and told everyone that she had found the Christ. They all came out to meet Jesus and were so relieved and excited by the things he said that they asked him to stay with them and teach them how to be believers in God. They needed forgiveness too, and they needed eternal life. Jesus did stay with them, and many of them received the living water Jesus offered them. Their hearts were cleansed, their souls were satisfied, and they received the gift of eternal life. Someday we will meet those people, and we will all have our own wonderful stories to tell about how Jesus saved us!

May 18

No Man Left Behind

*For the Lord will not abandon His people,
nor will He forsake His inheritance.*
Psalm 94:14 (NASB)

"I will never leave a fallen comrade." This statement, included in the *Soldiers Creed,* is a promise all soldiers live by. Since each warrior is a valued member of his unit, no man should ever be "left behind." This message in Psalm 94 is even more powerful for the soldiers in God's kingdom. "The Lord will not abandon his people."

It is so easy to fret over the evil in this world. Violence, chaos, and disunity are everywhere. We often worry about what may happen to us or to our loved ones. But God tells us to pay attention to his promise. Whatever we go through, God will not abandon or forsake us. God, in his lovingkindness, will hold us up. He will stand with us, comforting us in our joys and sorrows. Instead of deserting us, he will take us home! When our anxious thoughts seem to multiply, we can find comfort in this promise. Jesus is still in command of this world, and he is with us all the way. Whatever happens in this new year, it will be another opportunity to see how God provides for his children. King Jesus is faithful, so we can be sure that no child of his will ever be left behind!

May 19

"Online but Inaccessible"

*The name of the Lord is a strong tower;
the righteous runs into it and is safe.*
Proverbs 18:10 (NASB)

"The internet is inaccessible to many people with disabilities." A recent article published by the American Marketing Association estimates that marketers may be missing out on more than twenty percent of potential consumers due to the limitations disabilities pose. Though innovative website designers are providing the most dynamic experiences possible with flashing graphics, catchy music, and helpful subtitles, if a person has a visual or auditory disability, or is paralyzed and can't use a keyboard, he will be unable to access the wealth of knowledge being offered today. Even the most powerful cell towers in the world cannot overcome these disabilities which limit people's potential and restrict marketers' sales. Thank God that he is not limited or restricted in any way. This is clear in our verse for today.

"The name of the Lord is a strong tower." In the Bible, someone's name signifies his attributes. In this case, God's name signifies that he is a strong tower. Towers have always been a source of safety, and our God is a powerful, accessible, and willing refuge to go to when we need help. "Thou hast been a shelter for me," says the psalmist in Psalm 61:3. The problem is that we are severely disabled by sin, which makes God inaccessible to us. But God isn't a hoity-toity hunk of steel too high and too hard for us to reach. He's a real person who loves us so much he was willing to come down to our level and take on our sin. Jesus' death on the cross bridged the gap between our disability and his forgiveness. It makes God accessible to us, a place to run when we need help. The Lord is fully able to protect his righteous people. Until the time that we join him in heaven, the Holy Spirit lives in us, continuing to do away with restrictions to our access to God. He will be accessible every day until this life is over and we see Jesus, not on some computer screen, but face to face!

May 20

Songs

How can we sing the Lord's song in a foreign land?
Psalm 137:4 (NASB)

Songs tell stories, express emotions, and convey beliefs. They bring us back to another time. I can still remember the song "Cherish" sung by The Association in 1966 and played at sock hops around the country. These memories remind us about our lives, our struggles, and our victories. This verse in Psalm 137 reminded the Israelites of their captivity in Babylon, a time of great sorrow and lament.

The question posed in this verse is, "How can we sing the Lord's song?" How can we sing when we are defeated? How can we sing when we have been given bad news or when we lose our job? How can we sing when a friend or a family member dies? The answer is found in the gospel.

The Lord remembers and knows everything about your life and your situation. He cares how you feel because he loves you. This is especially good news if you are a believer. Don't forget what he has done for you. He saved you and rescued you from your sin. He has been faithful to you, keeping all his promises. He has a new home waiting for you where everything will someday be made right. How can you sing when your heart is breaking? The answer is to remember the love Christ has for you and thank him. Bask in his love and you will receive hope and a new song in your heart—a song of thanksgiving and promises to come.

May 21

Mediation

Therefore, I will allot Him a portion with the great,
And He will divide the booty with the strong;
Because He poured out Himself to death,
And was numbered with the transgressors;
Yet He Himself bore the sin of many,
and interceded for the transgressors.
Isaiah 53:12 (NASB)

Mediation is a process where a neutral third person called a mediator helps two parties discuss their differences and resolve a conflict. The process of mediation is voluntary since neither side is required to come to an agreement. The mediator does not decide the outcome, but merely focuses on important issues needed to reach a resolution. Isaiah 53 foretells the greatest mediator of all time.

The dispute is between a righteous God and rebellious sinners. God loves us sinners very much, so he appointed Jesus Christ to be our Mediator to resolve our conflict. He intercedes for us and pleads our case by offering himself as the solution. Because he lived a perfect life, he can make payment for our sins and resolve the conflict between us and God. When we accept his payment, the conflict is over and settled. We can live in peace with our holy, just, and loving Father in heaven.

May 22

Yoke of Slavery

*It was for freedom that Christ set us free;
therefore keep standing firm and do not be subject
again to a yoke of slavery.*
Galatians 5:1 (NASB)

A yoke is a wooden crosspiece that is used to control domestic animals. To use a yoke, you first fasten the yoke over the neck of two animals. Then you attach the yoke to a plow or cart you intend for them to pull. They don't have any choice in the matter. They must do as you command. So when this verse uses the word "yoke," it means bondage, enslavement, or oppression. In this passage, the word "yoke" is used to describe our slavery to sin.

"It was for freedom that Christ set us free" from our bondage to sin. Before we come to Christ, we are subject to the rule of our desires, the rule of our sinful habits, the rule of the destructive behavior of other people, and the rule of Satan (or the Evil One). We may want to live differently, but we are slaves to sin. Christ knew that trying hard doesn't really work well, makes us miserable, and usually doesn't last very long. But he declared that if you will entrust yourself to him, he will break that yoke of sin and release you to live your life in the freedom that comes from a loving relationship with him. Sure, we will sometimes fail to obey God. We won't be perfect until we get to heaven. But Jesus is there to forgive us when we ask. He reinstates us, so we  can go on learning and living in the freedom he gives. The good news is that Jesus has broken our yoke and offered us his amazing power to live a life of freedom from the slavery of sin.

May 23

Little Dainties

For my eyes are toward You, O God, the Lord;
In You I take refuge; do not leave me defenseless.
Psalm 141:8 (NASB)

We all have our little dainties. Mine is a hot loaf of bread. My wife prefers coconut cake. Dainties are delicacies. They are a delight to the eyes and delicious to our palette. Have you ever noticed how these little delights can capture your mind? David, in Psalm 141, understood this very well.

This verse challenges us to keep our eyes on the Lord. When my eyes are on Jesus, I am trusting him to satisfy me. I am finding true happiness in him and trusting God to never forsake me. If my eyes are not on him, it means that my trust is in something else. My focus is wandering to an alternative, something I believe will protect me, or at least bring me a little happiness and contentment. What is your dainty? Anything that takes your eyes off Jesus is a distraction. Dainties are wonderful, but be careful. Take refuge in Jesus. He is the only source of true satisfaction.

May 24

Michener Books and Chasing After the Wind

*The conclusion, when all has been heard, is:
fear God and keep His commandments,
because this applies to every person.*
Ecclesiastes 12:13 (NASB)

James A. Michener was an American author who wrote more than forty books. Most of them were family sagas covering the lives of many generations. Detailed history was incorporated into each of the stories. His first book, *Tales of the South Pacific,* won the Pulitzer Prize for fiction. Later on, it was adapted into the popular Broadway musical *South Pacific* by Rodgers and Hammerstein. My personal favorite Michener books include *Chesapeake, Alaska,* and *Texas.* What an incredible talent this man had in writing books! Solomon, king of ancient Israel, is another famous author. In fact, he has been acclaimed as one of the most prolific writers of all time. There has never been anyone like him in terms of his knowledge, wisdom, and search for the truth.

In the book of Ecclesiastes, Solomon tells his story. He was the King of Israel, prophet of God, and responsible for the building of the temple. Everything he did resulted in success. He had power and authority, fame and fortune, talents and skills, artistry, and best of all—wisdom. He had it all! Yet Solomon was not happy. He allowed his success to turn his heart away from the Lord. He chose to enjoy life to the fullest, but only for his own gratification. In his own words, Solomon said he was "chasing after the wind."

Jesus said, "I have come to give you life—life to the fullest." That means that Jesus makes our lives new and abundant, rich and satisfying. Trusting in the Lord for salvation gives us access to all kinds of riches that only come with a friendship with Jesus. If you don't know Christ, it doesn't matter how smart you are, how athletic you are, how wealthy you are, or how famous you are. In the end, it is all "chasing after the wind" without him. It took Solomon a long time to figure that out, but he finally did. When all was said and done, this was his conclusion: "Fear God and keep His commandments." Take it from Solomon, this is what life is all about!

May 25

Can You See?

*You have given a banner to those who fear You,
That it may be displayed because of the truth.*
Psalm 60:4 (NASB)

"O say can you see" is the opening phrase of "The Star-Spangled Banner" written by Francis Scott Key in 1814. He wrote these inspiring lyrics on the back of a letter. What inspired him? It was the sight of the American flag after Britain's bombardment of Fort McHenry. The Star-Spangled Banner was still standing in the morning after a long night of fighting. This banner represented the hope and freedom America offers its citizens. It represented the ideas and grand truths that we still celebrate today.

The God who rules all nations has given a banner too, to those who fear him. That banner represents something greater than one country. God's banner represents his worldwide kingdom. It is the banner of truth. Where do we find this banner of truth? In the pages of the Bible, God's Holy Word.

God has given the truth to those who fear him. We can celebrate God's truths because they are the source of eternal life, hope, and freedom. We can also *display* God's truths. Everyone needs to hear what Jesus Christ has done! He created this amazing world and filled it with awesome human beings. He stayed close to those human beings, even though every one of us has turned away from him and sinned. Finally, he came down personally and sacrificed his life to pay for our sins, so we could be forgiven. Now he offers people hope and freedom when they trust their lives to him. Jesus wants you to come to him for refuge. He wants you to turn to him for forgiveness, now and forever. And he wants you to lift him high for everyone to see.

Jesus was willing to be bombarded by the sins of the world, but three days later, he emerged victorious from his long night of death. Do you see Jesus now "by the dawn's early light"? He is the Light of the World, the Way to God, the truth, and eternal life.

May 26

Signet Rings

And you also were included in Christ when you heard the word of truth, the gospel of your salvation. Having believed, you were marked in him with a seal, the promised Holy Spirit, who is a deposit guaranteeing our inheritance until the redemption of those who are God's possession—to the praise of his glory.
Ephesians 1:13-14 (NIV)

Signet rings have been around for thousands of years. Wealthy men used these rings to seal correspondence or legal documents. The signet ring was different from other rings because it had an engraved or raised symbol on top that identified the owner. This could have been a name, initials, a title, or even a family crest. Whatever it was, the symbol identified the person and distinguished him from everyone else. The owner of the ring would seal the document by pressing his ring into melted sealing wax, making a permanent mark on the legal document or letter. This mark confirmed that the document was authentic.

Today, signet rings have been replaced by signatures. When you sign a legal document, a notary is required to be there to positively identify you and to witness the signing of the document itself. When this is done, the notary signs the document and stamps it with his official seal. The seal verifies that the signature is authentic. Verification is what these verses in Ephesians are all about.

Our status as believers has given us a new identity and a new inheritance. When you hear the word of truth and believe it, you are "included in Christ" and "marked in him with a seal, the promised Holy Spirit." In the very moment that you trust in Jesus, the Holy Spirit identifies you as God's possession and comes to dwell in you. God himself testifies that you are in his family. He has put a deposit on your life guaranteeing your inheritance as his own and that eternity with him is guaranteed. Signet rings and notaries serve an important purpose in our world, but the Holy Spirit of God dwelling in your heart is an indisputable guarantee. You are now a marked man or woman, a marked boy or girl! This truth calls for praise of our glorious God!

May 27

Left Behind

*And those who know Your name will put their trust in You,
For You, O Lord, have not forsaken those who seek You.*
Psalm 9:10 (NASB)

When the Vietnam War ended in 1973, there were still over a thousand Americans missing in action. Veteran groups committed themselves to making sure every American soldier was accounted for. POW bracelets engraved with the rank, name, and loss date were created to make sure no one was forgotten. Grieving families, friends, and the nation expected this. Nobody wants to be abandoned, left behind, or forgotten. This verse in Psalm 9 addresses the importance of God's name and assures us that he will never forget ours.

Names are important because they identify us and help people remember who we are. A name signifies a real person. Knowing the names of the Lord helps us know who he is and what he can do. He is all-powerful, all-knowing, all-wise, and omnipresent. He is sovereign and always keeps his promises. These attributes of God help us to trust him when life is difficult. And this verse tells us, "You, O Lord, have not forsaken those who seek you." Do you ever wonder if people will move on after you're gone, that you will be forgotten? Well, just remember that God will never forget you, abandon you, or forsake you. Your name is on his bracelet and in his heart. You will live forever in his presence! God knows you. You will never be left behind!

May 28

Sciatica Pain

*The Lord is good to those who wait for Him,
to the person who seeks Him.*
Lamentations 3:25 (NASB)

Over the last several years, I have started hearing about sciatica pain. Friends would tell me how awful this pain is. But it wasn't until I experienced it myself that I came to understand the full magnitude of this terrible back condition. Sciatic pain typically starts in the lower back and runs down the leg all the way to the bottom of your feet. It comes upon you suddenly and is agonizingly uncomfortable. It's like your body is screaming out to let you know that there is something terribly wrong! The worst thing about sciatica is there is nothing you can do to completely eliminate your discomfort. Your body seems to be solidly in control of the situation, so you just have to wait it out. For a person like me, this is difficult. I have a schedule to meet, and I don't have time to sit around and wait for my body to catch up with me. Do you get what I'm saying? Waiting is the hardest thing to do, and it is what I want you to consider in our verse for today.

The prophet Jeremiah, who wrote the book of Lamentations, began his ministry knowing that the message God wanted him to preach would be rejected by the people. His message was that God's people weren't being faithful to him. In fact, they had forgotten all about him. They had turned away from him to worship worthless idols which had never done even one good thing for them. God had blessed his people, protected them, and done miracles for them, but all they did was rebel against him.

Jeremiah knew the people wouldn't want to hear a message like that, and he would be ridiculed and persecuted. He also knew that if the people repented and turned back to God, God would forgive them and keep all his promises to them. God would never leave or forsake his people because he loved them so much. Jeremiah knew that God's love would convince them in the end. He knew the Lord is good to those who wait for him, for the person who seeks him.

    We, too, are called to seek God, to hope and to trust in him. This is my prayer for you today. If you have turned away from God, turn back. Search for him. He isn't far from you at all. I promise that if you go to him, you will never regret it. He is kind and gracious. He will be good to you.

May 29

Facebook

For the Lord has heard the voice of my weeping.
The Lord has heard my supplication, the Lord receives my prayer.
Psalm 6:8-9 (NASB)

Facebook gives us a good opportunity to update family and friends with all our current news. It even allows us to brag about our grandchildren! Recent studies confirm that Facebook profiles are an excellent way to boost your self-esteem without the risk of disclosing what is really in your heart, where you may be seriously hurting. We hide our hurts inside where no one can see that we are weeping. So Facebook becomes a facade by which we choose what we want others to know. But the verses for today do the opposite thing. King David opens his heart for everyone to see. He says that God has heard the voice of his weeping, that God knows exactly how he is feeling deep inside his heart.

Even though you may not acknowledge your hurts to others, you can trust that God hears it all: your crying, moaning, whimpering and sobbing, your supplications, and your prayers. The Holy Spirit understands what your tears are communicating. No words are needed, but it's always good to talk things over with him. He receives your prayers without criticism. He is sensitive to every tear, every request. He hears it loud and clear. We can take comfort in this fact: we have a Savior who weeps with us and receives our prayers without scorn or rebuke. No other person and certainly no Facebook page will ever do this for us!

May 30

Raising the White Flag

Do you not know? Have you not heard? The Everlasting God, the Lord, the Creator of the ends of the earth Does not become weary or tired. His understanding is inscrutable. He gives strength to the weary, and to him who lacks might He increases power.
Isaiah 40:28-29 (NASB)

Have you ever heard an exasperated parent say, "I'm raising the white flag"? This phrase means "I give up" or "I surrender." Actually, a white flag is an internationally recognized sign for ceasefire or to symbolize surrender. Raising the white flag is a sign that you feel totally overwhelmed or defeated. As parents, it seems like some days will never end. Cleaning messes, changing diapers, and negotiating fights are all normal routine. Total exhaustion is why so many parents get discouraged. The book of Isaiah gives us some helpful pointers to encourage us when we feel like we can't go on.

It is so easy for us to focus on the temporary and not on the eternal. By the time it is lunch time you have already changed three diapers, cleaned up spilled milk, and washed crayon marks off the wall. These temporary tasks are mandatory. Although it would be nice to sit on the porch reading the Bible or listening to music, it's not going to happen. The temporary is winning the war. But what happens if you change the mix? Maybe you get one minute to reflect on a Bible verse like Isaiah 40:28-29. You are reminded again of that which is eternal. This is how you combat discouragement. The good news in the Bible is given for the weary. Look to God's Word, and you will never need to raise the white flag.

May 31

Dachau Liberated

When the Lord brought back the captive ones of Zion, We were like those who dream. Then our mouth was filled with laughter and our tongue with joyful shouting; Then they said among the nations, "The Lord has done great things for them."
Psalm 126:1-2 (NASB)

On April 29, 1945, the US Army liberated Dachau, the first concentration camp established by the German Nazi regime. We will never fully grasp the feelings of these overworked, starving Jewish survivors. I imagine they must have thought the whole thing was a dream. But then their dream dissolved into joy and laughter. This transfer from captivity to euphoria is the picture you see in Psalm 126.

Every person is in captivity until he is rescued by Christ. We are captive to our own sinful nature and to the devil, who wants to destroy our lives. We are held in captivity by our doubts, our rebellion, our fears, and by the appalling love we have for our own pet sins. We want to be free; we even dream of being free. But we can't free ourselves; we need to be rescued. Jesus is the Savior, and he has a rescue plan. He wants to do great things for us. He is our ticket to freedom. He gives us the power to turn from our sin and the faith to receive his free gift of salvation. Is this true? Are you dreaming? No! It might feel like a dream, but when Jesus saves you, your dreams of forgiveness and freedom will come true. Then your mouth will be filled with laughter and your tongue with joyful shouting. God is waiting to do great things for you!

June 1

Golf, a Game of Contradictions

*I know that my Redeemer lives, and that in the end he will stand upon the earth. And after my skin has been destroyed, yet in my flesh I will see God; I myself will see him with my own eyes—
I, and not another. How my heart yearns within me!*
Job 19:25-27 (NIV)

A contradiction occurs when two statements on a topic cannot both be true at the same time. The problem is that some statements might *appear* to be contradictions when they are actually both true! If you have ever played golf, you will understand what I am saying. A good golf mentor will tell you that if you want to hit it hard, then you swing easy. If you want the ball to go up, you hit down on the ball. The tighter you grip the club, the less control you tend to have. If you make an adjustment in your swing and fail to make a corresponding opposite adjustment, the swing will go the wrong way. Are these statements true? Or are they contradictions? What we're missing here are some physics principles. If we could understand how physics works, the contradictions would disappear, showing that the statements are actually true. These supposed golf contradictions are good examples of what the prophet Job faced at a critical time in his life.

During this time, Job went through incredible suffering that most of us will never face. His friends counseled him by blaming him. "It's all your fault," they said. "You are the problem!" But their allegations contradicted *spiritual* principles Job knew about himself and about God. One principle was that he served a living God, who knew the truth about Job's innocence. Another was the fact that God was his Redeemer and would rescue him in the end. Things were tough right then. But even if Job was never vindicated in this life, even if he died, and his body was destroyed, he would someday stand again in his new body and see God face to face. Sometimes human eyes tell us something that contradicts the truth. Job's heart longed for the day when his Redeemer would stand with him and all seeming contradictions would be resolved—forever!

June 2

Who Are We Waiting For?

And it will be said in that day,
"Behold, this is our God for whom we have waited that He might save
us. This is the Lord for whom we have waited;
Let us rejoice and be glad in His salvation."
Isaiah 25:9 (NASB)

It seems like we are always waiting for something. We wait for graduation, then for a spouse, then a career, and then retirement. Why do we wait? Because there really is no other choice! We believe if we just wait, we will find contentment and joy in the end. But what happens when our expectations are not met? This is the case for most of us, isn't it? Life is full of twists and turns. Sometimes we get things we never expected. The prophet Isaiah expresses our situation.

God's people, in Isaiah's time, were waiting for the Messiah to come with salvation. He would forgive their sins and give them new life that would last for eternity. This new life would be better than anything else they might be waiting for. Knowing Jesus would fulfill all their expectations. Walking through life with Jesus would make them rejoice and be glad. Now, the waiting is over. Jesus has come, and no matter what else we're waiting for, he is the one who never disappoints. Knowing Christ gives us joy and makes us glad. The good news is that you don't need to wait for Jesus. Jesus is waiting for you!

June 3

Holding Hands

The steps of a man are established by the Lord, and He delights in his way. When he falls, he will not be hurled headlong, Because the Lord is the One who holds his hand.
Psalm 37:23-24 (NASB)

One of my wife's favorite memories involves our youngest daughter. She always wanted to hold hands when crossing the street or doing anything else. She would say, "You are my best, best, best, best, best, best friend." Holding hands is a sign of friendship and affection. This gesture is also one of God's many promises to us.

Our lives are not determined by fate but by Providence. God knows every step we take. He knows what is in your heart. If you trust in the Lord, he holds your hand. Since he is completely plugged in to your life, he is always active and never surprised. God knows all of your difficulties, struggles, and fears. When he promises that he will watch over you, he means it. He led by example all the way to the cross. Then in God's power he was raised from the dead. So when Jesus takes your hand, you know he is your best, best, best, best, best, best friend.

June 4

Whisper Game

O You who hear prayer, to You all men come.
By awesome deeds You answer us in righteousness,
O God of our salvation.
Psalm 65:2, 5 (NASB)

If you have ever played the whisper game, you will know how funny this game can be. You can play this game with several people or as many as you would like. A line is formed with all the players, and the first person in line will whisper a message into the ear of the second person in line. The next person will then whisper the same message into the ear of the third person. This continues until it reaches the last person in line. The last person in the line will then tell the entire group what the message is. I guarantee that the message the last person hears will never be the same as the one the first person whispered. So what is the point? Our hearing is often faulty, especially when we whisper. But thank goodness we have a God who hears all of our prayers exactly and never makes any mistakes.

You may not think that God hears you when you pray, but we know from this verse that he does! He hears every single prayer whether it is a thought, a whisper, or a shout! God promises his children that he hears it all and cares about everything happening in their lives because he loves them.

Now comes the best part of our verses for today. God answers us "in righteousness." Wait, are you telling me that God hears every prayer I send to him and that he answers every one of my requests? Yes, God loves you so much that he is going to give you an answer. His answer might not be what you expected. It might even challenge your behavior, require a change, or command you to do something you never thought possible, but it is always right, intended for your blessing and God's glory. I don't always know what is best for my life, but I'm thankful that God does. He only gives me what is best for my ultimate happiness and holiness. This truth is something to get excited about. When you are praying or reading God's word, God might whisper a good idea, a bit of wisdom, or an action in your heart. You will know when that happens. You can be certain that his message to you is true, and as long as what you are hearing agrees with biblical truth, you are good to go! That's because God's messages in the Bible never change and are always true—even when they go through all the people in your line!

June 5

Cities of Refuge

But let all who take refuge in you rejoice;
let them ever sing for joy, and spread your protection over them,
that those who love your name may exult in you.
Psalm 5:11 (ESV)

According to Old Testament law, anyone who committed a murder was to be put to death. For unintended deaths, however, God reserved six cities to which a killer could run for protection from "the avenger." These cities were designated as "cities of refuge." If someone was accused of murder, he could flee to one of these cities where he would be protected from retaliation and given a proper trial. If the evidence at the trial showed that the accused killed the person unintentionally, and did not intend to harm him, he would be sent back to the city of refuge for protection because he was not deserving of death. But if the evidence proved that the accused person killed his neighbor intentionally, the elders of his town would hand him over to the avenger for execution.

An accused but innocent person would be able to live under protection in the city of refuge until the death of the high priest. After that he was free to return safely and without fear to his own property. Cities of refuge were located throughout the country to avoid the shedding of innocent blood in the nation of Israel.

Cities of refuge point us to Jesus Christ. He is the person we can run to for protection from Satan, who pursues us and wants to destroy our souls. The problem is that we are all guilty of thousands of crimes against God and against each other, and we deserve to die. But God, in his love and mercy, doesn't want us to die, so he offers the perfect solution to our problem—Jesus Christ. If we run to Jesus, he will protect us from our avenger, Satan. Jesus himself took the penalty for every crime, every sin, I have ever committed. When I flee to Jesus for asylum, he spreads his protection over me. I am free and no longer counted as guilty. God has forgiven my sin because of what Jesus did on the cross. I can rejoice in what he has done for me. I can sing for joy because my Savior has promised to give me a home in heaven—the ultimate refuge from fear and death. This refuge is offered to everyone, but it is only effectual for those who turn from their sin and put their trust in Christ. So flee to Jesus. He is your only hope, your city of refuge. In Christ, you will be safe forever!

June 6

Postcards

O Lord, our Lord, how majestic is your name in all the earth!
You have set your glory above the heavens.
Psalm 8:1 (ESV)

After COVID struck, I started thinking about what I could do to encourage people I know. Sending postcards is one of the things I came up with. A postcard is a powerful tool. It is a quick and efficient way to send a message to another person. It allows you to make a point that is meaningful, sincere, and thoughtful without a lengthy letter. It is simple, unique, and appreciated since most people today never receive anything in the mail except junk. Along with this handwritten note, the receiver gets a picture. It might be a photo of an interesting site you are visiting, a funny picture, or a meaningful statement or quotation. The combination of a genuine note and an interesting illustration makes the postcard a blessing to the person who receives it. I've got to believe that when King David wrote Psalm 8:1, his note was like a postcard and a blessing to God as well.

This psalm was specifically addressed to the Lord. He is also called "Jehovah," and this name is referenced over 6,000 times in the Bible. King David's message is sincere and meant only for him. "Lord, how majestic is your name in all the earth!" You are awesome. You excel in everything you do. You are magnificent and exalted the world over! If these words were written on a postcard, God could have turned it over and seen a picture of the most brilliant stars with the moon overhead. That would have made a great postcard to God!

Would you like to know something? Another "postcard" has been sent. This time, it's from Jesus Christ to you. He is the one who loves you and is so kind to you. He is the one whose majesty is everywhere on display. Along with his picture is a personal invitation for you to come to him. Have you turned to Jesus Christ? Is he your Lord?

One last thing: your postcard is signed, "Love, Jesus"!

June 7

Vineyard Keeper

The Lord will protect you from all evil; He will keep your soul.
The Lord will guard your going out and your coming in
From this time forth and forever.
Psalm 121:7-8 (NASB)

Until the 1950s, there was a job in Europe called a "vineyard keeper." This job was temporary since it was only necessary during the season when the grapes ripened. However, it was a very important job. The keeper never took a weekend off or went on vacation. He was always "on duty." Duties included guarding the vineyards and protecting them from theft. The biggest enemy was the birds, who were always hovering, waiting to dip down and steal the fruit. If the keeper did not do his job well, the harvest would be destroyed, and the owner would not be pleased. This critical job is the focus of Psalm 121.

The keeper we are talking about here is the Lord, who made heaven and earth. His vineyard consists of all his children. Their purpose is to produce good fruit. The Lord is watching over and protecting every one of his children. He is on duty 24/7, every day of the year. His job is to keep their souls and guard against their predator, the devil. The Lord is so meticulous that he watches his child's every move from the time he "plants" him until the time he takes his soul to heaven. These are incredible promises to God's children. If you belong to Christ, wherever you go, he is protecting you, keeping your soul safe, and guarding your life. Understanding this promise is an encouragement to us when we are dealing with a worldwide pandemic that is attempting to steal our peace of mind. Every day, you can be mindful of the only keeper who will protect your soul forever. This will bring you joy as you journey through life.

June 8

Gifts

Thanks be to God for His indescribable gift!
2 Corinthians 9:15 (NASB)

When I purchase a gift for someone, I think long and hard about what will make him happy. Is my gift something he will value? Or will he just say, "Thanks!" because it's the polite thing to do? Is it a gift with no strings attached? Is it unexpected and a surprise? We spend a lot of time picking out just the right gift so the person we love will enjoy it. I think the apostle Paul, who wrote today's verse, was challenging us to thank God for the most incredible gift anyone could ever receive.

God set the standard when it comes to giving gifts. His gift to mankind is described in this verse as "indescribable"! God's indescribable gift was unexpected and has no strings attached to it. It is free for anyone who wants it, and its value is priceless. His gift, of course, is Jesus Christ, our Savior! It was the gift of Jesus' very own life, given so that you can live forever! This is a gift that only God could give. Jesus took every sin that weighs us down and makes us guilty, and he paid the price to make us forgiven and free. This precious gift demonstrates how much he loves us and wants us for his own.

Here's something else: when you receive God's indescribable gift, it's so big, you can share it with others who need his forgiveness too. This gift will probably be unexpected. Most people think they have everything they need. But the news you share will be just the right thing—the most incredible gift they could ever receive. Be generous! Share the good news! "Thanks be to God for His indescribable gift!"

June 9

The USS *Indianapolis*

*For the wages of sin is death,
but the free gift of God is eternal life in Christ Jesus our Lord.*
Romans 6:23 (ESV)

On July 30, 1945, the USS *Indianapolis* was torpedoed by a Japanese naval submarine. The ship sank in twelve minutes. Of the 1,195 crewmen aboard, approximately 300 men went down with the ship. Over the next four days, the remaining 895 faced exposure, dehydration, saltwater poisoning, and shark attacks. By the time they were found, only 316 men survived. This was the largest loss of life for any US Navy vessel in history. As of this writing, there is only one survivor left from that terrible catastrophe.

That all happened in the past, to the generation fighting World War II. But your generation is going to face life and death situations too, and sooner or later, whether we like it or not, we are all going to die. This fact is a hard pill to swallow, so most people don't like to talk about it. To make matters worse, we are all sinners, and the Bible tells us that the penalty for sin is *eternal* death. That means that not only are we all going to die, but that we need a Savior to rescue us from being separated from God—forever.

The wonderful thing is that we have that Savior in Jesus Christ. He is our hope. God offers forgiveness and eternal life to every generation of mankind. What we need to do is accept his free gift. He has promised to save every person who trusts his life to him. Jesus is throwing out a lifeline to you. The question is, "What are you going to do?"

June 10

A Good Reminder

You are good and do good.
Psalm 119:68 (NASB)

George Mueller was a 19th-century evangelist, missionary, and director of orphan homes in Bristol, England. He and his wife, Mary, were most noted for their work with orphans. Early in their marriage, they started caring for thirty girls. That number quickly grew to 130. By the time their work ended, they had cared for over 10,000 orphans. And the fact that is even more amazing is that they never asked for financial support from anyone, and they never went into debt. They prayed, and God provided for all those orphans! George and Mary were totally committed to their work, and their lives modeled this love. On February 6, 1870, after thirty-nine years of marriage, Mary Mueller died of rheumatic fever. George preached the funeral sermon for his wife not just to praise her, but to give thanks and praise to God. He preached, "I want to magnify the Lord in giving her to me, in leaving her to me so long, and in taking her from me to Himself." He wanted others to ponder the lessons of her life and most of all to see the truth found in Psalm 119:68: "You are good and do good."

The Muellers' relationship was based on their trust in Jesus Christ. They knew that God was good and knew that he only does what is good. They knew that God had blessed their union and that every day God gave them together was proof of his goodness. They made the most of their time together as they served the orphans, prayed together each day, and delighted in each other's love. Despite the fact that Mary struggled all her life with rheumatic fever, she knew the goodness of God. Even in her death, God demonstrated his goodness by releasing her from her suffering body and taking her to heaven to live with him.

This uplifting story is not at all unusual. The Bible and all of history are filled with stories of God's goodness. The ultimate act of his goodness was when he sent his Son, Jesus, to die for our sins. When you talk about the best person who ever lived, you are talking about Jesus.

June 11

Cut the Cord!

The Lord is righteous; He has cut in two the cords of the wicked.
Psalm 129:4 (NASB)

Have you ever heard anyone say, "Cut the cord"? This expression could mean to become independent from your parents and start paying your own bills. It could also mean to cut the umbilical cord with an abusive family member or friend. Most recently it means to cut the cord by canceling your cable or satellite service. These phrases are fairly new. But the Lord has been talking about cutting the cords of the wicked for a long, long time. We can see his cutting skills in Psalm 129.

What cords is God cutting? The Hebrew word for "cords" in this verse refers to ropes that bind the oxen to the plough. Sin destroys your freedom and your joy in life. It makes you a victim. The cords of the wicked are the snares and hidden traps that enslave you. So when God cuts the cords, he is breaking the power and control that sin has over you. The Lord is righteous and is offering you your freedom—freedom to do the right thing. When Jesus died for our sins and rose again, he cut the cords binding us. Will we accept this gift from God? I say, freedom from sin is too good to pass up!

June 12

Communication

*Long ago, at many times and in many ways,
God spoke to our fathers by the prophets,
but in these last days he has spoken to us by his Son.*
Hebrews 1:1-2 (ESV)

Communication is one of mankind's most important activities. People have always looked for ways to communicate with each other. In the past, people met each other in person or wrote notes and letters. Native Americans sent visual messages to each other in the form of smoke signals. When I was growing up, almost everyone sent birthday, anniversary, and Christmas cards. As time went on, people began calling each other on wired telephones they shared with their neighbors. Today we send emails, texts, and tweets on our smartphones and computers. All of these forms of communication satisfy a human need—to stay in touch with friends and relatives. Whether our message is good news or bad, we just want to stay in contact. God built this need in us when he created us because he is the great communicator and wanted a personal relationship with us. Our verse for today is proof of that.

"Long ago, at *many times* and in *many ways*, God spoke to our fathers by the prophets," communicating messages to mankind through symbols, dreams, and visions. He spoke to Moses in a burning bush and to the prophet Isaiah in a vision. God reveals himself through all the natural things he has created. God is always communicating how wonderful and powerful he is and is inviting us into a personal relationship with him.

When Jesus Christ came to earth, God pulled out all the stops. He spoke to us by sending his Son. Jesus was God in human form. He repeated his Father's past messages and explained them more fully. People could actually see Jesus with their own eyes, hear him with their own ears, touch him with their hands, and feel his healing hands when he touched them. Jesus was God's perfect communicator, a messenger of hope and salvation. Eyewitnesses like Matthew, Mark, Luke, and John wrote his words down and described his miracles, making it possible for the whole world to know God personally, to experience his forgiveness, and to be saved. God is still communicating. He's calling you and me and is waiting for our response. And when we respond with repentant hearts and put our trust in him, he doesn't put us on hold or ask if he can call us back. He hears us and welcomes us immediately. God is sending you a message right now. It is the most important message you will ever receive. Don't let his call go to voicemail. Don't tell him you will call him back. Answer his call. He will change your life!

June 13

You Deserve a Break Today

*Your attitude should be the same as that of Christ Jesus;
Who, being in very nature God, did not consider equality with God
something to be grasped, but made himself nothing,
taking the very nature of a servant, being made in human likeness. And
being found in appearance as a man, he humbled himself and became
obedient to death—even death on a cross!*
Philippians 2:5-8 (NIV)

McDonald's "You Deserve a Break Today" marketing campaign was launched in 1971. This catchy little song gives you permission to indulge in a fast-food meal at McDonald's. It encourages you to focus on yourself, relax a little, and let someone else do the work. "I need a break," we tell ourselves. "After all, I work hard and I *deserve* some rest!" We do need to take care of ourselves. But should "focusing on ourselves" be our top priority? Jesus didn't think so. And he is our model!

If anyone deserved a break, it was Jesus! Yet he spent his entire life considering the needs of others more important than his own. Serving his Father and serving humanity were *his* top priorities. Although he was equal with God and of the very same full nature as God, he did not claim any special privileges. He became a man with flesh and blood just like us. He even agreed to suffer and die on a cross, so we could be saved. He sure didn't *deserve* that! Jesus' attitude is refreshing and all too rare in our world today. Our attitude needs to be like his. We need to stop thinking so much about ourselves and start thinking more about others. In the end, God will remember our sacrifices and give us way more than we deserve!

June 14

"We Are Getting Old, Babe!"

Jesus Christ is the same yesterday and today and forever.
Hebrews 13:8 (ESV)

Have you looked in the mirror lately? When I was in my twenties, I ate just about anything I wanted. It seemed like I was always hungry. In my thirties, I noticed that my clothes were getting a little snug here and there. When I reached forty, I thought, "You know? My hairline seems to be receding—a little." At fifty, I had to go up to the next size for my pants. I was sure clothing manufacturers had snuck around and adjusted their sizes! When I reached sixty, I was suddenly surprised to see a big bald spot on my head. If that weren't enough, my legs and even my whole body seemed disturbingly stiff when I got up in the morning. Now that I'm in my seventies, the changes are coming quicker and are a little more discouraging. Even my lovely wife recognizes what's happening to me. She made me face a sad truth the other day when she said, "We are getting old, Babe!"

While our physical bodies are changing rapidly, the verse for today is super-encouraging. It tells us about someone who never changes. "Jesus Christ is the same yesterday and today and forever." Do we realize what that means? It means a lot of important things. For one, Jesus' body will never get old and feeble. He will never say, "I'd really like to help you, but I just can't do it. I'm too old." For another, he will never change his mind and say, "You know, I'm kind of tired of you. You're always messing up. I've decided not to be your Savior anymore." He doesn't change physically because he's immortal, and he doesn't change mentally because he is immutable. "Immutable" is a fancy word, but a good one to remember. Jesus' unchanging nature gives you complete assurance that he will never leave you or forsake you. Every promise he gives in the Bible is sure to come to pass.

I can't imagine what my life would be like if I didn't know this one true thing: "Jesus Christ is the same yesterday and today and forever"! Have you put yourself in his unchanging hands? Don't wait too long. We are getting old, friend!

June 15

Joints and Marrow

For the word of God is alive and active.
Sharper than any double-edged sword,
it penetrates even to dividing soul and spirit, joints and marrow;
it judges the thoughts and attitudes of the heart.
Hebrews 4:12 (NIV)

Osteology is the study of bones. If you were to study a bone, you would discover that it consists of three parts. The marrow is the very core of the bone. It is the spongy tissue where most of the red blood cells are produced. Bone cells surround the marrow. That is where the blood vessels are found. The last part is the outside membrane, which is a very hard substance called the periosteum. If you tried to slice between these three parts, it would be almost impossible, since they are fused together. It can be done, but only with the very sharpest knife or tool.

The book of Hebrews uses the example of joints and marrow to point out the power of God's word. Notice what the verse says: "the word of God is alive and active." It comes straight from the mind of God and is found in the Bible. Nothing God says is outdated or archaic. His words are meant for you and me, today. In this verse, the word of God is compared to a double-edged sword that is so sharp and so penetrating that it can divide your soul and spirit like a surgeon's scalpel divides a person's joints and marrow.

This verse also says that God's word is so powerful that it "judges the thoughts and attitudes of the heart." This is what we call "conviction of sin," and it can be a little scary. Our thoughts, our stinky attitudes, and everything we've been hiding are exposed to God's judgment. But God's surgery is actually our only hope! God is finding our sin and, in his love, he's cleaning it out. This only happens, of course, if we trust him and are willing to submit to his two-edged sword, his word. Trusting and submitting to Jesus' work in your life will save you from your sins. Remember, he loves you all the way down to the "joints and marrow" of your soul.

June 16

The Wheel of Fortune

But you, O Lord, reign forever;
your throne endures to all generations.
Lamentations 5:19 (ESV)

In 1975, Pat Sajak and Vanna White became the host and hostess of a popular television game show called *Wheel of Fortune*. The concept for this game is thousands of years old. In ancient cultures, the wheel of fortune symbolized the fickle nature of fate. The goddess Fortuna owned the wheel and would spin it at random, indifferent to the serious changes it would make in people's lives. For some, her spin could mean good luck; for others, it could mean misfortune. Fortuna didn't care; it was all just a game to her. This view of life, that things happen by chance, and that your personal fate has been determined by some impersonal force, still shapes human lives today. Many people see themselves as victims of fate, especially when the wheel spins and stops at "bankrupt." Many lives have been bankrupted by a belief in the power of fate! But is fate real? Does Fortuna exist? Is your life impacted by a mysterious, impersonal force? Jeremiah, the prophet, gave the answer to these questions in our verse for today.

The Lord reigns forever! God is the King of the universe. He isn't careless or indifferent. He is powerful and good. He's personal, and he cares about you. He is meticulously involved with the details of your life. These facts about God never change because God never changes. He's not fickle. He's immutable. As king of the universe, he is in control of all situations and uses them to call out to you to be saved, to be strong, to be at peace with him and your circumstances. Fate is a lie that will bankrupt your life. God is the truth and will make your life rich and full. God has a purpose for you, and when he sits on the throne of your heart, he will help you accomplish that purpose. Because God cares and never changes, because he knows your life is not just a game, you can know for certain that you are precious. Although Pat and Vanna make a good living spinning the wheel every day, their show will one day end. But the reign of the Lord will last forever!

June 17

Little White Lies

*O Lord God of Israel, You are righteous,
for we have been left an escaped remnant, as it is this day;
behold, we are before You in our guilt,
for no one can stand before You because of this.*
Ezra 9:15 (NASB)

*There are six things the LORD hates, seven that are detestable to him:
haughty eyes, a lying tongue, hands that shed innocent blood, a heart
that devises wicked schemes, feet that are quick to rush into evil, a false
witness who pours out lies and a person who stirs up conflict in the
community.*
Proverbs 6:16-19 (NIV)

Have you ever told a little white lie? *The Merriam-Webster Dictionary* defines one this way: a little white lie is "a lie about a small or unimportant matter that someone tells to avoid hurting another person." *The American Heritage Dictionary of the English Language* definition says it is "an often trivial, diplomatic or well-intentioned untruth." These definitions bring a question to my mind. How do we know for sure what is right and wrong? Who determines what is true? If we look around at our world today, it looks like people are choosing their own truths. People want to decide for themselves what is right and wrong. But the book of Ezra in the Bible tells us something different.

Here is the unvarnished truth: God is the one who determines what is right and wrong, and he is always right. If we want to know the truth, we must take a serious look at Proverbs 6:16-19. God says there that he hates lies—even the little white ones.

God never sugarcoats the truth, but we do. We make excuses, so we can feel good and justify ourselves. But if we make excuses, we are fooling ourselves. We are guilty before God, caught in sins that are detestable to him. If we believe that we can stand before this righteous God, we are sadly mistaken. When we see this truth, we are so thankful for what Jesus did for us on the cross. When we confess our sins to God, we are admitting our guilt and asking God for his mercy. This is how a person finds forgiveness and receives eternal salvation.

June 18

"Script Ohio"

*The pride of your heart has deceived you,
you who live in the clefts of the rock, in your lofty dwelling,
who say in your heart, "Who will bring me down to the ground?"
Though you soar aloft like the eagle, though your nest is set among the
stars, from there I will bring you down, declares the Lord.*
Obadiah 1:3-4 (ESV)

I was born and raised in Ohio for the first eighteen years of my life. This is where I learned about the intense football rivalries in the Big Ten Conference. Every Saturday we would watch a Big Ten football game and be entertained by our favorite marching band as they performed the traditional "Script Ohio." As the band played and marched across the football field, it would spell out the word "Ohio." The grand finale came when a lone sousaphone player marched onto the field to dot the *i*. By that time, the fans would be cheering in a frenzied state of excitement. Like the Ohio fans who took pride in their team and traditions, the nation of Edom took pride in its geographical location.

The nation of Edom was located in the high hills of Israel. The rocks are rough there. The peaks are almost inaccessible and are separated by deep gorges. The Edomites believed that their lofty position would keep them secure and that they had enough fields to provide food to make them self-sufficient. They were full of pride and thought they were invincible. But God had a different opinion.

The Hebrew word for *pride* comes from a verb that means "to boil up or seethe." The people in Edom were seething with pride. After a while, this pride boiled up into reckless arrogance, and they began attacking the nations around them relentlessly—especially the nation of Israel. They were ruthless and had no pity for God's people. They were sure they could get away with this aggression because of their superior location. They said in their hearts, "Who will bring us down to the ground?"

But God loved Israel and answered bluntly, "I will bring you down!" And God did bring Edom down. Nations Edom thought were their friends formed an alliance, pillaged Edom, and killed all the people there. The nation of Edom eventually disappeared. Pride destroys people and nations. Repentance and humility bring blessings from God. In the big picture, dotting the *i* in "Ohio" is not that important. However, trusting in the Lord is absolutely essential for eternal life!

June 19

Juneteenth

Therefore if you have been raised up with Christ, keep seeking the things above, where Christ is, seated at the right hand of God. Set your mind on the things above, not on the things that are on earth.
Colossians 3:1-2 (NASB)

In 2021, Juneteenth became a federal holiday in the United States. June 19, 1865 was the exact date when Union General Gordon Granger stood in Galveston, Texas posting an order to all the citizens that "all slaves are free." Even though President Abraham Lincoln had already issued his Emancipation Proclamation that legally freed three and a half million enslaved people in Confederate states, it was not until federal troops arrived to occupy Galveston that black men and women in Texas were given their first taste of freedom. This directive was only the beginning of this newfound status.

You will find a similar situation when you look at Paul's letter to the Colossians. These verses are an encouragement for Christ-followers who "have been raised up with Christ." These are the people who have accepted God's invitation. They are now in God's family. They have been given their spiritual freedom. They are no longer enslaved to a life of sin. They are free to pursue their new life and to enjoy the forgiveness and blessings they have in Jesus Christ.

But these Colossian believers found their new status hard to grasp. They struggled with God's life-changing truths. Paul's advice was to "keep seeking the things above, where Christ is, seated at the right hand of God." Seeking after Jesus is the key. This is where you find true freedom.

What occupies your thinking? Are you spending the bulk of your time on things that are only temporary? Or are you looking to your future home in heaven? What are you going to do? "Set your mind on the things above, not on the things that are on earth."

June 20

Mother Teresa

You are fairer than the sons of men; grace is poured upon Your lips; Therefore God has blessed You forever.
Psalm 45:2 (NASB)

Mother Teresa was an incredible woman! She was a nun and missionary who spent most of her life working with the poor in Calcutta, India. Her work with the destitute and dying earned her a Nobel Peace Prize. She wasn't perfect, but most people described her as a godly person because of her gracious words, sacrificial deeds, and all the love she poured out on so many people during her lifetime. Psalm 45 tells us about another person, who was prophesied in the Old Testament and then revealed in the New Testament as the very Son of God. Jesus Christ is that person. He *was* perfect, and in his perfection, he changed the world!

This verse describes Jesus as "fairer than the sons of men." Does this mean that Jesus was more handsome than anyone else? No, actually the Bible says, "He had no beauty or majesty to attract us to him, nothing in his appearance that we should desire him" (Isaiah 53:2 NIV). Physical beauty wasn't what made Jesus so special. It was the character of Jesus that made him fairer, more beautiful, than any person who has ever lived. The Hebrew word for "fairer" is actually doubled in this verse. It means Jesus' words and conduct were "fairer" to the max, perfect in every way. Jesus was the only person who never sinned, who met all of God's standards perfectly. There has never been anyone else like him.

Why is this so important? Because if Jesus had sinned, he would have his own guilt to pay for. He could never have paid for anyone else's sins. But because he was perfect, he was able to pay for your sins and mine. Those who trust in Christ's atonement are considered not guilty, fit to escape the judgment of God, and free to live with him forever. Jesus' perfect character and stunning sacrifice are reasons we love him so much, and God has blessed him forever.

June 21

Waiting for a Reunion

*Let the heavens be glad, and let the earth rejoice;
Let the sea roar, and all it contains; let the field exult,
and all that is in it. Then all the trees of the forest will sing
for joy before the Lord, for He is coming, For He is coming to
judge the earth. He will judge the world in righteousness
And the peoples in His faithfulness.*
Psalm 96:11-13 (NASB)

When I was a young soldier, my wife and I had many reunions. I was away so often. Sometimes I would be gone for a month without any communication (This, of course, was before cell phones and emails).

Waiting for these reunions brought excitement, joy, and relief as we reunited. Our promise to wait for each other was fulfilled. In Psalm 96, we see the excitement of creation as it awaits the return of Jesus Christ to Earth.

When Jesus comes back, he will dispose of everything bad and replace it with everything that is good. There won't be any more pollution in the sky or destruction on Earth. There will be no more toxins in our soil or pesticides that make us sick. The trees will be healthy and produce good fruit. All of creation will be glad and will rejoice in anticipation of his coming. The wait will be over. The mission to save us—complete! We will live in freedom without the fear of death. Everything will be made right again as the world stands before God. The bottom line is that he is coming. Will you be there? Will you sing for joy?

June 22

Bivouac

*The angel of the Lord encamps around
those who fear Him, and rescues them.*
Psalm 34:7 (NASB)

As soldiers in an infantry unit, we would frequently go on training operations. The training would last for several weeks. Living away from the military post, we would bivouac. A bivouac is an encampment of soldiers in the open air without tents. We remained in combat gear with our weapons during the duration of the entire training exercise, always under the vigilant eye of our commander. This state of readiness demanded our constant attention if we were to be successful. The same type of watchfulness is what we see in this passage in Psalm 34.

This verse is a promise for all those who fear or trust in the Lord. The angel of the Lord is Jesus Christ himself. When Jesus came to Earth, he was in bivouac. He was right there to reach out to the lost, to teach, and to heal. And he is with his people now. He will never leave us to fend for ourselves. The Lord himself encamps around us. He is not a distant commander living in a palace. He is on the ground alongside to rescue us, to protect, serve, and console us. What an encouragement to know that our Commander is watching over us right now!

June 23

Where Do You Want to Be Planted?

Blessed is the man who trusts in the Lord and whose trust is the Lord. For he will be like a tree planted by the water, that extends its roots by a stream And will not fear when the heat comes; but its leaves will be green, And it will not be anxious in a year of drought nor cease to yield fruit.
Jeremiah 17:7-8 (NASB)

The question of where to plant a tree is always important. Do you want the tree to make your yard look beautiful? Do you need more shade? Do you have the right kind of soil? And most importantly, will your tree have access to water? Water is crucial if you want a tree to flourish. Sometimes we forget about that. A tree can't survive without water. Jeremiah likens us to trees in Jeremiah 17.

If you choose to plant a tree in the desert, its chances for life are slim. If you choose to plant a tree by a stream, your tree will flourish. Jesus said, "I am the living water." Every day, you have a choice. Where are you going to plant yourself? By the Living Water, or in the desert of the world's lusts, greed, and power? Will you trust in Jesus, or will you trust in the promises of this world? Remember, if you choose to trust in Jesus, you will flourish. No matter what happens, you won't need to be anxious. Even in a drought, you will still be bearing fruit.

June 24

Friendship

*Be strong and courageous, do not be afraid or tremble at them,
for the Lord your God is the one who goes with you.
He will not fail you or forsake you.*
Deuteronomy 31:6 (NASB)

When I had a stroke many years ago, I understood what fear was all about. I could not understand what was happening at the time and could not communicate my fear to others. Fortunately, my wife completely understood my fears and became my advocate. Because I trusted her, I knew that she wanted what was best for me and would never do anything to harm me. Our relationship is more than a partnership or being a good spouse. It is about a special friendship we share with each other. We have a history together, and we share memories both good and bad. We would be willing to "take a bullet" to save the other. We know that our friendship is authentic and that neither of us would ever fail the other person or abandon our relationship. This type of relationship is what I want you to think about today.

Moses, in his last address, wanted to encourage the Israelite people. He knew huge difficulties were coming, and he knew the Israelites were terrified of the enemies that would come against them. So Moses commanded them, "Be strong and courageous," "for the Lord your God is the one who goes with you." Do you understand this promise? God, the Creator and most powerful force in the universe, "is the one who goes with us." He never fails or forsakes us. He is the one who is stronger than any enemy you will ever face in your life. He is more powerful than conflict, cancer, old age, and even death. These incredible facts about God are a reality for those who commit their lives to him.

What I'm saying is that God is the best friend a person could ever have. Even though God is the King of the universe and could never be compared to created beings like us, he invites us to be close friends with him. Jesus Christ will be your advocate. He will be your commander. He will be your companion as you journey through life. When I consider Jesus' invitation to me, I am simply amazed! This all-powerful God wants to be my friend. Life can be so hard, but God's friendship is what gives us peace, confidence, and courage. His love is what true friendship looks like.

June 25

Resplendent Quetzal

*You are resplendent with light,
more majestic than mountains rich with game.*
Psalm 76:4 (NIV)

The resplendent quetzal is a bird considered among the world's most beautiful because of its colorful plumage. These large birds are an unforgettable sight. They live in the mountainous, tropical forests of Central America. The birds often measure only fourteen inches from their bills to the base of their tails, but their magnificent tails can be another three feet long. The quetzal is Guatemala's national bird and is on its flag. If you ever see one of these birds, you will understand why the adjective *resplendent* is part of its name. The bird is truly impressive and stunning to see. In Psalm 76, the psalmist had only one word to describe God: *resplendent*!

In this verse, one of God's characteristics is compared to the "mountains rich with game." When mountains are rich with game, it means there are many wild animals that can be hunted for food. This is riches, power, and greatness for a man. This is glorious in the eyes of the world. God, however, is described as resplendent. When seeing the mighty acts of God, there is a perfect blending of two qualities: God is both glorious in holiness and excellent because of his deeds done in justice. He is truly impressive to behold.

I have never seen a quetzal bird, nor have I seen Jesus, but I have seen the power of his work to forgive sinners. I have seen his beauty in creation and have seen a person who has been transformed from a life of sin and despair to a life filled with hope in Jesus. This is truly stunning to see. If you want to see what resplendent looks like, I encourage you to examine the claims of Jesus Christ. I guarantee you that you will not be disappointed!

June 26

That's Not Fair!

When God saw what they did and how they turned from their evil ways, he had compassion and did not bring upon them the destruction he had threatened.
Jonah 3:10 (NIV)

Have you ever heard someone say, "That's not fair"? We've all said it, if we are honest with ourselves. Life's not fair. It is filled with many injustices. Children and adults both struggle with this reality every day. So what can we do about it? Are we going to run and hide from our troubles? Are we going to fight? Or do we just feel like giving up? The story of Jonah sheds light on this topic. I think it will encourage you.

Nineveh was a big city, but the people were wicked and violent. God commanded Jonah to go to Nineveh to preach against her sin and to warn the people about his judgment. But Jonah was afraid of the people there. What if they got angry and beat him up or killed him? Jonah was so afraid that he disobeyed God's orders and jumped on a ship going the opposite direction. As you probably know, that idea didn't work out very well! Jonah ended up in a huge storm, got thrown off the ship, and was swallowed by a big fish. It was in the belly of that big fish that he changed his mind and decided to obey God. The next thing Jonah knew, he was being vomited up onto dry land. (Pretty disgusting and a lesson in itself!)

Lying on the beach, Jonah got a second message from the Lord: GO TO NINEVEH! This time, Jonah went and warned the people to repent of their sins or God was going to destroy their city. Surprise! The people of Nineveh didn't kill Jonah; they all believed God and repented. Even the king commanded every person in Nineveh to turn from his wickedness and violence: "Who knows, God may turn and relent and withdraw His burning anger so that we will not perish" (Jonah 3:9 NASB). Sure enough, when God saw that the people of Nineveh turned from their wicked ways, he forgave them and changed his plans to destroy them. He gave them mercy instead of death.

Now comes the clincher to the story. Jonah looked at God's kindness, and guess what he said? THAT'S NOT FAIR! These are terrible people. They don't deserve God's mercy! But let me ask you. Was it fair for Jonah to run away from God? Was it fair for him to get saved from the raging storm and the fish's digestive system? Should he have been thankful for God's kindness and mercy? Here is the gospel: We rebel. God warns. We are sorry and repent. God forgives.

Unbelievable? Yes! Fair? Not really. Just? Yes! God's forgiveness is justified because Jesus took our death sentence and died on the cross in our place. Both Jonah and the wicked people in Nineveh experienced God's grace, and we can too. None of us deserves God's mercy. Our salvation isn't "fair." But I'll accept it. Won't you? It's a gift too good to pass up! Thank God. He is just!

June 27

I Give You My Word

*Even from eternity I am He, and there is none
who can deliver out of My hand; I act and who can reverse it?*
Isaiah 43:13 (NASB)

Have you ever heard someone say, "I give you my word"? This expression is a sort of vow, a way to say "I promise" or "I guarantee that what I'm saying to you will be done." It is usually given in good faith. Unfortunately, things don't always work out as planned. Sometimes, because we are human, we fail to keep our promises. But in Isaiah, we learn that there is one person who never fails.

This person calls himself "I am." He is Yahweh, God. He is the one who existed before creation. He reports to no one. Any action he does cannot be superseded. This means that no one can reverse any decision he makes. No one can undo it, prevent it, hinder it, or turn it back. Everything God does and everything written in the Bible cannot be reversed. The best example is our salvation. When you trust in Jesus for your salvation, his promises to you cannot be reversed. He will never fail to keep his vows. Only Jesus can truly say, "I give you my word."

June 28

Mourning into Dancing

*You have turned for me my mourning into dancing;
You have loosed my sackcloth and girded me with gladness,
That my soul may sing praise to You and not be silent.
O Lord my God, I will give thanks to You forever.*
Psalm 30:11-12 (NASB)

Have you ever had one of those mornings when everything seems to go wrong? Your child throws up on you when you are getting dressed for work? You oversleep and then get caught up in a traffic jam for an important meeting? These little annoyances cloud your day instantly. We get so caught up in the moment that we forget about what is really important in life. King David experienced these same emotions in Psalm 30.

He, like those who trust in the Lord for their salvation, discovered that our brief inconveniences are only a prelude to sustained joy and gladness. We have a God who loves us and only wants what is best for us. He will never give up on us. We have a God who turns our mourning into dancing. And yes, we have a God who takes away our sackcloth and gives us gladness. How could anyone be silent after experiencing Christ's forgiveness and mercy in his life? Forget about mourning, because we have a Savior who wants to dance with us!

June 29

Disambiguation

*The One forming light and creating darkness,
Causing well-being and creating calamity;
I am the Lord who does all these.*
Isaiah 45:7 (NASB)

Do you have any idea what the word "disambiguation" means? It is the act of making something clear. A television remote control offers a good example of this word. If you hold the TV remote, you are clearly the one in control. There is no ambiguity here. You are choosing what show to watch, the volume, and any of the other settings that suit you. You are in control of the entertainment. In Isaiah 45, God makes it absolutely clear who is in control.

The Lord is the one forming light, creating darkness, causing prosperity, and creating calamity. It is the Lord who does this. In other words, He is in control. He is all-knowing, all-powerful, sovereign, just, and merciful. There are no surprises with God. He knew all about COVID before it even hit. He is completely in control of what is happening in our lives. Yes, we would like to think that we have some control to shape outcomes and events to our liking. For those who trust the Savior, who loves us and wants the very best for us, the news is good. Jesus has the remote control of our lives!

June 30

Hatfield-McCoy Feud

*Behold, how good and how pleasant it is for
brothers to dwell together in unity!*
Psalm 133:1 (NASB)

This American feud between two rural families happened along the West Virginia and Kentucky border from 1863 to 1891. The Hatfields of West Virginia were led by William Anderson Hatfield, who fought for the Confederacy in the American Civil War. Most of the McCoy family also fought for the Confederacy. Asa Harmon McCoy, however, joined the Union's 45th Kentucky Infantry on October 20, 1863. He was captured by the Confederates and released to a Union hospital in Maryland after he received a gunshot wound to the chest. The feud started when Asa returned from the war and was murdered by a group of Confederates. Both families blamed each other for the murder, and the result was several years of retaliation. In Psalm 133, feuds are avoided and unity is achieved.

Whenever a Bible verse starts out with the word "behold," you'd better sit up and pay attention! Basically, it means, "Listen up! This is important!" What is the lesson the psalmist wants us to learn? It is good and pleasant for brothers to live together in unity. You might think, "Well, of course, that makes sense." It might make sense, but it's not what usually happens. The truth is that we are always finding ways to disagree with each other. And when we do, many people (even God's people) get angry and stop communicating. We make the mistake of not loving each other—of not wanting the best for each other. How can all of us live together in unity?

Jesus gave the answer when he commanded us to "love one another." It is hatred that divides us; it is God's love that unites us! Here, we see Jesus as the solution to our problem. He can save us from hatred and put God's love in our hearts. As God's people, we can model Jesus' love in our relationships with each other and the rest of the world. Jesus is the Savior. We find unity in him.

July 1

Begging in Baltimore

*Whoever oppresses a poor man insults his Maker,
but he who is generous to the needy honors him.*
Proverbs 14:31 (ESV)

When I drive to Baltimore, I quite often see people on the side of the road begging for money. Unfortunately, my antenna picks up signals and I start asking myself questions. Are these people really poor, or are they just collecting money to purchase alcohol or drugs? Does this person really need money for food and a place to live, or has someone hired him—someone who will take most of the money himself? Do I lock my door and look the other way, or do I roll down my window and give him a dollar? Situations like this are complicated. Are there better ways than handouts to help the poor, or should I take this opportunity and share what I have on hand? In any case, this verse challenges us to look beyond ourselves.

There are valid needs around us every day. When we choose to close our eyes to those who are poor, we insult our maker. He is the maker of both the rich and the poor. He is also the one who has blessed us with the ability to share our blessings with others. God owns everything and uses us to bless others. It is one thing to be careful where we put our money. It is another when we actually oppress the poor by overlooking their needs when God is giving us the opportunity to help, when we spend money with no regard for the needs of the poor, or when we undercut them by not paying them adequately for their work. Oppressing the poor is an insult to God who made them. Being generous to the poor shows that we care what God thinks and are choosing to be generous for his honor and glory. God knows if you are generous or greedy.

It might be a good idea to have a talk with God about how you can contribute to the welfare of people in need. He might surprise you with answers you've never thought of. He might even bring you people who need your help. Will you open your hand to the needy? God has been generous with you. Will you be generous to others? Will you give to others in the name of Christ? If we follow Jesus' example, we will help acquaintances, people on the side of the road, missionaries who need our support, and organizations that stand for truth. We will give to our church. It takes wisdom to know where to start helping and a willing heart to start giving to others. Remember, this is what God requires of you. Generosity honors God.

July 2

Car Restoration

*As for me, I said, "O Lord, be gracious to me;
Heal my soul, for I have sinned against You."*
Psalm 41:4 (NASB)

Have you ever thought about restoring a classic car like a 1966 Chevrolet Corvette, or how about a 1965 Pontiac GTO? It's not easy at all to bring a classic car back to its original state. These cars have lost their luster with plenty of dents, scratches, and scrapes. It takes a lot of work to restore them. It also requires a huge investment in time, know-how, and money. Even if you could make the investment, you would still have to depend on getting substitute parts when you need them. King David never saw a restored 1966 Corvette, but the Bible verse for today sounds a lot like a request for something more important—a restoration of his soul.

David knew he had sinned against Almighty God, and that sin was serious business. God is the King of the universe. Rebelling against the King is treason in the ultimate sense of the word. When we start to understand the gravity of our sin, we begin to understand David's request for healing. He was asking God to forgive him, to restore him, and to repair their relationship. This is what true repentance looks like. It is admitting you have sinned, just like David did in this verse. It means asking God to be gracious to you and to forgive you. It is receiving his forgiveness and being thankful that God is so gracious. It is knowing you are forgiven because God always keeps his promises. Thank goodness God doesn't keep a rap sheet on his children! One of these days we will stand before him. But no worries there. We will stand before him with our new bodies and our new souls totally restored by Jesus Christ!

July 3

Lost and Found

For this son of mine was dead and is alive again;
he was lost and is found.'
So they began to celebrate.
Luke 15:24 (NIV)

Did you know that the most common lost items are keys, cell phones, credit cards, and ID cards? If you have ever lost one of these, you know exactly how it feels. How about losing one of your children in a crowded mall? Yes, that was me! I lost one of my children while shopping at the mall one day. My son was actually hiding in a coat rack and did not respond to my calls. The panic I felt was overwhelming. I started screaming, running around, and crying out to him hoping he would answer. The feeling of loss made me feel crazy. Fortunately, my little one saw my fear, heard the urgency in my voice, and came out of the rack smiling. I didn't know whether to punish him or hug him! All I knew was that I was relieved. I am sure that many of you have also experienced this feeling.

Jesus told three lost-and-found stories. They are recorded in Luke, a book in the New Testament. The three lost items were a sheep, a silver coin, and a beloved son. Each of these stories is easy to relate to. We all know how we feel when we lose something that is precious to us. Jesus' third story, though, is the most striking. It is about a lost child, a son. Jesus is teaching us that each of us is precious to him, but that all of us are lost until he finds us. Many of us are hiding, thinking life is just a game. But Jesus knows the truth. We are in great danger, so he urgently calls out to us. He might be calling out to you right now. It's time to heed his call and come out of hiding! Do you know that when a person comes to Christ, God's angels in heaven celebrate? God the Father celebrates too! We were dead, but now we are alive. We were lost but now we are found!

July 4

Gospel Music

I will sing of lovingkindness and justice, to You,
O Lord, I will sing praises.
Psalm 101:1 (NASB)

Gospel music expresses the struggles and problems we face every day. The lyrics encourage us to trust in Christ's promises. Whenever we combine good music with the gospel, we feel closer in our walk with the Lord. This was the psalmist's desire in Psalm 101.

The focus of this verse is on two of the Lord's attributes—his lovingkindness and his justice. Understanding both of these attributes is the key to a vital relationship with God. It was God's love that caused him to leave the glories of heaven, take on a human body, live as a servant, and die to pay the debt we owe for our sins. And it is God's justice that declares us "not guilty" even though we deserve to be punished. God's justice is satisfied because our penalty is paid! When we sing about this, we are letting God's free gift of salvation marinate in our hearts. The more it marinates, the more we experience the love of God. It's impossible to get enough of his love. So sing praises to the one who is loving and kind, the one who walks with you in your journey through life.

July 5

Capture the Flag

My shield is God Most High, who saves the upright in heart.
Psalm 7:10 (NIV)

Capture the flag was one of my favorite games growing up. This backyard game can actually trace its roots back to the Civil War. Every military unit had a regimental flag with a unique symbol or color that the soldiers could easily spot on the battlefield. In the heat and smoke of the battle, the regimental flag was the rallying point for the soldiers in each unit. It directed soldiers and marked their advances in battle. Enemy soldiers would concentrate their fire onto the standard-bearer (the person holding the flag) because they knew this was the area of primary attack. If that person were hit and the flag went down, another soldier would immediately pick up the flag. If the flag was captured during the battle, every soldier knew the war was over. The regimental flag was a symbol that embodied the honor, spirit, and heritage of each regiment.

As Christians, we have a symbol too. It is not a flag. It is a person. He is known as our rock, our fortress, our deliverer, and our shield. In this verse, we learn that our shield is God Most High.

Each of us is in a spiritual battle. Satan is fighting to control our minds and hearts. If you aren't a believer yet, he wants to control your thoughts and turn you against the God who loves you. The outcome of this war will determine your eternal destiny. It is a life-and-death battle.

If you are a believer, Satan is fighting to control you, too, by putting doubts in your mind and trying to tear you away from your relationship with God. But our shield is God Most High. He is the one we rally to in the heat of battle. He is our protection, the only one who can save us from Satan's power. He will give us strength to be victorious. He will lead us all the way to heaven. Jesus is our standard-bearer. Without a doubt, no one will ever capture his flag!

July 6

Little Tomato Girl

*Let us not lose heart in doing good,
for in due time we will reap if we do not grow weary.*
Galatians 6:9 (NASB)

I think that God must smile when he sees an old man teaching a little girl how to plant tomatoes in a garden. The little girl asks many questions of her PopPop and watches and obeys every command given to her. "You pull out all of the weeds and throw out any rock or branch in the garden. We will till the soil until it is very fine and level it all out. Then we will add some good topsoil and spread a couple of bags of cow manure over the garden." When the little girl understands what cow manure is, she smiles and says, "I want to do it." Once the garden is ready, we go to the local nursery and carefully select the tomato plants she desires. When we come home, she learns how to space each plant, how to dig the holes, how to carefully prepare each plant, and how to water each one thoroughly. Now it is time for God to give the sun and rain. It is God's time to make it grow. The little girl waits and waits until four long months have passed. Then she says what she has been waiting for, "Can I eat this tomato now?" This true story is also our story in the Bible.

If we have trusted in the Lord as our Savior, he does not want us to lose heart in doing good or grow weary of loving people. He knows our weaknesses and doesn't want us to be discouraged and give up hope. He knows that life can be challenging, even very difficult, but he has promised us a positive outcome. It's a lot like my story about the little tomato girl. God must smile when he sees us trusting his promises and not giving up. He must chuckle when we wait and wait and finally reap the rewards of our labors. Maybe he laughs when he sees that little girl popping two or three cherry tomatoes into her mouth—all at once!

July 7

What Haunts You?

Cast all your anxiety on him because he cares for you.
1 Peter 5:7 (NIV)

*Do not be anxious about anything, but in everything,
by prayer and petition, with thanksgiving, present your requests to God.
And the peace of God, which transcends all understanding,
will guard your hearts and your minds in Christ Jesus.*
Philippians 4:6-7 (NIV)

Salvation belongs to the Lord.
Psalm 3:8 (NASB)

Do you ever wake up in the middle of the night worrying? What are you struggling with? Are you angry with someone, or is someone angry with you? Are you worried about that chronic pain you feel or the results of the MRI your doctor ordered? Are you concerned about your mounting financial burdens? How are you going to pay all those bills? Our minds can become completely obsessed with a problem, and in the middle of the night, it just won't go away. It haunts us. We feel hopeless. Our problem seems way too big and impossible to solve. It might not occur to us that God has a solution or that he even cares. Yet this verse tells us to cast all our cares upon God because he cares for us. Another verse like it says that if we trust in God, his peace will guard our hearts and minds in Christ Jesus.

I'll ask you again: do you ever wake up in the middle of the night worrying? Remember God, who cares. Remember God, who is powerful and will help you. Throw your cares on him, trust him for solutions, and go back to sleep. He will work in you if you trust him, and he will resolve your issues in time. "Salvation belongs to the Lord"—salvation from sin and salvation from worry. Trust him! You are in his hands!

July 8

Lying Lips

In my trouble I cried to the Lord, and He answered me.
Deliver my soul, O Lord, from lying lips, from a deceitful tongue.
Psalm 120:1-2 (NASB)

Lying Lips is a 1939 American film about a woman named Elsie, a popular nightclub singer. Elsie is accused of murdering her aunt, and because of a series of lies and deceit, she is convicted and sent to prison. This movie contains everything we typically see in real life: love, romance, jealousy, murder, lies, and deceit. Although this movie was made over eighty years ago, it is still relevant to us today. Our world is full of trouble caused by lying lips. The psalmist knew this when he prayed to God, asking him in Psalm 120 to deliver him from lying lips and from a deceitful tongue.

Because we live in a world filled with sinners who lie, cheat, murder, and only think about themselves, we yearn for someone who offers us hope. We yearn for someone to make things right and to give us a better future. In this passage, God answers us: "Yes, I know that the world is broken and filled with sorrow and pain, but if you trust in me, I will deliver you and free you. I have overcome all sin and offer you joy eternally. Yes, I chose you to be in my family, and I will not forget the promise I made to you. You belong to me, and I will rescue you."

This broken world will be fixed when Christ returns to bring us home. I recommend the movie *Christ on the Cross*. It's one you don't want to miss!

July 9

People-Lover

Who is a God like you, who pardons sin
and forgives the transgression of the remnant of his inheritance?
You do not stay angry forever, but delight to show mercy.
Micah 7:18 (NIV)

My wife is a "people-lover." How do I know? I hear her and our children and grandkids as they talk on the phone about the news of the day. She always reminds them how much she loves them. I see it when she invites neighbors over for breakfast, or when she takes time to encourage someone she doesn't even know. I watch it as she cooks a meal for a needy family. I see it when she purchases little gifts for every grandchild on every special holiday and birthday, never forgetting any of them. These gifts and words of encouragement resonate with everyone who experiences them. People-lovers speak a language of genuine love. The prophet Micah had strong warnings about God's judgment, but he also spoke of the hope we have in God who delights in showing us his mercy. God is the people-lover of all time!

How do I know? Micah tells us in our verse for today. God delights in being merciful. He finds incredible joy in forgiving our sins. God reinforced this fact many times in other encouraging passages in the Bible. Then God actually came himself in the person of Jesus Christ to demonstrate his people-loving skills. Jesus showed his compassion every day as he healed the sick, gave sight to the blind, cast out demons, and raised the dead. The climax of God's love came when Jesus willingly suffered and died on the cross to pay for our sins. We deserved condemnation, but Jesus offered us mercy instead. The amazing thing is, he was delighted to do it!

I often wonder what Jesus looked like. He was a simple man, physically-speaking. But in his actions, he looked just like God, because he *is* God—God, the people-lover! And now, he is inviting the people he loves to come to his upcoming celebration in heaven. He doesn't want any one of you to miss this magnificent event!

July 10

The Gospel Midpoint

Praise the Lord, all nations! Extol him, all peoples!
For great is his steadfast love toward us,
and the faithfulness of the Lord endures forever. Praise the Lord!
Psalm 117 (ESV)

What is the shortest chapter in the Bible both in the number of verses and words? The answer is Psalm 117. This chapter is also the middle chapter in the Bible. The 595th chapter has 594 chapters before it and 594 chapters after it. I wonder if this is a coincidence. Psalm 117 is recognized as the gospel midpoint, and it just happens to be a clear summary of God's good news to us.

Verse two tells us that God's love toward us is great. "Great" sounds like an understatement when we consider all he has done for us! A companion word might be "extravagant"! God's love toward us is so extravagant that he sent his one and only Son to die for us. It's so extravagant that when we sin, and come to him with a repentant heart, he forgives us—every time! God's love for us is also steadfast or unwavering! This means he will never get tired of us, lose interest in us, or kick us out of his family. God isn't temperamental like that. We can always count on him. But that's not all!

Verse two also tells us that God's faithfulness endures forever. This fact means that God's faithful promises will never end for those who commit their lives to him. The truths in these verses are everlasting. They are the gospel in a nutshell. And when we wrap our minds around the gospel, we can say from our hearts, "Praise the Lord!" How amazing that this verse is smack dab right in the middle of the Bible. There's a reason for that. I'm pretty sure both you and I will never forget it!

July 11

A Tornado in Ohio

My soul is cast down within me; therefore I remember you....
Deep calls to deep at the roar of your waterfalls;
all your breakers and your waves have gone over me.
By day the Lord commands his steadfast love,
and at night his song is with me, a prayer to the God of my life....
Hope in God.
Psalm 42:6-8,11b (ESV)

Many years ago, we took a car trip to western Ohio to visit my family. If you have ever traveled through Ohio, you know that the land is very flat with a lot of cornfields, silos, and occasionally—a tornado. On our way to visit my sister, we had an unexpected encounter with one of those tornados. If you have never experienced one, I can tell you, it is terrifying. The sky turns black, the winds swirl around you, and it comes up so fast, you don't know where to turn. In the countryside, it's hard to find a place to hide, so you hurry to the closest safe place you can find. In our case, it was a barn. We parked next to it, and all we could think about was whether we were going to die. The wind was howling so loudly, and the van we were in was shaking and rocking so hard that we felt that we would be swept away. The only thing we could do was to pray and ask God to save us. This appears to be how the psalmist felt in Psalm 42. He uses the example of a roaring waterspout breaking over him to describe the distress, even the panic, he is feeling.

All of us face "tornados" at some point in our lives. It could be a medical emergency, a financial decision, a spiritual crisis, or problems we face emotionally. Whatever the tornado, it turns our life upside down. The interesting thing to note in these verses is that the storms we face all belong to God and are under his control. So, we might ask, if God is loving, why does he allow bad things to happen? The answer is that God uses hardship to grab our attention, to show

how much we need him and *how much he loves us!* The Lord knows about the fierce storm you are facing. He also knows if you trust him. "Hope in God." He is your lifeline. He is ready to command his steadfast love. He is there to reassure you and give you a song at night—even when the tornado has come upon you.

July 12

Eat Your Veggies!

How can a young man keep his way pure?
By keeping it according to Your word.
Psalm 119:9 (NASB)

Maybe your mom was right when she told you to eat your veggies! Why? Most doctors tell us that if we want to live healthy lives, we need to exercise and eat plenty of veggies. That's right! A diet that includes plenty of vegetables reduces the risk of chronic problems like heart disease, stroke, and some types of cancer. Veggies provide nutrients vital for the health and maintenance of your body. They also lower blood pressure, diminish the risk of digestive problems, and help to stabilize your blood sugar. The top benefit, in my opinion, is that veggies help keep your appetite in check, making you feel full more quickly.

We chuckle sometimes about our moms' words of advice, but as we grow older, we find that many of their words contain valuable guidance for life. The same can be said for our verse for today. The question in this verse is a good one: "How can a young man keep himself pure?" This question can be asked at any time, in any culture. Temptations to sin come to all of us, but young people are particularly vulnerable, especially in today's world where standards are changing so quickly, and current thinking pushes young people into moral confusion. How is it possible to remain pure, to lead a lifestyle that pleases God?

Thank God, he has given us the answer. We keep our way pure by knowing God's Word and living according to it. The Bible is filled with valuable guidance for life. The more closely people live in accordance with God's guidance, the wiser and purer they will be. Like filling your body with veggies, fill your heart with God's words. The Bible contains the spiritual nutrients you need to know the truth and maintain your spiritual health. Following God's commands seriously reduces the risk of chronic sin! You might say, "But I don't like eating vegetables *or* following God's commands." That's where Jesus comes in. When you trust your life to him, he sends the Holy Spirit to live in your heart. The Holy Spirit changes your "likes" and rearranges your life. He gives you the desire and power to be pure.

This is the simple truth found in the gospel. Trust God, eat your veggies, and keep God's commandments! That's the way to keep your way pure!

July 13

Refreshments

*Come to Me, all who are weary and heavy-laden,
and I will give you rest.*
Matthew 11:28 (NASB)

If you have ever attended an eight-hour training meeting in a dimly lit conference room with no windows, you will understand what sheer joy is when the leader announces it is time for refreshments. The cookies, fruit, and snacks immediately rejuvenate your whole body and put a big smile on your face. Refreshments renew your energy and give you a sense of well-being. In Matthew's Gospel, Jesus invites us to come for refreshments as well.

Our journey in life is hard, marked by struggles, failures, and the consequences of sin. Weariness and the burdens of life can be overwhelming at times. Here, Jesus gives us a simple promise. Come to me if you have a heavy burden, and I will give you rest. Jesus is offering us refreshment, satisfaction, and contentment when we trust in Him. Jesus is the simple answer. He offers himself as our refreshment. He gives us hope. This is good news. It puts a smile on our face.

July 14

Disabled People

And large crowds came to Him, bringing with them those who were lame, crippled, blind, mute, and many others, and they laid them down at his feet; and He healed them.
Matthew 15:30 (NASB)

In 2021 the World Health Organization (WHO) reported that there were more than one billion disabled people in the world, which accounts for about fifteen percent of the population. I was surprised to find that such a large number of people are disabled. Over 250 million are blind or visually impaired. Almost 500 million are deaf or have hearing loss. About 200 million have an intellectual disability. And over 75 million need a wheelchair on a daily basis. Jesus knew all about this situation as reported in the gospel account of Matthew.

Large crowds came to see Jesus, and they brought their disabled friends and relatives with them. Why would so many people seek out Jesus? When you are broken, you need a healer, and this is what Jesus offered. He was a breath of fresh air for those who sought God for hope and healing. When we come to Jesus in humility, he heals our brokenness and releases us from our misery. This is good news for every living soul.

July 15

The Atomic Bomb and the Cross

But God shows his love for us in that while we were still sinners,
Christ died for us.
Romans 5:8 (ESV)

On July 8, 1941, Japan declared war on the United States. Japan fought America in the Pacific Theater for the next three and a half years, resulting in over 426,000 American casualties: 161,000 deaths; 248,316 wounded; and 16,358 captured. Japan refused to surrender under any conditions, so there was no foreseeable conclusion to Japan's imperialism and cruelty. US forces had to make a decision that would end the war. In July 1945, the US Department of War issued their estimates for casualties should the US invade the Japanese islands. Such an invasion would result in a staggering 1.7 to 4 million American casualties, including 400,000 to 800,000 US soldiers dead, and 5 to 10 million Japanese dead. A land war was out of the question. America used the atomic bomb, instead, to bring an end to the conflict.

The atomic bombings of the Japanese cities Hiroshima and Nagasaki shocked the world. Over seventy percent of the buildings in these cities were destroyed; more than 140,000 people died. But to continue this evil war was not an option. Even though we are saddened by the Japanese people's losses, the impact of the atomic bombs resulted in the defeat of an imperialistic empire and the end of World War II.

There is another event that struck the earth around 2,000 years ago. This event made a bigger and better impact than any bomb could. It was the coming of Christ. Jesus' perfect life, his example, his teachings, his healing, and his love for all people elevated people's understanding of what it means to be human and what it means to be good. His death and resurrection defeated Satan's evil empire and won the war against sin and death. Jesus' impact was worldwide.

It has transformed individual lives and shaped entire nations and civilizations. "God shows his love for us in that while we were still sinners, Christ died for us." The death of Christ was shocking, but it brought an end to the conflict between God and humanity. Satan's imperialism and cruelty were over. The door to God's love and power opened. Jesus' impact on the world was the apex of history. His life, death, and resurrection were not the end, but only the beginning for anyone who puts his trust in him. This good news is the best thing that has ever happened!

July 16

Passing the Baton

Therefore, since we are surrounded by so great a cloud of witnesses, let us also lay aside every weight, and sin which clings so closely, and let us run with endurance the race that is set before us, looking to Jesus, the founder and perfecter of our faith.
Hebrews 12:1-2 (ESV)

I have never participated in a track meet. I am slow and have never liked running. But when I watch the relay races in the Olympics, I am fascinated. I notice certain strategies that give me clues about which team will win. Little things like starting the race off with the second fastest runner and saving the fastest runner until the end make a big difference. But passing the baton is probably the key strategy if a team is going to win. Every pass must be precise, smooth, and perfectly timed. All of us are running the "race that is set before us." This verse in the book of Hebrews gives us important tips for running the race of life.

We all want to be "winners," but if we have committed our life to Christ, our idea of a "winner" has probably changed. We're just thankful to be on God's team and want to be the best runner possible. We know his team will be victorious, but we just want to do our part. This verse gives us key strategies to help us as we run.

The first is to "lay aside every weight" that clings to us so closely. That's all the extra stuff in our life that distracts us from the race. The second is to lay aside every sin, those attitudes and habits that entangle you and cripple you from running well. Don't let sin weigh you down. This race is long and demands determination. Following the strategies in this verse will enable you to run the race with endurance. The most important thing to remember is to look to Jesus. He is the one who chooses us for his team and trains us to be good runners. A close relationship with him is our true goal. Being on his team gives you the privilege of passing the baton to your children, grandchildren, to everyone you know! Knowing Christ and passing the baton is our goal and passion—the very purpose of our lives!

July 17

The Longest Bridge

For there is one God, and one mediator also between God and men, the man Christ Jesus, who gave Himself as a ransom for all, the testimony given at the proper time.
1 Timothy 2:5-6 (NASB)

Over the last twenty years, there have been many new bridges built around the world. Innovative designs have made it possible to span incredible distances. The longest bridge in the world is the Danyang-Kunshan Grand Bridge in China, which opened in 2011. This structure is a remarkable 102 miles long and runs between Shanghai and Nanjing. The longest bridge in the United States is Lake Pontchartrain Causeway in southern Louisiana. It is also the longest bridge in the world that runs continuously over water, and it does so for almost twenty-four miles. Each of these incredible bridges makes it possible for people to travel from one side of a chasm to another. Bridges, in effect, bring two sides of a chasm together. This is also the function of a mediator.

A mediator is a person who intervenes between two parties to restore peace and friendship. Jesus Christ is the mediator between God and mankind. Because we are sinners, there is a huge chasm between us and God. Having peace with God is a "bridge too far." God is inaccessible to us. But because God loves us, he sent Jesus to die on the cross. Jesus' death paid the price for our sins and made peace with God possible. Jesus became the bridge between us and God. As our mediator, he makes us friends with God and secures a place for us in God's kingdom. With one foot firmly planted in heaven and the other on Earth, Jesus became the longest bridge ever. The wonderful thing is that the invitation to cross the bridge is free, and so is our friendship with God!

July 18

Shooting Stars

Lift up your eyes on high and see who has created these stars,
The One who leads forth their host by number,
He calls them all by name;
Because of the greatness of His might and the strength of His power,
Not one of them is missing.
Isaiah 40:26 (NASB)

Have you ever seen a shooting star and wondered what happened to it? Did the star fall to the earth? Is it gone forever? Shooting stars are actually small pieces of rock or dust that hit Earth's atmosphere from space. This fast-moving rock becomes so hot that it glows as it moves through the heavens. Astronomers call shooting stars meteors. Meteors burn and fall to the ground. But stars don't. Stars stay exactly where God has placed them. So not one of them is missing. The prophet Isaiah gazed at the stars just as we do and pondered God's claim.

God's claim is justifiable and quite simple. God created every star in the heavens. He knows how many stars there are, and he has given them all a name and their place in the sky. Not one of them is missing. When I think about this truth, I am honestly blown away. Our God is powerful and awesome. Yet most people look at the stars and never stop to think about how they got up there. We get so caught up in meaningless topics like shooting stars that we miss out on the greatness of God. God created stars to show us his brilliance and his mighty power. He created them to grab our attention and make us want to worship him. Why did he do this? Because he loves us and wants us to enjoy a relationship with him forever. The next time you look up to enjoy the stars, consider the love the Savior shines on you.

July 19

Strawberry Preserves

O Lord, You preserve man and beast.
Psalm 36:6 (NASB)

I love strawberry preserves! This chunk of fruit is the real deal. It is not fruit juice in jelly or the pureed fruit in a jam. No, this is whole fruit, best enjoyed on crispy toasted bread or combined with creamy peanut butter on soft bread. Preservation is the process of keeping the fruit intact with no damage or decay. So we get to enjoy the gift of strawberries even when the fruit is not in season. When you read Psalm 36, it is not difficult to conclude that God is the one who preserves our lives.

God "preserves both man and beast." This word *preserves* is derived from a word meaning "save" or "rescue." It signifies the preservation and protection of life. God is the creator of all life. And he is the one responsible for the growth and sustenance of life. Think about this for a moment. It is God who preserves every human being. He also preserves every kind of beast known, every type of bird, every variety of fish, and even all of the armies of insects. All of God's creation is included in this claim. He is the giver of life, the one responsible for all of its growth, and most definitely the sustainer of life.

When we consider the magnitude and extent of God's creation and sustenance, we stand in awe. Every single creative act of God points to his sustaining love, his faithfulness, and his patience with us. Every breath is a gift from God and reflects how much he loves us. So the next time you enjoy strawberry preserves, thank God who is keeping you alive and blessing you.

July 20

Back-Up Plans

My soul waits in silence for God only; from Him is my salvation.
Psalm 62:1 (NASB)

In his book *Next Man Up*, John Feinstein takes an inside look at an NFL football team over a one-year period of time. He interviews multiple players and coaches to understand their mindset and prescription for success. One of Feinstein's conclusions is that every player and coach needs to be thoroughly prepared for the game. No one is exempt from injuries, and there are always going to be unexpected situations that change the strategy of the game. This means that every plan must be detailed and include players, coaches, plays for the game itself, and every possible scenario that may happen in the game itself. Back-up plans are a requirement if you want to have a championship team.

When I think about back-up plans, my mind immediately goes to all of the possible "what-if" questions. What if I don't back-up my pictures in the computer and my computer crashes? What if I don't have car insurance and then get involved in an accident? Or what if I don't have medical insurance and I discover I have prostate cancer? All of these types of what-if questions can happen in a person's lifetime. None of us is totally prepared when disaster strikes. How about you? When you are faced with an emergency, do you have a back-up plan?

Looking at Psalm 62 and considering what the author wrote, it becomes apparent that, for him, there was only one viable plan for this life and for eternity. His plan was a conscious decision to trust in God alone. This doesn't mean he didn't carefully plan for solutions to life's problems, he just didn't obsess over them. He knew his life was in God's hands. What he did do was make a conscious decision to trust in God for his eternal salvation. He decided to "wait in silence for God only." He knew God was the only source of his salvation.

Your eternal destination is precarious if you haven't made that conscious choice. What do you really believe? Is there anything that you can do to save yourself? What other plan can save you? You need to make a decision.

What I can tell you is that the Bible clearly states that there is only one option that will deliver you from your sins and save you. There are no alternatives or back-up plans in this area. Your only option is Jesus Christ. He is the only one who willingly died for your sins. He is the only one who could make the perfect sacrifice for you. And he is the only one who can offer you forgiveness. Jesus is the only one who can give you this exclusive offer. Since none of us knows the future, why not accept his generous offer now and follow him?

July 21

Leprosy

*And so Jesus also suffered outside the city gate
to make the people holy through his own blood.*
Hebrews 13:12 (NIV)

Leprosy is another name for Hansen's disease. It was the most dreaded disease in ancient times. It was incurable and a death sentence for anyone who contracted it. This bacterial infection ravages the skin with deformities and destroys nerve endings so that a person loses all feeling in his extremities. Over time, muscle tissue deteriorates, the person becomes paralyzed, and body parts may even rot and fall off.

Lepers were banished from society and forced to live in leper colonies until the 1940s, when a cure was found to treat the disease. After that, most countries abolished their compulsory isolation policies. However, despite medical breakthroughs, old stigmas and fear of contagion still exist in some countries today. Living in isolation, separated from the rest of society, lepers have always been outsiders.

Our Bible verse today tells us about the extreme measures Jesus took in his day to rescue outsiders. Jesus hung out with tax collectors and sinners, expelled demons, and healed the poor and disabled. One good example of his power and goodness was his reaction to meeting a man with leprosy. No one touched a leper; the disease was highly contagious. But when Jesus met this leper, he was filled with compassion. He reached out and touched him, and the man was healed immediately. At that moment, he stopped being an outsider and was able to be reinstated as a member of his community. You can read about this miracle in your Bible in Mark 1:41-42.

Jesus Christ does the same for us. He sees we are unhealthy and under the sentence of death. He sees we are outcasts of his kingdom, and he is filled with compassion. When he reaches out to touch us, we are healed, forgiven, and made full members of his eternal family "through his own blood," shed for us. Receiving Christ, we are no longer outcasts. We are insiders, members of God's glorious Kingdom!

July 22

Christmas in July

*Since therefore the children share in flesh and blood,
he himself likewise partook of the same things,
that through death he might destroy the one who has the power of
death, that is, the devil, and deliver all those who through fear of
death, were subject to lifelong slavery.*
Hebrews 2:14-15 (ESV)

Christmas in July is not an authorized holiday, but for many people it is a great time to celebrate a second Christmas and to enjoy entertainment, small gatherings, seasonal music, and shopping. It's an opportunity to renew the "Christmas spirit." Businesses especially appreciate the whole idea since it generates sales of Christmas goods and makes room for next year's inventory. Christmas in July is a good celebration because it reminds us of the most important event in history—the incarnation. I know, *incarnation* sounds like a fancy word, but stay with me. This is important!

The incarnation happened when God's Son, Jesus, emptied himself of his privileges, came down from heaven, and became a human being. He was conceived by the Holy Spirit, and consequently, he was born 100% human and 100% God. During his life on Earth, he experienced all the hardships and temptations we humans experience, but he never sinned. Since he was perfect, he had no sin debt to pay. So when he died on the cross, his death was able to pay the debt for our rebellion and save us from eternal condemnation.

We had absolutely no ability to save ourselves, so Jesus offered himself as payment and secured the gift of eternal life for us. Our part is to choose life, repent of our sin, and gratefully accept the gift that cost Jesus his life. This is great news because we no longer need to fear death. We are all going to die physically, but Christ is also giving us the opportunity to rise physically to a brand-new life with him in heaven. This is the good news of the incarnation. It is why we celebrate Christmas in December and again in July. I say, Christmas is worth celebrating anytime! So let me take this opportunity to wish you a very Merry Christmas!

July 23

Searching for Palladium

*O Lord, you have searched me and you know me.
Search me, O God, and know my heart; test me and know my anxious thoughts. See if there is any offensive way in me, and lead me in the way everlasting.*
Psalm 139:1, 23-24 (NIV)

Palladium is a chemical element with the symbol Pd and atomic number 46. It is a rare and lustrous silvery-white metal that has a melting point of 2,831 degrees Fahrenheit. The largest use of palladium today (over half) is in catalytic converters. Other uses include dentistry, blood sugar test strips, aircraft spark plugs, surgical instruments, and classical flutes. It is also used by the pharmaceutical industry to aid developers in bringing new drugs to market. Because of its useful properties, palladium is extremely valuable. This metal is thirty times rarer than gold, which makes it one of the most expensive metals on the planet. But elevated traces of this element in medicine can cause serious problems in our bodies, so every means must be used to test for palladium in medicines and remove it. In Psalm 139, we see God searching for the "palladium" in our hearts.

David writes, "O Lord, you have searched me and you know me." That fact is pretty astounding and a little scary! God knows everything about me, and too often, when he searches, he finds sin in my heart. Sin is like palladium; it produces undesired effects. Since we are precious to God, our hearts must be purified. Jesus paid a high price to purify your heart. He gave his very life for you!

July 24

Unemployed!

Or do you think lightly of the riches of His kindness and tolerance and patience, not knowing that the kindness of God leads you to repentance?
Romans 2:4 (NASB)

I have been officially unemployed two times in my life. In both cases this economic hardship resulted in hidden blessings I never expected. God always has a way to bless his children. This passage in the book of Romans challenges us to look at things, like unemployment from a different perspective. Many would view these uncertainties as God's punishment or discipline.

The verse today is asking us to reconsider what God is doing. Do you realize that God's kindness, tolerance, and patience are leading you to repentance? Even in the midst of unemployment, God shows his love in new, unconventional ways. Hardship forces us to view our relationship with God, family, and friends differently. God is working and blessing his people around the world. His good news is not hidden. He is right now encouraging us not to fear, but to trust in him. So whatever the situation you are in today, look around. You may see some hidden blessings from God!

July 25

Pay the Price

*And I will betroth you to me forever.
I will betroth you to me in righteousness and in justice,
in steadfast love and in mercy. I will betroth you to
me in faithfulness. And you shall know the Lord.*
Hosea 2:19-20 (ESV)

When you use the expression "pay the price," you can mean one of two things. First, it can mean that a person will suffer the consequences if he does something risky or morally wrong. The second meaning is that you are willing to "pay the price" for something you desire. The phrase in the Hebrew language is the word *aras*, "to betroth." In our culture, it means to become engaged. The passage we are looking at today is an allegory comparing a man who loved a woman with God who loves his people.

The story starts with God's love for his people, the Israelites. God loved his people so much that he betrothed himself to them. Just one problem: the Israelites were unfaithful and adulterous. They repeatedly cheated on God, forgetting him, worshipping idols, and committing crimes of sexual perversion, violence, and child sacrifice. God was grieved by their unfaithfulness, but he still loved them. He wanted to convince his people to be true to him, to practice lives of purity and devotion. He wanted to bless them. So God turned to the prophet Hosea with a dramatic plan. He commanded Hosea to marry a promiscuous woman named Gomer. She would repeatedly be unfaithful to Hosea and break his heart, but God told Hosea to speak tenderly to her, to "pay the price" and buy her back when she was unfaithful, and to renew his marriage vows to her. This story of patience and mercy illustrates God's love and forgiveness to his people. This love is astonishing! Israel deserved divorce, but three times in today's passage God told Israel, "I will betroth you to me." God wanted Israel to know with certainty that he loved her and would "pay the price" to get her back.

This story describes all of us before we become believers in Christ. Like Gomer, we are all unfaithful to God. But God pursues us anyway with his proposal to bless us and make us his own—forever. Jesus Christ has already "paid the price." Will you accept his gift of salvation? You really can't afford to pass up his offer. This is the good news of Jesus Christ.

July 26

The Potter's Hands

Your hands made me and fashioned me; Give me understanding, that I may learn Your commandments.
Psalm 119:73 (NASB)

Watching a potter turn a lump of clay into a beautiful ceramic bowl is quite impressive. The potter's hands are the key ingredient for success. The dexterity and sensitivity of the human hand cannot be replicated. A hand has over thirty muscles, twenty-nine flexible joints, and thousands of specialized nerve endings that provide a world-class sensory system. This incredible system can immediately discern the difference between hot and cold and can easily distinguish smooth and rough surfaces. The combination of the potter's hands and skill working together create unique designs that can only be achieved by the creator himself.

God is the perfect example of a potter. His hands created every human who has ever lived, and each one is a unique masterpiece, capable of great good but also capable of evil. That is why the psalmist penned this request to God, "Give me understanding, that I may learn your commandments." The psalmist was asking for help. He wanted to understand how God works in our lives.

God uses his commandments to guide and motivate us, to make us beautiful and capable of great good. Knowing this gives God's people a desire to learn his commandments and a sense of awe and purpose. As we surrender to God's work in our lives, as we yield to his commandments, he molds us into vessels that show the world his power and wisdom. It is this wisdom that forms us. It is his hands that shape us to love and serve him. Only God's hands can craft us. Surrender to God! "Learn his commands"!

July 27

Nothing Is Certain Except Death and Taxes

For I am convinced that neither death, nor life, nor angels,
nor principalities, nor things present, nor things to come, nor powers,
nor height, nor depth, nor any other created thing,
will be able to separate us from the love of God,
which is in Christ Jesus our Lord.
Romans 8:38-39 (NASB)

In one of his last letters, Benjamin Franklin gave a quick update about the Constitution's ratification and the beginning of the new United States government. Franklin wrote, "Our new Constitution is now established, everything seems to promise it will be durable; but, in this world, nothing is certain except death and taxes." He then concluded by observing that his own health was so poor he could not hold out much longer.

What Franklin didn't realize is that there are promises that are even more certain than death or taxes: God's promises for his redeemed children. Absolutely nothing can separate us from the love of God. Jesus loved us so much that he sacrificed his life so that we would never die, so that we could live forever. He was willing to give up everything, just for us. Jesus' love is certain. Does his sacrifice convince you? Death and taxes will end someday, but the love of Jesus Christ our Lord will endure forever.

July 28

Balance Sheet

*For God has not destined us for wrath,
but for obtaining salvation through our Lord Jesus Christ,
who died for us.*
1 Thessalonians 5:9-10 (NASB)

A balance sheet is used in financial accounting to provide a summary of an individual's or an organization's financial balance. It is used to provide a snapshot of your assets and liabilities. When all of the numbers are computed, you have a statement of your net worth. But financial numbers don't tell the entire story. This is true in life as well. We like to add up life's circumstances to make sure we get a fair shake. It makes us feel good when everything is in balance. But are our lives ever in perfect balance? In Paul's first letter to the Thessalonians, we find the reason why the numbers in our lives rarely add up.

In the first part of this verse, God tells us that we are not destined for wrath. God is not sitting in heaven trying to make our lives miserable or punishing us for every little mistake we make. He is not adding up the negatives. He wants to bless us, not harm us. He wants to give us the gift of salvation. The good news for you is that when Jesus died on the cross, he took on all your liabilities. When you trust in him for your salvation, you only get the assets. So when God sees your balance sheet, your net worth is priceless!

July 29

Change of Status

For you are all sons of God through faith in Christ Jesus.
Galatians 3:26 (NASB)

A change of status can refer to anyone who wants to change a name, a permanent residence, marital status, or immigration status. The required documents can include detailed application forms, passport-style photos, travel documents, receipts, letters of recommendation, a marriage certificate, job-offer letters, and other miscellaneous items. The bottom line is that if you want to change your legal status, you'd better be prepared for a lengthy process that will cost you both time and money. It's different if you want to change your status with God. This verse in Galatians tells you all he requires.

God gave us his law to reveal his standard of righteousness. We have all broken God's law, so we are all guilty. We know it, and God knows it too. There is no way to change our status with God and enter his kingdom. We can't fill out some forms, pay some fees, get recommendations, or send him a photo. The only way to change our status is to put our faith in Christ. Jesus came to Earth to deliver us from condemnation. He offers us a change in status from guilty to not guilty. We no longer need to be under the death sentence. We can receive eternal life because Christ Jesus has paid the fine for all our sins. The best thing? Our change in status is free! There is no cost involved. When you turn from sin and put your faith in Jesus, you become a child of God. Your status is permanently changed from condemned prisoner to heir of God.

July 30

Sophisticated Braggadocio

Every day I will bless You, and I will praise Your name forever and ever.
Psalm 145:2 (NASB)

It is difficult to be around braggarts. They want everyone to know what they did, who they know, and how important they are. Direct bragging is obnoxious and turns people off. However, it is much easier to be a "sophisticated braggadocio." This is the art of indirect bragging. Sophisticated braggadocios reveal little things about themselves that make them look and feel superior. They would never admit the fact that they don't have it all together. It would be too hard to take an honest look at themselves and admit they aren't better than everyone else. The psalmist wasn't a braggart. He knew he wasn't perfect. David knew he needed a Savior. This is why he wrote Psalm 145:2.

This verse is all about praising the Lord. Jesus is the central figure. What he did is good news. His accomplishments are breathtaking! He lived a perfect life, sacrificed his life for us, and offers it as payment for our sins. Jesus' life, death, and resurrection is the central event of history! This is why we bless him, and why we will praise him forever and ever.

July 31

Time Out

For his anger lasts only a moment, but his favor lasts a lifetime;
weeping may remain for a night,
but rejoicing comes in the morning.
Psalm 30:5 (NIV)

When I was growing up, the concept of "time out" did not exist. My disobedience and rebellious actions against my parents' authority usually resulted in a few whacks with a paddle or a whipping with a belt. Today, many parents use "time out" to impose a temporary suspension of play activities for the child who is misbehaving. Time out is a disciplinary measure that gives the child time alone so he can consider his disobedience. If the infraction is big enough, it might even result in the child being sent to his room for the rest of the night to think about what he did. Repentance usually results in tears, hugs, and forgiveness. This verse hits home for the child of God who has been disobedient to his heavenly Father.

David was well aware of his sins against God. This resulted in a heartfelt confession when he disobeyed and in genuine repentance (turning away) from the sin he committed. Since God knew David's heart was sincere, his discipline was only temporary. David knew that God never holds a grudge. He is compassionate and gracious, slow to anger, and abounding in love. He knew God's favor lasts for a lifetime. God's lovingkindness is extended to us even though we don't deserve it. When you turn to your heavenly Father and say, "Forgive me," he always does! You will never lose God's love. Our "weeping may stay for the night, but rejoicing comes in the morning."

August 1

Follow Jesus

Then Jesus told his disciples, "If anyone would come after me, let him deny himself and take up his cross and follow me."
Matthew 16:24 (ESV)

"I Have Decided to Follow Jesus" is a hymn originating from India. The lyrics are based on the last words of a man in Garo, Assam. During the last great revival in Wales, nearly 150 years ago, Baptist missionaries were sent to India to share the good news of Jesus Christ in northeast India. The tribes who lived there were primitive and aggressive headhunters. Naturally, these missionaries were not welcomed. One missionary, however, succeeded in converting a man and his family to Christianity. This man's faith was contagious, and as a result, other villagers also made decisions to follow Jesus.

The village chief was not happy about this new situation. He called the man who was the first convert and demanded that he renounce his faith in public or face execution. This man who truly believed said, "I have decided to follow Jesus." Being completely enraged, the chief ordered the execution of both of his children. Now the chief asked, "Will you deny your faith? You have lost both of your children. You will lose your wife too." But the man replied, "Though no one joins me, still I will follow." The chief then ordered the execution of his wife. Now the chief gave this man one last opportunity to deny his faith and live. His last words were, "The cross before me, the world behind me. No turning back."

What happened next is a true miracle. The chief was so overcome by this man's faith and his family, that he, too, made a confession of faith to follow Jesus Christ. The song we sing today is the last words of Nokseng, a man from the Garo tribe of Assam. It is also the song of the Garo people.

This verse in the book of Matthew is a straightforward invitation that Jesus extended to his disciples, and now we, too, are included.

If you want to follow Jesus, you need to deny or renounce yourself. It is a kind of death notice to self. And when you take up your cross, this is an absolute surrender to God. It means you are willing to die to follow Jesus. It is a call to self-sacrifice. There is no turning back when you make the decision to follow Jesus Christ! What are you going to do?

August 2

Names

But now, thus says the Lord, your Creator, O Jacob,
And He who formed you, O Israel,
"Do not fear, for I have redeemed you;
I have called you by name; you are Mine!"
Isaiah 43:1 (NASB)

A person's name is his identity, so most expecting parents spend hours, even days, deciding on the name to give their new baby. Should we name him or her after a grandparent, a special friend, or maybe even a season of the year? The list of possible names is endless. When you look at cultures around the world, you will see that for some, the naming process is fixed. For others, it is totally unconventional. This Bible passage tells us that God knows the name of every person in the world. At times, I forget the names of my own kids! But God knows and remembers each person by name.

This verse in Isaiah includes a command, "Do not fear." This is the most repeated command in the Bible. Why? Because all of us are full of fear! Man's biggest fear is death; but God, in his mercy, thought of a plan to take that fear away. It wasn't that we deserved his kindness. We were enemies of God. We deserved to die for our sins. But God sent his only Son, Jesus, to die in our place. By his death, Jesus paid the debt we owed. He redeemed us and claimed us as his own. If we put our trust in him, we no longer need to fear death.

The God who created you before you were born knew everything about you. He knew your name. He knew where you would be born and the number of days you would live on this earth. He knew how many hairs you would have on your head and the number of tears you would shed. He knew about all your hopes and fears. The good news is that if you trust in Christ, God says, "I have called you by name; you are mine!" What a wonder it is that God claims you as his own!

August 3

Neuschwanstein Castle

Walk about Zion, go around her, number her towers, consider well her ramparts, go through her citadels, that you may tell the next generation that this is God, our God forever and ever. He will guide us forever.
Psalm 48:12-14 (ESV)

If you were to go to Neuschwanstein Castle, in Bavaria, you would experience the amazing view of one of the most picturesque castles in the world. This palace in the German Alps was commissioned by King Ludwig II of Bavaria in 1868. It was also the castle from which Walt Disney got his inspiration to create the Sleeping Beauty Castle in Disneyland. When you take a tour around this European castle with its towers and unbelievable scenic view, you are left speechless. If you go inside, however, you will be surprised. King Ludwig never completed his project. There are only twelve rooms that are finished! Maybe he became exhausted and decided that the outside of the castle was good enough. Whatever happened, we are disappointed that he didn't give as much care to the inside of his castle as he did to the outside. When I thought about this story, my thoughts went to Psalm 48.

This psalm is about a beautiful city with majestic towers, incredible palaces, and an impregnable fortress. God is building this city. It is the kingdom of his people, and it is absolutely awesome! First, it is blessed with plenty of defenses—towers, ramparts, and citadels. God will always defend his people from their enemy, the devil. Next, it is beautiful. God's people make it beautiful, especially if they are living in the castle, close to God. Your relationship to God will determine what you see. If you reject God, there will always be fear, and in the end there will be anguish. For those who come to God, believing, there will always be amazement and joy. This city is great and awesome because God is great and awesome. He not only builds a kingdom that is beautiful on the outside, but he finishes his work by making his people beautiful inside too.

The Neuschwanstein Castle provides a good example for our own spiritual journey. Each of us is going to walk through life. Even though you may look good to those around you, what really matters is what is going on in your heart. What will you tell your grandchildren on the walking tour of your heart? Will they know that God is your God forever and ever? What do you want them to know about you? Will they see his beautiful work in your heart? I hope they will find the finishing touches of King Jesus in you.

August 4

Rescue Operations

For the Son of Man has come to seek and to save that which was lost.
Luke 19:10 (NASB)

Rescue operations involve saving lives or the urgent treatment of injuries after a devastating accident. In most cases, medical personnel with a high degree of training perform rescue operations. Rescues may include the use of animals like dogs and horses, vehicles like ambulances and helicopters, and special tools like the "jaws of life." What I find interesting is that, whether they are rescue squads or volunteers, each person is willing to risk his own life to save another. Although there are many extraordinary stories, there is one particular account that happened over 2,000 years ago. It was the epitome of all rescue operations. You can read about it in the book of Luke.

Jesus volunteered to come to Earth for one specific purpose. He knew all about the difficulties and risks involved, but he felt it was a most worthy cause. His mission was to seek out and save the lost. The operation was well thought out. Every detail was carefully planned, and every person to be rescued was included. Jesus came for the needy, the prisoner, the shut-in, the student, the lawyer, the CEO, the restaurant worker. He came for all who would repent of their sins and put their trust in him. His purpose was to save his people from a bitter end. His gift to us is eternal life. I am so thankful that Jesus was willing to lay down his life so I could be rescued. This is what I would call a successful rescue operation.

August 5

Making His Mark

*Now faith is being sure of what we hope for
and certain of what we do not see.*
Hebrews 11:1 (NIV)

How do I know when my grandchildren have visited me? I know because I see their fingerprints on the storm door and the glass on the coffee table. I see the crumbs on the kitchen floor from a cookie or cracker. I see the pillow or bedspread wrinkled up like someone was jumping on the bed. All of these little signs tell me that my beloved grandchildren were here to hug me and spend some fun time with me. These little signs are marks of the confidence they have in my love and forgiveness. Think on this verse today as it speaks of faith as well. It is faith in God.

We have faith that God exists and loves us because he shows himself so clearly in the world he created. Look around! His "fingerprints" are everywhere. They tell us God is powerful, wise, and good. They tell us we can put our confidence in his love and forgiveness even though we can't see him right now. This certainty helps us live to honor him. It keeps us on the right track and fortifies us when difficulties come our way.

I haven't seen God face to face yet, but I know what he has promised in the Bible. If I trust him for salvation, he will forgive my sins and take me to his home someday. This is "what we hope for" and what faith is all about. Even though we cannot see him right now, he has given us every reason to believe in him and trust him with our lives. Faith is confidence that God exists and is really there for me.

August 6

Wonderful Masterpieces

For You formed my inward parts; You wove me in my mother's womb.
I will give thanks to you, for I am fearfully and wonderfully made;
Wonderful are your works,
And my soul knows it very well.
Psalm 139:13-14 (NASB)

Leonardo da Vinci's *Mona Lisa* is probably the most popular painting in the world. It is considered a masterpiece. But even this great treasure of art is not as valuable as one human being. That's because each person is a masterpiece of God. God put a heart in each body that beats 100,000 times a day. Each body produces twenty-five million new cells—every day. If each person's DNA were uncoiled, it would stretch out ten billion miles! Besides that, each person is unique; no one else is exactly like you. Your fingerprints, DNA, and personality can never be duplicated. When the psalmist considered the intricacies of his own body, he was overwhelmed.

His response? Thanksgiving and praise! "I will give thanks to you, for I am fearfully and wonderfully made; wonderful are your works, and my soul knows it very well!" How blind we are not to recognize ourselves for what we really are—masterpieces of God! Yet so often, we take this truth for granted. Instead, we should see ourselves as instruments of God, reflecting his glory and drawing others into a relationship with him. What a privilege this is to be masterpieces of God!

August 7

Disappointments

*Though the fig tree should not blossom and there be no fruit on the vines, Though the yield of the olive should fail and the fields produce no food, Though the flock should be cut off from the fold
And there be no cattle in the stalls, Yet I will exult in the Lord, I will rejoice in the God of my salvation.*
Habakkuk 3:17-18 (NASB)

If you have lived even a few years of life, you will understand about disappointments. You don't have to be an old person to get it. We live with disappointing news every day. Sometimes our favorite team loses. Maybe our children take the wrong path, or someone we trust breaks a promise. We've all been through it. There's no way to avoid unhappiness, suffering, even tragedy. This was the story facing Habakkuk, who lived during a terrible time in Hebrew history, the decline and fall of the nation of Israel.

Uncertainty and fear must have consumed Habakkuk. He knew that Israel's unfaithfulness to the Lord would result in destruction. And he knew that Israel's fall would make life devastating for God's people. This could be our story, as well, when life isn't going as planned. But Habakkuk chose to do an amazing thing. He chose to trust God, and he chose to rejoice. Even though he had no idea what would happen next, he made a decision to walk by faith, to not become bitter. In fact, it was just the opposite for him. He would hang in there, because he was choosing to believe in God for the final outcome. Habakkuk's final outcome was heaven, where Jesus Christ is King and nothing goes wrong—forever and ever. Do you have this confidence when disappointments come your way? I will exult in the Lord!

August 8

In Over Your Head

Then Hezekiah took the letter from the hand of the messengers and read it, and he went up to the house of the Lord and spread it out before the Lord. Hezekiah prayed before the Lord and said, "O Lord, the God of Israel, who are enthroned above the cherubim, You are the God, You alone, of all the kingdoms of the earth. You have made heaven and earth."
2 Kings 19:14-15 (NASB)

Hezekiah was the King of Israel when the Assyrians besieged Jerusalem in 701 BC. The Assyrian army was relentless and cruel. They had the newest and most destructive weapons of their time. When Hezekiah got a threatening letter from the Assyrian King, Sennacherib, he knew he was "in over his head." The phrase "in over your head" means that you are deeply imbedded in a situation you can't possibly manage to resolve. This threat was too much for him to handle. So what did he do? He went up to the house of the Lord and spread the threatening letter out before God. Then he prayed. He acknowledged God's absolute kingship over all the kingdoms of the earth—including Assyria. God was in charge. He had the power to disrupt the Assyrian attack and give the victory to Israel. Hezekiah prayed to the Lord and praised him for his sovereignty. He trusted God for Israel's deliverance. And God did deliver Jerusalem. That night, the angel of the Lord went out and put to death a hundred and eighty-five thousand soldiers in the Assyrian camp. Sennacherib broke camp and withdrew his forces.

We will never be surrounded by an Assyrian army, but many times we feel we are in over our heads. We might be struggling in an unhappy marriage. We may be trying to get back in touch with our wayward son or daughter. We may be experiencing a budget crisis or a failure in business. Whatever the situation, we need to spread it out before the Lord. He is the King, and he has the power to deliver us, to change everything. A person who trusts in God will never be "in over his head."

August 9

Repetition

Oh give thanks to the Lord, for he is good;
for his steadfast love endures forever!
Psalm 118:1 (ESV)

All first-grade students know that two plus two equals four. Children know that *b* follows *a* in the alphabet. And when learning a musical scale, you know that B is higher than A. Each of these simple facts is learned through repetition. If you repeat something enough times, it sticks. Repetition causes an imprint on the brain. God uses repetition throughout the Bible, but especially in Psalm 118.

The phrases "he is good" and "his steadfast love endures forever" are repeated several times in this psalm. God does this to emphasize the truth about his faithful character. He wants us to know beyond a shadow of a doubt about his grace and mercy. Grace is getting what we don't deserve: forgiveness and a transformed life. Mercy is *not* getting what we *do* deserve: judgment and punishment for our sins. God repeats this good news many times in the Bible. He is making sure we learn it and understand it. He wants us to know without a doubt that his grace and mercy can forgive even the most rebellious sinner. Forgiveness, forgiveness, forgiveness, forever, forever, forever! These are nice words to hear repeated! Even little children can understand them and give thanks to the Lord!

August 10

Joni Eareckson Tada

No, in all these things we are more than conquerors through him who loved us. For I am sure that neither death nor life, nor angels nor rulers, nor things present nor things to come, nor powers, nor height nor depth, nor anything else in all creation, will be able to separate us from the love of God in Christ Jesus our Lord.
Romans 8:37-39 (ESV)

Joni Eareckson Tada is the founder of a ministry that reaches out to disabled people around the world. Joni grew up in Sykesville, MD. In 1967, she suffered a diving accident which made her a quadriplegic. Initially, Joni suffered from severe pain and feelings of depression, but within two years, she taught herself to paint beautiful pictures, holding a brush between her teeth. Since then, she has become a gifted artist, written over forty books, and recorded her own radio shows and music albums. In addition to these accomplishments, she has established family retreats for disabled children and become a well-known speaker. When I pondered her work, I was struck with a question. How could a teenage girl, who has been given the news that she is paralyzed for life, go on to triumph over this tragedy?

The answer to this question can be found in our verse for today. Read it again. Although Joni cannot walk or take care of any of her personal needs, she has been energized by the loving relationship she has with Jesus Christ. Anyone who has met Joni can see that she is "more than a conqueror." God is working powerfully to give her a life filled with joy and purpose. Following Jesus doesn't mean your life will be easy. It does mean that your life can be filled with wonder, beauty, and meaningful achievements. And he promises heaven, where he will make all things new.

August 11

A Man Cave

For while I was passing through and examining the objects of your worship, I also found an altar with this inscription, "TO AN UNKNOWN GOD," Therefore what you worship in ignorance, this I proclaim to you. The God who made the world and all things in it, since He is Lord of heaven and earth, does not dwell in temples made with hands; nor is He served by human hands, as though He needed anything, since He Himself gives to all people life and breath and all things.
Acts 17:23-25 (NASB)

Have you ever been to a "man cave"? If you have, you will probably see all the colors, trinkets, and pictures of a man's favorite sports team. Man caves are often in the man's basement, where many of his friends come to watch the game of the week. Whether a gentleman knows it or not, his cave is advertising what he is proud of and what he stands for. When the apostle Paul visited Athens, he observed that Greek men were proud of their many gods and stood by their altars.

There was one altar that really piqued Paul's interest. It was inscribed, "TO AN UNKNOWN GOD." Paul used this altar to show the Greek people what *he* was proud of and whom *he* stood for. He was proud of the one true God who made the world and everything in it, the ruler of heaven and earth. He stood for the God who is too big to dwell in little altars on Grecian hills, who doesn't need any help from "human hands," and who "gives everyone life and breath and everything else"! Paul warned them that this "Unknown God" would judge their sin, that they needed to repent, and that their "Unknown God" was actually Jesus Christ. This information was so new and compelling that people wanted to learn more. "We want to hear you again on this subject," they said. Paul's clear and confident proclamation brought Jesus and eternal life to many people in Athens.

August 12

Dreaded Reality

*Jesus said to her, "I am the resurrection and the life;
he who believes in Me will live even if he dies,
and everyone who lives and believes in Me will never die.
Do you believe this?"*
John 11:25-26 (NASB)

Death is the dreaded reality we would all like to avoid. But everyone knows this is not possible. Every hour almost 7,000 people die around the world. Every day 165,000 people die. The yearly total is nearly sixty million. Death comes to everyone—the young, the old, the rich, the poor, the good, and the bad. Death can strike any person at any time. No one lives in this world forever. Is there no hope for a future life? Has anyone ever defeated death? Jesus answered this question in the Gospel of John.

In these verses, Jesus Christ makes a bold claim. He says, "I am the resurrection and the life. If you believe in me you will never die." What did Jesus mean by that? We just said that no one lives forever, and it is true. No one lives forever—in this present world! But Jesus is talking about another time and another world—heaven. Our bodies might die for now, but each of us has a soul that will never die. That soul includes our spirit, our personality, our mind, emotions, conscience, and sense of self. Your soul lives on even when your body dies; and if you belong to Christ, both your body and your soul will be resurrected someday. Jesus came to Earth to abolish our final earthly destruction. He proved that we can live forever when he rose from the dead himself. Because he conquered death, there is no need to fear death any longer. What Jesus was asking is, "Do you believe me?" Well…do you?

August 13

Where Is He?

He is not here, but He has risen.
Luke 24:6 (NASB)

Many years ago, my wife, Faith, and I spent a few days in a large cabin-type hotel in Colorado. This hotel had a common bathroom. In the middle of the night, without Faith realizing it, I got up and went out to this bathroom. While I was gone, she reached across the bed and realized I wasn't there. This realization completely startled her. Where is he? What has happened to him? This is exactly what the women thought when they realized that the stone guarding the tomb of Jesus' body had been rolled away.

These women who had come to love Jesus so much were completely startled. Where is he? What has happened to him? We saw him being crucified on the cross. We saw him die. What did they do with his body? The answer came when two angels appeared and answered their questions. "He has risen!" they said. Can you imagine their astonishment? Jesus was alive! When you talk about the best news of all time, this is it. Jesus proclaimed that he came to save sinners, and he did. He promised that he would conquer death, and he did. And if you ask me where he is now, don't be startled by the answer. He is alive! He sits at the right hand of his Father in heaven, and his Spirit is alive in my heart!

August 14

Limited Access

*Who may ascend the hill of the Lord? Who may stand in his holy place?
He who has clean hands and a pure heart.*
Psalm 24: 3-4 (NIV)

I would venture to say that most of us have never met a king or even a president. You can't just call them or send them an email and expect an appointment. They are very important and access to them is limited. Even if you were fortunate enough to land a meeting with them, you would most likely encounter a number of obstacles before the meeting. Things you could say and do before the meeting and even during the course of the meeting would be determined in advance. Access would be limited and rare.

In our verse for today, the writer brings up some very important questions. "Who may ascend the hill of the Lord? Who may stand in his holy place?" Do we just show up and automatically land a meeting with God? The answer is clear: No! Only clean people with pure hearts can approach God. But we are all sinners with hearts that have rebelled against God. None of us is pure enough to expect a meeting with the King of the universe. In fact, in our state of impurity, we could only expect his judgment and our condemnation.

But God, in his love, is eager to meet with us and has made a way to cleanse our hearts so we can come to him. The Bible tells us we can draw near to God with full assurance, having our hearts sprinkled to cleanse us from our guilty consciences. Jesus purifies our hearts when we confess our sins to him and put our trust in him. He is able to do this because he lived a perfect life himself, died a death we deserved, and shed his blood, which washes away our sins. His invitation is to come to him and be saved. This means we now have unlimited access to God the Father. Are you keeping your appointment with him? He will change your life!

August 15

What Does Love Look Like?

He who did not spare his own Son but gave him up for us all, how will he not also with him graciously give us all things?
Romans 8:32 (ESV)

What does love look like? How would you describe it to someone? Well, you might want to talk about physical attraction, the joy of companionship, and the feeling of openness and respect. Or you might describe it as honesty, faithfulness, or empathy toward a loved one, feeling the other person's pain as your own. One of the things I think about is a willingness to sacrifice anything for the person you love. As parents, we love our children so much we would willingly give up our lives for them. But consider this: would you be willing to give up the life of one of your *own* children so that a child from another family could live? This question leads us to consider the unbelievable sacrifice God made for us as recorded in the book of Romans.

This verse tells us that God "did not spare his own Son but gave him up for us all." This is what true love looks like! God was willing to give up the life of his one and only Son so our guilt could be forgiven. God's Son was the only person perfect enough to serve as a substitute for our sins, and Jesus was willing to suffer and die a terrible death to pay the price and bring us into his kingdom. Just let that fact sink in. Jesus did this for you and me so we could become members of his kingdom, be transformed, and live forever. The amazing thing is that he did this even though we don't deserve it. Do you want to know what love looks like? Look at God, the Father, and his Son, Jesus Christ. They are love personified! They are pure love!

August 16

The New York Foundling Asylum

*In love he predestined us for adoption to himself
as sons through Jesus Christ.*
Ephesians 1:4-5 (ESV)

Around 1880, there was a huge wave of very poor immigrants who abandoned children that they could not care for. The sisters at St. Peter's Convent on Barclay Street in New York City would regularly find a baby who was left on the doorstep of their convent. As a result of this need, Sister Mary Irene FitzGibbon convinced the church to open an asylum for these children. On October 8, 1869, Sisters Irene, Teresa Vincent, and Ann Aloysia began operating out of a rented house. They received an infant the very first night it was opened. Sister Irene placed a white wicker cradle in the foyer of the home and kept the front door unlocked so a desperate mother could leave her child there. The sisters' only request was that if a mother left a baby she would ring the bell by the front door so the little one could be brought upstairs with the other babies. In that first month, forty-four others followed. "Today the New York Foundling is one of the city's oldest and most successful child agencies." (NYFoundling@rubenstein.com)

The passage in Ephesians today concerns love and adoption. We are all spiritual orphans. As a result, many people feel alone in this world and abandoned. But God has not left us that way! He loves us so much that he has provided a way for us to be adopted into a new family—his family!

God determined before the world was even created to adopt us as his own sons and daughters. If you turn away from being alone and an orphan, and if you trust in the love of Christ for your salvation, God will adopt you into his family. God knew his plan would cost him dearly. He would have to give up Jesus, his one and only Son, to pay the penalty for our sins. He was willing to do that, and Jesus agreed wholeheartedly. Jesus was the only one who could pay our debt of sin and legitimately adopt us. Because of God, we don't have to be orphans anymore. We can have a new standing as sons and daughters, legal heirs of the King of the universe. No longer orphans, we are children of God!

August 17

Tear Catcher

You have taken account of my wanderings; put my tears in Your bottle. Are they not in Your book?
Psalm 56:8 (NASB)

A tear catcher or "lacrymatory" is a small bottle made of blown glass that was used to collect the tears of people in mourning. These small ornamental containers could be carried or hung around the neck. In the Victorian era, they became popular because people at that time were suffering so much with death and mourning. During the American Civil War, the wives of soldiers in combat would save their tears in these small bottles to show their devotion to their husbands. If a husband died, his wife would sprinkle her tears on his grave on the first anniversary of his death. This action marked the end of her mourning period. A tear catcher is also mentioned in this verse today as an encouragement for anyone who has ever suffered to the point of shedding tears.

Believe it or not, God takes notice of your sadness, your pain and suffering, and your heartaches and weariness. He is even concerned when you wander away from him and suffer the consequences of going astray. He sees every teardrop that falls from your eyes, and he has collected every one of those tears in his bottle of remembrances. You may think that nobody cares, but God cares. He has been with you every step of the way and has recorded every trial in his book. Your life is precious in his sight.

Why do you think that God displays such great tenderness and mercy to his children? Because he loves us! If he was willing to send his own dear Son to Earth as a payment for your sin, he must really care about you. So don't linger on in your sorrow. Let God's Spirit comfort you. And remember one more thing: in God's new world, our sorrows will be turned to joy, and our tears will be turned to laughter. God will wipe away every tear from our eyes. He will make all things new!

August 18

Raising Children

*Cast your burden upon the Lord and He will sustain you;
He will never allow the righteous to be shaken.*
Psalm 55:22 (NASB)

Raising children is so hard. We want the very best for each one of them. Because we love them, we many times take on burdens that don't belong to us. We worry and fret over their future. We are anxious because of our lack of control over the most simple situations in their lives. This verse offers an alternative to all our anxieties.

God is saying, "Take your burdens and cast them on me!" Our control in life is always limited and temporary. What we are doing is putting God in control, and he can handle any situation a lot better than we can! God gives us a promise that he will sustain us. He will never allow a person who is trusting in him to be defeated. Casting our burdens on God is a decision we make. This is what it means to walk in faith. This is believing that our Savior knows what is best for our children and what is best for us. Jesus knew all about burdens. Don't forget that he took every one of them on himself when he died for us. We offer him our burdens; he offers freedom from fear in exchange. We never have to be shaken with anxiety. God is able to take care of everything!

August 19

Hurricane Katrina

Peace I leave with you; my peace I give to you.
Not as the world gives do I give to you.
Let not your hearts be troubled, neither let them be afraid.
John 14:27 (ESV)

In 2005, a historic Category 5 Atlantic hurricane struck the southeastern United States. Hurricane Katrina caused over 1,800 deaths and more than $125 billion in damage. When catastrophes like this happen, what goes through your mind? Why would God allow this to happen to these people? Why would God allow this suffering? Maybe you would question God, asking, "Don't you know that some of these people belong to you?" Anytime we have an unexpected tragedy like this, we question God. We want to know why. Today's passage is a promise Jesus Christ gave to his disciples and all of his followers that addresses things just like this.

Jesus promises to give peace to those who trust in him. The peace he was promising was not an exemption from suffering, conflict, and trials. Jesus himself was very troubled by his own impending crucifixion. The peace he was referring to was Christ's confidence in his heavenly Father's love and approval. Our world can only give false peace when we have unexpected tragedies like a hurricane. Jesus had total confidence in his Father's plan and knew his power. This is why he was able to move forward with this crisis without fear. This same peace was the source offered to the disciples. The promise of peace is what he offers those of us who believe in him. It is the only thing I know of that provides true encouragement and hope when a Katrina strikes.

August 20

Splitting a Granite Boulder

*Tremble, O earth, before the Lord, before the God of Jacob,
Who turned the rock into a pool of water,
the flint into a fountain of water.*
Psalm 114:7-8 (NASB)

When our next-door neighbors started building their new home a few years ago, they discovered a large granite boulder right in the middle of the foundation. This, of course, was a major problem. For the next week, we woke up at 7:30 a.m. sharp every day to the drilling and pounding on this huge rock. By the end of the week, the rock had been removed, and the foundation for their home was well-established. Splitting this granite boulder was an incredible project that required many days of labor and significant costs to complete. In Psalm 114, we read about God splitting a huge rock with no effort at all.

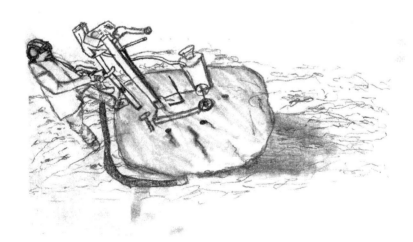

The Israelites had just escaped from Egypt and were on their way to the promised land. But they hit a serious problem. There they were, about 600,000 people, out in the desert with no water to drink. Moses asked God what to do, and God told him to strike a rock. It sounded a little foolish, but to everyone's surprise, the rock broke open and out came springs of fresh water. The water was so plentiful that it created a pool and became a source of pure, refreshing water for the people of God. While this sounds impossible to us, it was no big deal for God. The natural world still takes orders from God. When I ponder this, my awe factor increases significantly. God, who created this earth and commands all of nature, is the same God who came here to deliver us from sin and transform our lives. He holds power over death and grants his people eternal life. Thinking about this makes me realize that nothing is impossible with God. If he can split a boulder, he can save you and me!

August 21

Chewing the Cud

*But his delight is in the law of the Lord,
And in His law he meditates day and night.*
Psalm 1:2 (NASB)

Have you ever wondered why cows chew the cud? Cud is softened food that is regurgitated from the stomach back to the cow's mouth. There, it is slowly re-chewed and finally swallowed for good. Cows must chew their food this second time before it is fully digested. Cows spend almost eight hours a day chewing their cud. It is an indicator of a healthy animal. It also relaxes a cow and helps her produce more milk.

Are you wondering what chewing the cud has to do with a verse in the Bible? Chewing the cud is a great word picture for what believers do when they meditate, day and night, on the law of the Lord. When you meditate on God's word, you are thinking deeply and often about what it says and how it could apply to you. It's like you are mentally "chewing the cud." It's not just a quick look, so you can check it off your list. It is a prolonged stare to examine and think about what the Holy Spirit is teaching you. The more you chew on God's Word, the more you will be encouraged and comforted, convicted and challenged. The more you chew on God's Word, the more you will grow as a Christian and be transformed to be more like Jesus Christ.

You will also produce spiritual food for others to enjoy! People who meditate on God's Word are a blessing to others. They nourish others with their words of wisdom, and they teach others how to be right with God. Chew on God's Word. Learn what pleases him and obey him. Draw near to God. Love him with all your heart and meditate on his words. They are your daily bread. They will keep you, nourish you, and sustain you.

August 22

Permanent Change of Station

For He rescued us from the domain of darkness,
and transferred us to the kingdom of His beloved Son,
in whom we have redemption, the forgiveness of sins.
Colossians 1:13-14 (NASB)

When my wife and I received PCS (Permanent Change of Station) orders for our first military move, she cried for three months. The Army had decided that they would transfer us from Ft. Riley, Kansas to Wiesbaden, West Germany. Unfortunately, we didn't have an option. A transfer like this means many things: a new home, new friends, a new language, new customs, new foods, and a new commander—a dramatic change in every area of life. We moved and adjusted to all the changes beautifully, and we enjoyed our tour in West Germany.

This little story gives us a picture of what happens when God saves us. He is offering us a Permanent Change of Station—a rescue from the kingdom of darkness and a transfer to the kingdom of his dear Son. In this case, we are faced with two options. Do we prefer to stay in the old kingdom where we are living in darkness, enslaved by sin and guilt? Or are we willing to be transferred to the kingdom of light, where we will live free, redeemed, and forgiven? Our choice to be rescued will mean many things. Because our new commander is Jesus, there will be significant changes in every area of our lives. There's no need to worry, though. We'll adjust beautifully, and we will enjoy our forever citizenship in the kingdom of God's beloved Son!

August 23

An Even Exchange?

Surely our griefs He Himself bore, and our sorrows He carried;
Yet we ourselves esteemed Him stricken, smitten of God, and afflicted.
But He was pierced through for our transgressions,
He was crushed for our iniquities; The chastening for our well-being fell
upon Him, And by His scourging we are healed.
Isaiah 53:4-5 (NASB)

In retail sales, a customer is often allowed to return an item that does not satisfy his expectations. The reasons for his return may include size, color, cost, or the working condition of the item. The retailer may exchange the product for a different one or just give the customer a refund. In some cases, the seller will not allow a refund. Each store dictates the policy for exchanges. The prophet Isaiah wrote about an important exchange between the Messiah and mankind in the Bible.

God created mankind just perfect. The Bible says that God saw the people he had made and declared them "very good"! But mankind fell into sin, and ever since then, no one has even come close to living up to God's expectations. God could have given up on us, returned us, or exchanged us for a better model. Instead, Jesus became human himself, lived up to his Father's expectations perfectly, then took the punishment for all our sins so we could be healed. Jesus Christ, the Messiah, agreed to carry our griefs and sorrows, to be stricken and afflicted. He changed places with us so we could get credit for His perfect life. This was never an even exchange. Jesus was willing to take all my sorrows and exchange them for joy. He was willing to experience death in exchange for my eternal life! Jesus was pierced, crushed, and punished so that I could be forgiven. And the best thing is that Jesus loved us so much that he made this exchange of his own free will! How could anyone ever refuse an exchange like this?

August 24

Symbol of an Arm

O Lord, be gracious to us; we have waited for You.
Be their strength every morning, our salvation
also in the time of distress.
Isaiah 33:2 (NASB)

If you have ever seen a picture of an arm in an advertisement, you can be certain that this symbol probably means strength, power, or influence. The Bible says that God arms his people with strength. The reference to *arm* is used more times in the book of Isaiah than in any other book in the Bible. The Assyrians were threatening the people of Jerusalem. The prophet Isaiah prayed that God's arm of strength would be with them every morning.

This prayer reveals the heart of a person who waits and trusts in the Lord. He understands that God will show his grace when he calls out. This is a person who wants the Lord's strength. He knows that only God can help him every day. And he knows that only God's salvation can help us in our times of distress. The prayer of a humble person who loves the Lord will always be heard. God will always respond with grace and strength. God's arm will give us this strength every morning.

August 25

To-Do List

*My heart is steadfast, O God; I will sing,
I will sing praises, even with my soul.*
Psalm 108:1 (NASB)

A to-do list is a list of tasks and errands that you want to accomplish by the end of the day. Sometimes I take a piece of scrap paper or a Post-it note to serve as my memory aid. I have even used napkins to take notes on during lunch. The bottom line is that you want to complete these items because they are important to you. King David, in Psalm 108, names an item that should be on every person's to-do list.

As the King of Israel, David had many tasks to complete each day. His heart was steadfast, dedicated to making time for the most important tasks. The projects that pleased God were "must-do" projects. Prioritizing was a conscious decision on David's part. If you read this verse, you can see his top priority. It was singing praises to God. He was determined to give time and effort to appreciating and honoring God. Many times he did this in public ("among the peoples"). He wanted a close relationship with God, and he wanted others to praise him too. When we thank and praise God, he reveals himself to us. So when you are planning a to-do list today, let me encourage you to jot down "praise Jesus" on your Post-it note.

August 26

Who Gets the Credit?

Unless the LORD builds the house, its builders labor in vain. Unless the Lord watches over the city, the watchmen stand guard in vain. In vain you rise early and stay up late, toiling for food to eat—for he grants sleep to those he loves.
Psalm 127:1-2 (NIV)

When you work really hard on a project or in your job, it is nice to get credit for your efforts. Praise and recognition (and maybe even a bonus) let you know you are appreciated for a job well done. But what happens when someone else comes along and takes credit for your hard work? You feel robbed. "That was *my* work," you say. "*I'm* the one who should be getting the credit!" But think about it for a moment. Is that absolutely true? This verse in Psalm 127 gives us a better understanding about who should get the credit, and it uses two real-life examples.

"Unless the Lord builds the house, its builders labor in vain." I like to look at it this way: I can build a life for myself, a career, a home, a family, a smart financial portfolio. I also know that all of these things could be gone in an instant. Unless the Lord builds my life, all my work is in vain. The same thing can be said about guarding our cities and nation. Our government and our military can stand watch for us, but it is impossible for them to guarantee our safety. Only the all-powerful, all-knowing, all-wise God can do that!

Now back to the question of who gets the credit. Who builds our lives? Who guards our cities? Jesus Christ! He is the one who is worthy of honor, and he is the one who should get our praise. Don't become a slave to your personal ambitions, staying up late, getting up early, always looking for recognition—and that bonus. God is the one who determines these things. Appreciate him for his good work, and give *him* the glory. Then lie down and get a good night's rest! Your worth is secure when it is based on the work God is doing in you. Just remember, he is the one doing the great job, so he is the one who deserves the credit!

August 27

Difficulties

Is anything too difficult for the Lord?
Genesis 18:14 (NASB)

In 2015 I had a major stroke that affected the left side of my brain. My speech was gone, and nobody could understand what I was talking about. As I lay in my bed night after night, all I could think about was, "Will I ever be able to speak again? Would this stroke impair me for the rest of my life?" Difficult questions like these are something to grapple with. But I knew the Bible contains plenty of accounts of God's mighty power. These accounts encouraged and challenged me to hang in there.

One good example of God's mighty power can be found in Genesis, the first book in the Bible. This story is about a couple named Abraham and Sarah. God made a promise to them that within a year, Sarah would give birth to a son. This seemed impossible since Sarah was ninety years old and Abraham was one hundred, both way past the age of childbearing. They had a hard time believing that such a thing was possible. But God responded to their doubts with the question, "Is anything too difficult for the Lord?" And sure enough, within a year, Sarah gave birth to a son! They named him Isaac. He became one of the great patriarchs of the Jewish nation.

So what is my point? My point is that nothing is too difficult for the Lord. There are no difficulties that God cannot overcome. We can't put God in a box. His power is unlimited, far beyond anything we could ever imagine. In fact, God uses impossible situations to accomplish his plans, bless his children, and bring glory to himself.

Knowing this story and many others gave me the confidence I needed to trust God and do my part. My dear wife, Faith, found an experimental program for victims of stroke and enrolled me. No one knew if this program would help, but for my treatment, I spent the next several months reading the Bible many hours each day, five days a week, writing down notes and discussing them with my therapist. And you know what? God gave me back my ability to speak! Since then, he has blessed my life in so many ways. If you have never trusted in God in a big way, trust him now. His answer for you might involve a lot of effort on your part, but he is true to his promises. I challenge you to check him out. Trust in him and obey his guidance. Faith in God will change your life forever!

August 28

Resumes

He does not delight in the strength of the horse;
He does not take pleasure in the legs of a man.
The Lord favors those who fear Him,
those who wait for His lovingkindness.
Psalm 147:10-11 (NASB)

Resumes are a formal "smiley." We want a job, so we put on our best face: "I accomplished this task. I have a lot of experience and education. You should pay attention to me. I am the perfect person for this job." This is the way the world operates. Pointing out your credentials and area of expertise can help make you successful. But Psalm 147 puts a limit on our claims for success.

It's not that God pooh-poohs our strengths and skills. And it's not that God underrates our education and experience. The problem comes when we fail to acknowledge that all the things we're so proud of are simply gifts from him. It comes when we start trusting our own strengths and skills, when we take the credit for ourselves and think we can handle our lives without God. It's when we take delight and pleasure in ourselves and leave God out. Power, athletic skill, beauty, brains, awards, and degrees mean nothing without the blessing of God. He is not impressed with our fancy resumes.

The Lord favors the person who fears him, who relies on him, and who waits humbly for his lovingkindness. The world's standards for approval do not impress God. God's stamp of approval comes to those who give him the credit he deserves. This is how we get God's smiley face: trusting Jesus.

August 29

"Make Your Bed"

The fear of the Lord is the beginning of knowledge.
Proverbs 1:7 (NASB)

"The first thing you do in the morning defines your day!" This quote is from Admiral William McRaven, a retired Navy SEAL. He is the author of the best-selling book *Make Your Bed*. This book is an outline of the top ten lessons he learned during his distinguished career. The first lesson is simple but profound: begin each day by making your bed. If you do this each morning, your first task will be accomplished. Starting your day with this success encourages you to complete the next task and so on.

How do you start your day? Drinking a cup of coffee? Reading your emails? Exercising? Taking a shower? Planning the day? Solomon, the successful king of Israel, made this wise recommendation: "The fear of the Lord is the beginning of knowledge." If you don't want to waste a single day of your life, start each day with God. The fear of the Lord will give you the knowledge you need to accomplish the rest of the tasks of the day. Fearing the Lord doesn't mean that you are terrified because God is getting ready to zap you. No, fearing the Lord is about awe, respect, and reverent obedience. It is treating God as your Creator, King of the universe, and Lord of your life. It's giving him top priority in your life. Failing to reverence God is a big mistake! If you want true knowledge, the starting point is seeking God and reading his words in the Bible. Just like learning to read requires you to learn the alphabet, learning God's Word is the foundation for living a life that pleases God. It will encourage you to accomplish the tasks God is calling you to do. Making your bed is a good thing to do in the morning, but the fear of the Lord will define your life forever.

August 30

Waiting for the Other Shoe to Drop

Therefore there is now no condemnation for those who are in Christ Jesus.
Romans 8:1 (NASB)

In the late 19th century, tenements in New York City were designed with bedrooms on top of one another. This meant that noisy neighbors could make sleeping difficult for the people in the bedroom underneath them. One of the most common sounds occurred when working folks came home late at night. It was the sound of a heavy work boot hitting the floor. The neighbors living below probably woke up, sighed, and waited for the other boot to drop, so they could go back to sleep. This is the origin of the funny little saying, "We're waiting for the other shoe to drop." It means some negative event has occurred and another is sure to follow. An example would be, "They laid off a couple of people at work today. Now we're all just waiting for the other shoe to drop."

This way of looking at things is a common tool of the devil. It's called fatalism, the belief that the world is ruled by a random, impersonal force that couldn't care less about the individual. Belief in fate steals our joy without our even knowing it. It whispers to us that life is bad, it's going to get worse, there's no hope, and we probably don't deserve to be happy anyway. This way of thinking can condemn us to despair unless we know Jesus Christ as our Savior. This verse in Romans tells us the truth about the one who truly rules the world and what he can do in our lives: "Therefore there is now no condemnation for those who are in Christ Jesus."

    If you believe in Christ and trust him with your whole heart, God will never condemn you. God isn't an impersonal force. He is a real person who is full of compassion and loves to help us. First, Jesus paid the price for your sins and pleads your case before his Father in heaven. The Father willingly forgives you when you sin because forgiveness was his plan all along. Then, he fills our hearts with joy and blessings, not condemnation and despair. In other words, he involves himself in our day-to-day lives and gives us wisdom and strength to deal with life's difficulties. God's gifts of forgiveness and help are offered to all who receive them. We either choose to trust in Christ or we choose what the world offers—fate, negativity, and despair. The thing to remember is that in Jesus, there is absolutely, positively NO CONDEMNATION! God will never say, "Well, you almost made it to heaven, except for the time when you…." In other words, you'll never need to wait for the other shoe to drop!

August 31

Peace, a Misunderstood Word

*Peace I leave with you; my peace I give to you.
Not as the world gives do I give to you.
Let not your hearts be troubled, neither let them be afraid.*
John 14:27 (ESV)

When you look up the word *peace* in the dictionary, you will discover several definitions. Peace is the absence of war, an agreement or treaty, freedom from quarrels and disagreement, law and order, inner contentment, calm, and serenity. Some would say that peace is getting away from everything. Take a trip to Hawaii and lie on the beach. Change your circumstances and go where nothing bothers you at all. I would submit to you that this meaning of the word *peace* is misunderstood because it is only temporary. Jesus addressed this word right before he was crucified on the cross.

"Peace," he said, "I leave with you; My peace I give to you." Peace is a gift from God. It has little to do with the circumstances of our world. Jesus had peace even when he was going through his last trial. Peace came from being confident of his Father's love and approval. God gives this same peace to his children when they trust and obey Him. Confidence in God is what calms our hearts. We know that Jesus overcame death, and because of God's mercy, we will too. Lying on the beach in Hawaii might give temporary peace, but only Jesus can give permanent peace, rest from our troubles, and hope for the future.

September 1

Shepherd's Responsibilities

*Come, let us worship and bow down, let us kneel
before the Lord our Maker.
For He is our God, and we are the people of His pasture
and the sheep of His hand.*
Psalm 95:6-7 (NASB)

One of the world's oldest occupations is shepherding. This job includes a wide range of responsibilities. Sheep are needy and not very smart, so they need a lot of care. Their digestive systems are sensitive, so shepherds must lead their sheep to safe pastures and avoid plants that can make their sheep sick. Sheep need safe water too. Sometimes, in the Middle East or during a draught, water is hard to find. Good shepherds find still waters because lambs are fearful little animals. Sheep tend to stray. A good shepherd will search until he finds a lost sheep and will rescue him from danger. Predators love to eat sheep, so a good shepherd is protective, vigilant, and brave. Psalm 95 tells us that we are the people of God's pasture and the sheep of his hand.

The shepherd we are talking about is the Lord Jesus Christ. He even referred to himself as the Good Shepherd. He is the one who assumes the role of leading, feeding, watering, rescuing the lost, and protecting his people from their predator, the devil.

Are you in his flock? Then worship and bow down, kneel before the Lord your maker.

He is your God! You belong to him! You can relax because your shepherd knows you and is watching over you. When Jesus is your shepherd, you have nothing to fear. Your shepherd knows you and always looks out for you.

September 2

Great Reversal

*Then Hannah prayed and said, "My heart exults in the Lord;
My horn is exalted in the Lord, my mouth speaks boldly against my
enemies, Because I rejoice in Your salvation.
There is no one holy like the Lord, indeed, there is no one besides You,
Nor is there any rock like our God."*
1 Samuel 2:1-2 (NASB)

An Old Testament woman named Hannah was unable to have children. At the time that she lived, barrenness was not only a bitter disappointment but an invitation for insults. Hannah's husband loved her very much and felt sorry for her, but others were not so kind. Years went by, and Hannah was beside herself. Sometimes she cried so hard, she couldn't even eat. Finally one evening, she completely broke down, crying bitterly as she prayed to God to give her a son. And sure enough, in the course of time, God graciously answered her prayer, and she became pregnant with a baby boy, Samuel.

Samuel grew up to be a prophet, an important spokesman for God. Hannah was privileged to be his mother. And, as an extra blessing for waiting so long, God gave Hannah three more sons and two daughters. This is a story of a great reversal. It begins in heartache and ends in joy. This godly woman took her troubles to the Lord and trusted in him. It was not her physical circumstances that brought her victory. It was God, who heard her when she cried and answered her prayer. This biblical account is an encouragement to all who feel that their situation is hopeless. Nothing is impossible. Never stop praying, and God will answer your prayers—sometimes in ways you didn't really ask for or never could have dreamed!

Of course, the most amazing reversal of all time was when Jesus died a terrible, humiliating death on the cross only to rise from the dead three days later. He proved that nothing is impossible for those who trust in his power. The good news is that Jesus can reverse your course in life. In fact, those who trust in the Lord will always win in the end!

September 3

Full-court Press

I press on toward the goal for the prize of the upward call of God in Christ Jesus.
Philippians 3:14 (NASB)

A full-court press is a basketball strategy in which the defense applies pressure to the offensive team the entire length of the court before and after the inbound pass. This maneuver includes attempting to deny the initial inbound pass or trapping ball handlers either in the backcourt or at mid-court. The full-court press is strenuous and exhausting for both teams. This same type of pursuit is mentioned in the book of Philippians as an encouragement to believers.

Once we realize that our only hope is found in Jesus, we eagerly pursue him. We run to him for our salvation, and we trust him completely. Our lives are all about knowing him better and being on his team. Nothing else matters when you are running for the prize awaiting you in heaven. Trusting in Jesus gives you strength to press on. Jesus knows your heart, appreciates your efforts, and will be waiting for you at the finish line to celebrate the victory.

September 4

Wooing my Beloved

*The steadfast love of the Lord never ceases;
his mercies never come to an end; they are new every morning;
great is your faithfulness.*
Lamentations 3:22-23 (ESV)

When I first met my future bride, I was intrigued by her sense of humor and great conversation. Our dates were spent talking, eating, having fun, and getting to know one another. I seldom got to see her because of our locations, but as our relationship continued, we started to trust one another. Finally, I got bold and proposed to her. I wanted to have a permanent relationship with her based on love and faithfulness. But the commitment God has for his children is far greater than mine.

God loved us so much that he was willing to come to Earth just to rescue us from our sin and rebellion. When we trust in him, our relationship with Jesus is firmly established. Every morning he shows us new mercies. His love and compassion for us never ceases, never fails, and is never exhausted. I think that Jesus actually looks for new and creative ways to show us his love. Our relationship grows as we trust in him. What an incredible blessing it is to know that Jesus is reinforcing his commitment to us by pursuing us every day. Wow! This is what I call wooing my beloved!

September 5

"Standing on the Promises"

Listen, my dear brothers:
Has not God chosen those who are poor in the eyes of the world
to be rich in faith and to inherit the kingdom
he promised those who love him?
James 2:5 (NIV)

Russell Kelso Carter grew up in Baltimore, Maryland where he graduated from Pennsylvania Military Academy (PMA) in 1867 with a civil engineering degree. He was a star athlete serving as a pitcher on PMA's first baseball team. He was also an excellent student. After graduating, he taught natural sciences and chemistry at his alma mater. During his career, besides teaching, he became an ordained Methodist minister, musician, and songwriter, and he later became a physician. When Carter was thirty years old, he developed a critical heart condition that threatened his life. All of his doctors told him there was nothing they could do for him, so he turned to God in faith for his help and healing. This was a turning point for him when he fully committed his life to Jesus Christ as his Savior. From this time on, the Word of God became a reality in his life. Over the next several months, Carter's health returned and his heart was healed. One of the songs he wrote, "Standing on the Promises," became a popular hymn sung by Christian believers around the world.

You can find God's promises on every page of the Bible. Some people believe the promises of God number between seven and eight thousand. One of these promises is found in James 2:5. This promise says that if you love Jesus Christ, you will inherit the kingdom of God. The promise is given to those who are poor in the eyes of the world. The poor in this verse are those who recognize their spiritual bankruptcy. They know that they are sinners and know that they don't have it all together. They are broken people who need a Savior.

The promise is given to all people: poor, rich, men, women, all races, and all ages. The only condition for the promise is that you must love Jesus. If you do, you will be rich in faith and your inheritance will be entrance into God's kingdom. Now that is some promise to encourage you. God is offering you eternal life, healing from your brokenness, and a relationship with Jesus. This is a promise to not pass up. Carter accepted this promise and rejoiced when he stood on the promises of Christ.

September 6

In God's Presence

*Surely you have granted him eternal blessings
and made him glad with the joy of your presence.*
Psalm 21:6 (NIV)

Whenever I traveled on business, I was always eager to get back to my wife and children. Kisses, hugs, small gifts, and getting caught up on all of the latest news were things I looked forward to. But I have got to say that the best thing about our reunions was just the joy we had in being in each other's presence again. At that moment, gladness was the only thing that mattered. When I thought about this, I realized that there is an incredible sense of freedom when you experience the love your family members have for one another. We accept each other with all our warts and weaknesses. King David wrote about this sense of freedom in our verse for today.

David loved being in the family of God. He clearly understood the unlimited love God had for him. In his words of praise, David lists the kindnesses God has shown him: granting him his heart's desire, rewarding him with rich blessings, and giving him a long life with victories over his enemies. But the greatest joy David had was being in God's presence.

Jesus died so you, too, could experience the joy of God's presence. When you believe in Jesus, confess your sin, and ask for God's forgiveness, you are born into God's family, and the Holy Spirit comes to live within you. From that time on, you are in God's presence. You are free from bondage to your sinful past. And you can come to him again and again to be cleansed from your sins. God doesn't hold a grudge against you. When you confess your sins, he doesn't even remember them anymore, and you are free to experience God's presence in your life. What a feeling it is to be right with God!

September 7

Facial Recognition

*Man looks at the outward appearance,
but the Lord looks at the heart.*
1 Samuel 16:7 (NIV)

Development of facial recognition systems began in the 1960s. Since that time, use of this technology has become widespread. Although fingerprint and iris recognition are more accurate than facial biometrics, this technology is still the most popular form of matching a human face against a database. While identification and categorization of human faces is a handy tool that saves time and is valuable for security, it is useless when it comes to recognizing the condition of the human heart. Only God can do that.

The Bible says, "Man looks at the outward appearance, but the Lord looks at the heart." In other words, only God knows the real you! That might frighten you, but it can comfort you too. God is the only one who knows what you've gone through and what you may be going through right now! Heartache, rejection, betrayal, disappointment, abandonment, abuse—God knows your heart, and he cares.

This verse makes two important points. It spurs us on to be better people, and it tells us that God is understanding and compassionate when we fail. Come into the light of God's scrutiny. Let him point out your weaknesses and imperfections. Then receive his compassion and forgiveness. That's why God sent Jesus. That's why Jesus died. And that's why we love him so much!

September 8

Barbie Doll

*Beloved, do not imitate what is evil, but what is good.
The one who does good is of God;
the one who does evil has not seen God.*
3 John 1:11 (NASB)

In 2020, Mattel sold $1.35 billion worth of Barbie dolls and accessories. This 11-inch plastic doll, which looks like an adult woman, was created by Ruth Handler. In one of her trips to Europe in 1956, she saw a German doll named Bild Lilli, who looked like an adult blonde bombshell. Handler purchased several of these dolls and gave one of them to her daughter and some to her toy maker to get their feedback. Handler's daughter, Barbie, loved the doll, and the rest is history. "Barbara Millicent Roberts" was officially created and launched on March 9, 1959. Since that time over one billion Barbie dolls have been sold, making it one of the most popular dolls in the world. Barbie has become a model for what little girls admire: a perfect body, perfect hair, a beautiful face, flawless skin, and fancy clothes.

Of course, little girls don't think about the fact that she has no brains, no personality, and zero character. They forget that she's just a piece of plastic with nothing special to distinguish herself except her looks. With Barbie dolls, it's all about physical appearance and nothing about her inner character. Now, I must admit that Barbie dolls aren't evil in themselves. In fact, some movies depict her as a kind person. However, "Barbies" have set an unrealistic standard for femininity in our culture, and they have actively determined what many girls want to be like. Our Bible verse today admonishes us to be very careful about whom we choose to imitate.

Should physical beauty be our top concern? Not if we look at the negative consequences that come along with it: pride, jealousy, competition, ridicule, eating disorders, low self-worth, and maybe even suicide. These are some of the fruits of focusing on one's outward appearance instead of one's inward character. This verse says to focus on what is good. That means what is true and honorable, what is just and pure, what is confident, but also kind. These are the traits God is looking for. These are the traits that make us good people. Do you want to know what is good? The standards of this world are never the best measure of a person's worth. Instead, Jesus Christ should be our model. He didn't appear to be someone the world would admire. But when you love Christ and obey his commands, you are imitating the best person who ever lived, and you are becoming more and more like him. He is the only one I know who is authentically good. He is the opposite of a pretty plastic doll.

September 9

Johnny Appleseed

He who supplies seed to the sower and bread for food will supply and multiply your seed for sowing and increase the harvest of your righteousness.
2 Corinthians 9:10 (ESV)

John Chapman, better known as Johnny Appleseed, was an American pioneer nurseryman who introduced apple trees to Pennsylvania, Ohio, Indiana, and Illinois. When his family moved to Ohio, John began his apprenticeship as an orchardist growing apple trees. Since apples were a viable way for pioneers to support their families, apples were seen as a good money-making business. When Chapman was twenty-six years old, he started his first apple orchard. For the next forty-five years, he was "a gatherer and planter of apple seeds." This hard-working business entrepreneur traveled over 100,000 square miles of Midwestern wilderness as he encouraged settlers to raise apples. Although this became one of the primary reasons for his legend, his earnest appeal to remember the importance of God and his reputation for generosity served as an incredible example for thousands of people. What a role model he was—planting seeds of generosity, devotion to God, and good deeds to others. Oh, to see more people like Johnny Appleseed today!

This verse in 2 Corinthians is a reminder and a promise for God's people. God "supplies seed to the sower and bread for food," and he is the one who "will supply and multiply your seed for sowing." The seed that God gives is not just for your physical food alone, but it is spiritual food. It is opportunities that God provides for you. God wants you to be a sower. He wants you to plant good seeds of hope, to invest in the lives of others, and to offer his grace. He wants you to be a blessing to others.

Isn't this what Jesus Christ did when he became the ultimate example by laying down his life for mankind? This is what sowing is all about—when you plant little seeds of the good news. Just as Johnny Appleseed's generosity gave so many people happy hearts, God has promised to you that he will "increase the harvest of your righteousness" when you give yourself away by serving others. This is your opportunity to be generous!

September 10

Beyond Timbuktu

From the end of the earth I call to You when my heart is faint;
Lead me to the rock that is higher than I. For You have been a refuge
for me, A tower of strength against the enemy.
Psalm 61:2-3 (NASB)

I bet if anyone asked you where Timbuktu is located, you might say that it is somewhere "at the end of the earth." Well, that's not true! Timbuktu is actually a city in the western African nation of Mali and is located on the southern edge of the Sahara Desert. But for most of us, it is beyond our reach. It is too difficult to travel to and probably the last place you would visit. This makes it seem like it *is* the end of the earth. But the truth is that Timbuktu can be reached. It is not impossible to do.

When you look into Psalm 61, King David, who wrote this psalm, must have felt like he was at the end of the earth. Actually, he was at the end of himself and completely overwhelmed. He was paralyzed with fear and felt like he was dying. Have you ever felt that way? Maybe you're in a difficult marriage, have an addiction problem, health problems, or financial troubles. Whatever it is, you feel like you are out of options. You have no place to turn. Your situation is beyond your control.

But David knew he had another option; he called out to God. He cried out to his heavenly Father because he knew that God would hear him. He knew there was no place on Earth where his prayers would not be heard, and he knew that there is no impossible situation when God is involved. Because David trusted in his Savior, he knew that there was no place on Earth that God's love cannot reach.

Let me encourage you today. If you find yourself completely perplexed and exhausted, go "to the rock that is higher" than you. Jesus Christ is that rock, solid and protective, the only true refuge and tower of strength against the enemy that is overwhelming you. He hears all of your prayers. It doesn't matter if it is a silent pleading prayer or even a shout of anger. He hears and cares about you. Just remember that there is never a place beyond the love of Jesus, not even Timbuktu!

September 11

You're in the Army Now!

*For there is no distinction between Jew and Greek;
for the same Lord is Lord of all,
bestowing his riches on all who call on him.
For "everyone who calls on the name of the Lord will be saved."*
Romans 10:12-13 (ESV)

I got off the bus one hot summer afternoon in June 1969 and was quickly introduced to a man who was wearing a "Smokey the Bear" hat. He was screaming at me and all the other men to get off the bus and drop our bags. As soon as we did, this man told us that he was "god," that we were in the Army now, and we had to do anything he ordered—regardless! "Do you understand me?" he asked. Now, this introduction was nothing I had expected. He continued to rant, "You cannot talk; you cannot eat; you cannot sleep unless you are given approval." What was I to do? I was just like all the other enlistees in the Army. It didn't matter where I came from or the color of my skin. No one cared about my education or any other distinctions. I was in the Army now, and the drill sergeant was telling me exactly what to do if I wanted to be successful. So what did I do? I said, "Yes sir!" I knew that joining the Army was going to be difficult, but I was looking forward to the privilege of serving my country and being a success.

If you consider my little story, you might get a hint of what it means to be a member of *God's* army. We're not talking about a God who screams and rants, but we *are* talking about a God who gives orders. Obedience to God's orders satisfies his requirements and makes us good soldiers, successfully serving in his kingdom. It doesn't matter where you come from or the color of your skin. Your history or the ways you have distinguished yourself don't matter. The fact is that all of us are sinners. We have rebelled against God and deserve to be judged. But God the Father loves us so much that he sent his Son to pay the price and rescue us from eternal punishment. Jesus Christ has saved countless numbers of people from the penalty of their sins. He is "Lord of all who call on him" for salvation. Be assured, "Everyone who calls on the name of the Lord *will be saved.*" Will you call on the name of Jesus? He will hear your call if it comes from your heart. Join his army and follow his orders. Then you will have the privilege of serving successfully in the kingdom of God.

September 12

Honey from the Rock

But I would feed you with the finest of the wheat,
And with honey from the rock I would satisfy you.
Psalm 81:16 (NASB)

The lives of bees consist of making honey, pollinating crops, building their hives, and protecting them. It is not uncommon to see wild honey bees make a hive in a rock. Rocks provide far better protection during storms than nests in soil or wood, and they provide protection from parasites. The bees can also stay safe while they are busy making luscious honey. This simple explanation of why bees choose to make their home in rocks makes perfect sense to me. God has given bees the natural ability to know the best place to locate their hive. As a result, honey is one of our blessings.

I see Psalm 81 as a reminder that God has always wanted what is best for mankind. Unfortunately, we often choose to ignore what God has promised to us. We choose to not listen and to rebel against his commands. We go our own way because we think it will be better for us. We choose to pursue "strange gods" that only want to enslave us. We think we will be free, but we end up spiritually bankrupt and unsatisfied. When I look at what the world offers, it is easy to conclude that this life is lacking.

Take a moment now and look at this verse. God is saying that he will "feed you with the finest of the wheat, and with honey from the rock I would satisfy you." God will feed your spirit and satisfy you from the rock. Jesus Christ is the Rock. He is the source. He is the one who offers forgiveness from your sins and provides eternal life. If you follow Jesus, you will be satisfied. This is the only way. Go to the Rock and you will find the most luscious honey in the world!

September 13

Ambush

*You have enclosed me behind and before,
and laid Your hand upon me.*
Psalm 139:5 (NASB)

An ambush is a military tactic that has been used for thousands of years. The ambush is a surprise attack on someone from a concealed position. The trap is always planned in detail, well-rehearsed, and established in a specific location to destroy or capture enemy soldiers. When you are caught in an ambush, you are totally surrounded. There is no place to go. It's a very frightening situation. On the other hand, it can be the best thing that ever happened—if you are ambushed by God!

The Bible says that we have rebelled against God, so we are his enemies. But his love for us is so strong that even while we were still sinners, Christ died for us. But how does he make us his friends? His tactic is to ambush us. His mission is to capture our hearts! This often comes as a surprise! Suddenly, God is in front of us and behind us. We can't get away! We try to avoid him, but he has planned every detail, and he will win us over!

We can thank God for his mission to ambush us. I thank God he has captured my heart!

September 14

A Few Handbreadths

*Behold, you have made my days a few handbreadths,
and my lifetime is as nothing before you.
Surely all mankind stands as a mere breath!*
Psalm 39:5 (ESV)

Do you have any idea what a handbreadth is? It is a space equal to the breadth of the hand or palm. The Bible mentions the handbreadth as a unit of measure. In the Talmud, it is equivalent to four fingers' width. The mean size of an Army glove is 3.5 inches. So when you look at this measurement, it is approximately 2.5 to 4 inches or the breadth of a hand for most humans. This little tidbit of information is what the Bible tells us about man's brevity of life.

God has made our days "a few handbreadths." In other words, our lives are short. We have a limited number of days. Some of us may live seventy or eighty years. In rarer cases, some may even live ninety or one hundred years. But when you stop to consider how many days you have left, you begin to realize that life is really quite short. We are mortal, and compared to God, our lifetime is "a few handbreadths" or "a mere breath"!

The writer of this verse challenges us with an important truth. Every day is a gift from God. The handbreadths we have been given are the extent of our story, and each of our stories is unique, one of a kind. What story are you leaving behind? What are you doing with the precious days you have left? Let me challenge you to consider your relationship with Jesus Christ. Following Jesus makes every day meaningful. He will challenge you to know him better and love him more. He will use you to bless the lives of other people as you reach out to them in love and service. You still have so much to offer in your time on Earth. Jesus will give you purpose and joy as you make every one of the days you have left count for eternity. Surrender your remaining days to God. He will give your life purpose, and you will be rewarded eternally.

September 15

Irrevocable Trust

Behold, I received a command to bless: he has blessed, and I cannot revoke it.
Numbers 23:20 (ESV)

An irrevocable trust agreement is a legal document that allows the transfer of a person's assets into a trust. It is irrevocable in the sense that it cannot be modified, amended, or terminated without the permission of the grantor's beneficiaries. The advantage of setting up an irrevocable trust is that it minimizes estate taxes, so the beneficiaries will be able to keep more of their inheritance. Trust agreements mirror a spiritual truth found in the book of Numbers.

When God gives a "command to bless," that blessing cannot be revoked. It is an irrevocable trust. This was the case when Balak, king of Moab, wanted a heathen prophet to curse the Israelites. The nation of Israel was God's chosen people, and he had promised them an inheritance—the land of Canaan. God was transferring that land to the Israelites, and no king or prophet could modify, amend, or terminate God's intent. His "command to bless" could not be canceled or reversed.

This Old Testament account is given to remind us that God's promise to bless his people is irrevocable. God is faithful; he never changes his mind and always gives good gifts to his children. What an encouragement it is to know that all your sins can be forgiven. God's gift of forgiveness is being offered to you, and his gift to you is irrevocable!

September 16

The Whole Ball of Wax

The law of the Lord is perfect, restoring the soul.
Psalm 19:7 (NASB)

There are several stories about the origins of the expression *the whole ball of wax*. None of these stories are certain, and the connection to wax is unknown. But we do know that in the 1880s, American newspapers used this expression to mean "the whole thing" or "the whole matter." (I would probably call it "the whole enchilada"!) This expression is a good way to think about the law of the Lord in Psalm 19:7.

The law of the Lord is the whole deal or the whole package. It includes the Spirit, the Word of God, the doctrine of God, and most certainly the gospel. All of these together form God's perfect revelation. There are no redundancies and no omissions in it. Of course, the heart of God's revelation is the gospel. God reigns, God saves, and God transforms people's lives. If you embrace these truths, everything changes because the good news of the gospel is "the whole ball of wax."

September 17

Keys for Rest

"I will feed My flock and I will lead them to rest,"
declares the Lord God.
Ezekiel 34:15 (NASB)

In Phillip Keller's book, *A Shepherd Looks at Psalm 23*, he says that it is nearly impossible for sheep to lie down and rest. In order for this to happen, four things must occur:

1. They must have a sense of freedom from anything frightening like a dog or coyote.
2. They should be free from tension or stress between the sheep in the flock.
3. Aggravations caused by flies or pests should be eliminated if possible.
4. They will not lie down if they are hungry.

What is significant here is that the shepherd is the only one who can provide the circumstances that will relieve the sheep of their anxieties.

The Bible says that people are like sheep, so people need a shepherd too. Fears of disease and death, tensions and stress in our relationships with others, aggravation caused by a world of imperfection, a hunger for love and acceptance—what we want is relief from all these anxieties. Will we ever find rest? Ezekiel says, "Yes!" We can find rest in the Lord God, Jesus Christ!

Jesus Christ is the Good Shepherd. He is the only one who can calm our fears and free us from anxiety. He feeds our hearts with his promises in the Bible. He guides our steps and leads us to a place of rest. This rest is found in trusting Jesus for everything. He is what we've all been waiting for. Our Good Shepherd will give us peace now and forever.

September 18

Those Who Can Sympathize

Therefore let us draw near with confidence to the throne of grace, so that we may receive mercy and find grace to help in time of need.
Hebrews 4:16 (NASB)

Anyone who has had cancer knows about fear, anticipation, and hope. Survivors are usually the best ones to offer encouragement. They have been there and done that. Survivors know the difficulties and struggles cancer patients will face. They will offer practical advice that is not sugar-coated. This passage in Hebrews refers to a person who is a lot like one of those cancer survivors.

Jesus is the person we are talking about. He can sympathize with all of our weaknesses. He lived in a body and in a world a lot like ours. He knew what it was like to be tempted, though he never sinned. He knows what it is like to be tired and hungry, to be scorned and betrayed. Grief is not something new for Jesus. He knows all of our struggles and has experienced each one of them himself. When he invites us to draw near to his throne, he is offering us mercy and grace: mercy to find forgiveness, and grace to overcome our difficulties. What a blessing it is to know that although we fail, we can always come to God's throne for forgiveness and help in our time of need.

September 19

The Elliptical Machine

The Lord is my portion.
Psalm 119:57a (NASB)

Many years ago, I met a man whom I would see regularly at the gym. We usually were on the elliptical machine at the same time. A fifty-minute workout gives you many opportunities to get to know someone. If you ask a few questions, you may quickly discover a person's name, job, interests, and maybe even something more. In my first conversation with this man, I learned all about a company that was listed on NASDAQ. In our continuing conversations, it became apparent that this man spent most of his day checking his investments in the stock market and reading articles that would give him more insight into his ultimate goal, to become a rich man. All his thoughts, energy, and affection centered on this one thing. If you want to know what is important to people, listen to what they like to talk about, and watch how they spend their time. This verse in Psalm 119 tells us volumes about what was important to King David.

When David proclaimed, "The Lord is my portion," he was stating what was most important to him. As King, David had everything most men dream about: wealth, power, and fame. But what was his main topic of conversation? It was the wonder and joy of his relationship with the God of the universe. His relationship with the Lord was his ultimate treasure. When we read these words of David, it challenges us to think about our own lives. What are my goals each day? How am I spending my precious time and resources? Is my goal in life merely getting rich? Is it a favorite hobby? Is it simply entertaining myself? It is easy to focus on things that will pass away and forget the things that will last forever. Your relationship with God is what is really important since you will spend eternity *with* him—or *without* him. What is *your* portion? The time to decide is right now. Seek after God. Open up the Bible and ask God to reveal himself to you. God says, "If you seek me with all your heart, you will find me." Who knows, after fifty minutes in God's Word, you could actually meet Jesus!

September 20

Peace of Mind

The steadfast of mind You will keep in perfect peace, because he trusts in You. Trust in the Lord forever, for in God the Lord, we have an everlasting Rock.
Isaiah 26:3-4 (NASB)

What gives you peace of mind? Is it your bank account or owning your own home? Is it a good report on your physical or the fact that you don't have cancer? Maybe it is a teenager driving home safely from a date or seeing your child graduate from college. Whatever it is, it stops you from worrying about a particular problem or difficulty. This verse in Isaiah does the same kind of thing for believers.

The promise is made to all people who rely on the Lord. Christ will hold you fast. No matter how many times you fail, he will not give up on you. No matter how many times you turn your back on him, he will keep his promise to you. And no matter how many times you lose your way, he will bring you back. Jesus does this because he truly loves you and delights in you. When you take hold of this gospel truth, you will find peace of mind. You have an everlasting Rock who will hold you fast.

September 21

Bird Watching

Look at the birds in the air, that they do not sow, nor reap nor gather into barns, and yet your heavenly Father feeds them.
Are you not worth much more than they? And who of you by being worried can add a single hour to his life?
Matthew 6:26-27 (NASB)

When I go on a hike, I am always amazed by the sights and sounds of the birds. Their colors, size, chirping noises, whistles, and croaks are a tribute to the Creator. Soaring in the sky or singing atop a tree, they seem to love life. They are filled with joy with no visible stress in the world to bother them. Their Creator feeds them every day without question. They have no worries or concerns because God cares for them. This observation about birds was given to us in the Gospel of Matthew.

We could learn so much from these little birds if we could just be still long enough. It is so easy for us to race through life trying to make the next appointment or deadline. Life is so fast and chaotic that we never have time to enjoy the little things. All around us, God is at work feeding the birds and faithfully taking care of the universe. He is aware of every single thing happening right now. Nothing escapes his notice. When a sparrow falls to the ground, he knows. But look at us running around chasing after things that really don't matter at all. We have a God who loves us so much and values us much more than the birds! Yet we fret and worry over the non-essentials. Ultimately, few things I worry about are going to matter. The only thing that will matter is whether we have a relationship with the Savior. The next time you take a hike, relax in the knowledge that he loves you and cares for you.

September 22

Besieged!

The cords of death entangled me; the torrents of destruction overwhelmed me. The cords of the grave coiled around me; the snares of death confronted me. I call to the Lord, who is worthy of praise, and I am saved from my enemies. He brought me out into a spacious place; he rescued me because he delighted in me.
Psalm 18:3-5,19 (NIV)

Floyd James Thompson was the longest-held American POW in the Vietnam War. He was an Army Special Forces soldier serving as a Green Beret when he was captured on March 26, 1964. Thompson survived the crash of his observation plane when it was downed by enemy small arms fire. He was the only one to survive, but he broke his back and was quickly captured by the Viet Cong, where he was besieged with torture, starvation, and isolation. He wasn't allowed to talk to other Americans for over five years. His captors relentlessly attempted to make him admit that what he was doing as an American soldier was criminal. He refused and was beaten, choked, hanged by his thumbs, handcuffed, and shackled in leg irons. It's hard to imagine the abuse this man endured. His was a living nightmare. Finally, in March 1973, Thompson was released with other POWs, ending nine years in captivity.

An individual is under siege when he (or she) is surrounded by enemy forces and cut off from help or supplies. In our verses for today, King David writes about a time when he was besieged by his enemies, what it was like, and how he was rescued. You and I will probably never be besieged like Thompson or King David, but many times, we can be under siege by the difficulties of life. Broken relationships, depression, anxiety, financial hardship, and even our own feelings of guilt can overwhelm us. We feel we are surrounded by impossible circumstances with no one to help and no one to supply what we so desperately need.

But how we feel and what is actually true can be two very different things. King David might have felt alone, but he knew the truth. The God of the whole universe delighted in him and was willing to intervene. He could go to God and find forgiveness for his sins and the power to overcome them. He could find peace with God to calm his anxious heart. He could ask God for supplies to meet his needs. He could trust God, who never betrays his children or breaks his promises to them. He believed that God would rescue him and bring him out of his circumstances and "into a spacious place." And that's exactly what God did! God offers to do all these things for you too. He can release you from your captivity. Your living nightmare can finally be over!

September 23

Opinions

Let them praise the name of the Lord, for His name alone is exalted; His glory is above earth and heaven.
Psalm 148:13 (NASB)

If you were to look into how many US Congressional bills had unanimous vote approval, you would find those bills are rare. How many people do you know who share the same opinion? Sometimes the issue looks so obvious, yet there is usually at least one person who will not agree. This truth is actually one of the most important strengths of our nation. We value differing opinions. In Psalm 148, however, we learn a critical truth: there must never be differing opinions on what God has clearly taught in his Word.

God did a superb job when he developed a plan for this planet. It was good and well thought out. And when he created people, he communicated his plan. The plan is this: he alone is above Earth and heaven. He alone is the Creator, the Lawgiver, and the judge. No one is allowed to have a different opinion from God's. He's the boss. We must understand this simple fact.

This is a bit upsetting to us, isn't it? We have always believed we are entitled to our *own* opinion. And we've gotten so independent and prideful, we think our opinions are the only thing that matters. We think we know better than God! We are so focused on ourselves, that we fail to exalt him. We want our rights, and we will fight for them. We rebel and go our own way, and we make up our own gods to worship. But Jesus Christ came to Earth to rescue us from this foolish thinking. He offers us the truth, and it's time to get on board. We will all be faced with the same question when our lives end. Sure, we get to have our opinion. And what will it be? Will you choose eternal life with Jesus? Or will you choose another way? If we believe the truths in God's Word, we get the best of everything God has to offer. We get a Savior, Jesus Christ the Lord.

September 24

The Promise

He has remembered His covenant forever,
The word which He commanded to a thousand generations,
The covenant which He made with Abraham,
and His oath to Isaac.
Psalm 105:8-9 (NASB)

Have you ever made a promise to someone you love? "I am taking you out for ice cream next Wednesday." "I am going to take you to Disneyland when you turn ten years old." This kind of promise is often made during a casual conversation. You intend to keep the promise, so there's no need for a signed contract or binding agreement. Promises like these are something a person remembers and looks forward to with great anticipation. If we forget our promise or fail to keep it, our loved one will be seriously disappointed. It might be difficult to regain his trust. The God of the Bible never forgets. He always keeps his promises. We see that clearly in our verses for today.

God's covenant is a promise he gives to the ones he loves. His promise is to be our God, our Father, our provider and protector, our Savior and closest friend. This promise wasn't just for Abraham, who lived way back in ancient times. It extended to Abraham's children and their children, and it extends right up to the present day. He has taken an oath to be faithful and true to our children, our grandchildren, and all future generations who put their trust in him.

God put his signature on the contract when he took on a human body, came to Earth, died for our sins, and rose from the grave. There are no exceptions or limitations to his promise, so you can count on God. He will never fail. His ultimate promise? "I am taking you to heaven when you die. You are going to live with me forever!"

September 25

Now That Is a Big Door!

*I am the door; if anyone enters through Me,
he will be saved, and will go in and out and find pasture.*
John 10:9 (NASB)

The world's largest doors are the doors of the NASA Vehicle Assembly Building at the Kennedy Space Center, on Merritt Island, Florida. Space shuttles are big, and that is the reason why you need big doors. The doors are 456 feet high, and it takes forty-five minutes to completely open and close them. The doors are the same height as the world's tallest roller coaster and almost three times the height of Niagara Falls. In John 10, Jesus compares himself to a door.

Why would Jesus do this? Doors provide access to something. Jesus is the door you must go through to gain access to salvation. What Jesus is saying is that if you want to be saved you need to trust in him for your salvation. If you trust in him, he will open the door to heaven, and you will be included in the family of God. There is only one door big enough to give you this access. When Jesus sees your heart, you are given free access to the pasture of fullness of life and eternity. A big door means a great King and a great Savior who gives access to all who run to Him.

September 26

Mert's Potato Salad

Blessed be the God and Father of our Lord Jesus Christ, who has blessed us with every spiritual blessing in the heavenly places in Christ.
Ephesians 1:3 (NASB)

Growing up in the Midwest, I have always loved potato salad. When I first started courting my wife, my future mother-in-law, Mert, served me her special potato salad. When I tasted it, I was simply amazed. Her salad was far better than anything I had ever eaten. When talking to my wife about how it was made, I learned about all the correct ingredients and the steps to make it just right—little things like not letting the potatoes cool down too much before peeling off the skin. Also, I learned to let the salad sit in the refrigerator for one day before eating it. All these details contribute to making it one of my favorite foods. Mert's potato salad is, in my opinion, a little taste of heaven. This is exactly what Paul was talking about in the book of Ephesians.

Jesus Christ blesses us with every spiritual blessing when we follow him. It is only given to those who trust in him. Each blessing is a foretaste of our relationship with Jesus. Just like Mert's potato salad, Jesus assembled all the ingredients needed to bless our lives. He was willing to do what it would cost to save us from our sins. He took all the steps necessary to bless us with every spiritual blessing. Gifts like adoption, redemption, forgiveness, and other items we cannot buy were all included to give us a new life and a future home in heaven. Just like Jesus did, he gave us the best because he loves us.

What a blessing Mert was because of her love for Jesus and her special recipe which I now enjoy!

September 27

A Carpenter's Level

Let the nations be glad and sing for joy;
For You will judge the peoples with uprightness
And guide the nations on the earth.
Psalm 67:4 (NASB)

If you have ever had to hang a picture on the wall or had to install a countertop, you would have discovered how important a carpenter's level is. This popular tool is a necessity in determining whether a surface is flat. To use this level, place the tool on the surface of the frame or the countertop. In the level itself, there are usually two or more small vials that have a bubble and liquid in them. The vials will have markings that indicate when the bubble is in the center of the vial. If the bubble is centered, it is true vertical or true horizontal. In other words, it is plumb, upright, or in balance. How do you know this? Your eyes will tell you if it is crooked, slanted, or lopsided. Much like this simple carpenter's level, today's verse illustrates a simple truth about God.

God "will judge the peoples with uprightness and guide the nations on the earth." God is sovereign and just in all of his dealings with mankind. He is upright, fair, equitable, and impartial all of the time. God is the only standard for what is right and wrong in this world.

Do you want to know if your life is centered or plumb? Examine your heart. Look at your motives, attitudes, priorities, deeds, and words. Once you do that, look at God's standard. Guess what happens when you do that? All of a sudden you realize that your life is slanted and lopsided. Why? Because we are sinners and have broken God's standards of righteousness.

This is not the end of the story, however. God was gracious to us and sent his Son, Jesus, to dwell with us. He offers each of us the gift of forgiveness. He will take your brokenness and center the bubble in your life. He levels your life and gives you the Holy Spirit as your guide. Do you want to know why I am glad and sing for joy? I am forgiven!

September 28

Been Down That Road Before!

The Lord is the one who goes ahead of you; He will be with you. He will not fail you or forsake you. Do not fear or be dismayed.
Deuteronomy 31:8 (NASB)

How many times do we think, "I have been down that road before, and I don't want my children to make the same mistakes"? We want the very best for our kids. We're even willing to help them clean up the garbage they've accumulated, if necessary. The amazing thing is that our heavenly Father feels the same way about all of his children. He wants the very best for us, no matter where we've been or what we've done. This verse from Deuteronomy was Moses' charge to Joshua and the people of Israel. It's also a verse for us!

We like to think that we lead the way, but God has already been there and done that. God is way ahead of us. He is the true pathfinder. And here is God's promise to encourage your heart: God will be with you, and he will never fail you or abandon you. In other words, he is with you on your journey. He sees where you are and knows what is happening to you right now. He never loses sight of you. He knows when you are struggling, and he hears your complaints. You need not fear or be dismayed at all. The good news for you is that Jesus has been down that road before. He knows what lies ahead. Yes, he knows about your fear of death, COVID, or anything else that worries you at night. What a blessing to know that King Jesus is the one who leads the way!

September 29

Ticker-Tape Parades

But thanks be to God, who always leads us in triumph in Christ, and manifests through us the sweet aroma of the knowledge of Him in every place.
2 Corinthians 2:14 (NASB)

The term *ticker-tape parade* originated in New York City on October 28, 1886 during the dedication of the Statue of Liberty. Ticker tape was the paper output of ticker-tape machines used in brokerages to provide updated stock market quotes. The term *ticker* was the sound made by the printing machine. The shredded paper was used in parades to honor heroes and celebrate special occasions. Two of the largest parades ever included General Douglas MacArthur after the Korean War and astronaut John Glenn in 1962. Roman generals and their troops had similar parades when they came home from successful military campaigns. These parades were called triumphal marches. They fascinated and dazzled the Roman crowds.

In the verse for today, Paul describes our lives with Christ as triumphal marches. Jesus, our general, has achieved victory over the devil by his death on the cross, and he's on the march home. His victories are adding new people to God's kingdom every day. As we march with Christ, *we* are celebrating God's victory of grace in our hearts, and *the world* is catching the sweet aroma of Christ. His love, his joy, his peace, and his goodness are on public display for all to see. When a person trusts in Christ for his salvation, he joins God's victory march, celebrating Jesus, who conquered death and gave us eternal life. No confetti is needed for this parade, only the sweet aroma of the knowledge of Jesus!

September 30

Biltmore House

But will God indeed dwell on the earth?
Behold, heaven and the highest heaven cannot contain You,
how much less this house which I have built!
1 Kings 8:27 (NASB)

In 1889, George Vanderbilt began construction on the Biltmore House in Asheville, North Carolina. By the time it was complete, it was the largest home in America, spanning 175,000 square feet of space. The 250-room home includes thirty-five bedrooms, forty-three bathrooms, and sixty-five fireplaces. Adjacent to the home are seventy-five acres of gardens designed by the famous landscape architect, Frederick Law Olmsted. Today it is still family-owned, but it has become a tourist site for others to enjoy.

In the book of 1 Kings, we learn that King Solomon built an extravagant house too. This house became known as "Solomon's Temple" and is one of the wonders of the ancient world. But at the dedication of the temple, Solomon asked a serious question: "Will God actually come here and dwell on the earth?" Even the highest heaven, even the entire universe could never contain God! The answer Solomon got surprised him. Yes! God would dwell in Solomon's house—for a while. But he had an even better plan. God would come to live on Earth as a human being in the person of Jesus Christ! When Jesus dwelt on Earth, he didn't live in a lavish temple. He didn't even own a home! While he was here, he suffered in every way a human being can suffer. He was poor, homeless, ridiculed, and rejected. He even suffered a violent death. Jesus lived a humble life, but the words he preached changed the world. His words were simple, challenging, and life-changing. His death purchased our salvation. Jesus is still dwelling on Earth today. His Holy Spirit lives in the body and heart of every person who puts his trust in him. And what's more, nothing can compare with the spectacular home we will share with him forever at the end of time. This is really good news!

October 1

"He's Got the Whole World in His Hands"

Tremble before Him, all the earth;
Indeed, the world is firmly established, it will not be moved.
Let the heavens be glad, and let the earth rejoice;
And let them say among the nations, "The Lord reigns."
1 Chronicles 16:30-31 (NASB)

This traditional gospel song was published in 1927. It became an international hit in 1957 when it was recorded by English singer Laurie London. As the title tells us, God has the whole world in his hands. These words have been a source of comfort for people all over the world. Many verses of the lyrics have even made it popular with little children: "He's got the little bitty baby in his hands," "He's got my brothers and my sisters in his hands," or "He's got the sun and the rain in his hands." No matter which verse you are singing, the message is clear—God reigns!

"The world is firmly established, and it will not be moved." God didn't establish the world just to throw it away! He established it to reign over it, and he is intimately involved with his people. What an encouragement to know that God is governing all of creation, and he loves us and is involved with us personally. No matter what turmoil or chaos we see in the news today, the world is firmly established by God, and therefore it cannot be moved. We learn from this that God has a purpose for this world and for each of us, and he will accomplish what he has set out to do. He is never frustrated. He is in charge. We should tremble before a God like this, but we can also rejoice. No doomsday for us! God holds the whole world in his hands, so we have hope and a future! What a privilege it is to be included in God's purpose and future plans! It causes us to sing with confidence and joy, "He's Got the Whole World in His Hands"!

October 2

How Many Times?

*Therefore you are no longer a slave, but a son;
and if a son, then an heir through God.*
Galatians 4:7 (NASB)

My wife and I are truly blessed to have seven grandchildren. We are proud of all of them. I am constantly amazed by the number of times she tells our grandchildren that she loves them. How many times does she hug and kiss each one? How many times does she buy them little gifts? How many times does she encourage them with little comments like, "You can do it!" How many times does it take for all of these kids to know that they are loved, appreciated, and accepted? Is it 100 times, 1000 times, or 10,000 times? These questions remind me of the many times and many ways God says, "I love you!" to his people.

Jesus came to the earth to offer the gifts of forgiveness and eternal life to everyone who receives it. When we receive these two gifts, we get another—the gift of a new identity. We are no longer slaves to sin. We are beloved sons and daughters of God. And if we are his children, we are also heirs of God's kingdom. If you think about this for a while, it can be life-changing. So back to the question I posed: How many times does it take for you to believe? How many times have you experienced God's work in your life? How many times has he provided for your needs? How many times does he bless you each day? And how many times does he offer you forgiveness? Is it 100 times, 1000 times, or 10,000 times? We tend to forget his blessings until we remember the cross. That's how we know we are beloved.

October 3

Special Treasure

*For the Lord has chosen Jacob for Himself,
Israel for His own possession.*
Psalm 135:4 (NASB)

There are many reasons to praise God, but this one is especially awesome. It says that the Lord chose Jacob for himself, to be his own possession. Why is this so awesome? Because Jacob was a sinner, just like you and me. Jacob represents every one of us! Does anybody you know deserve to be counted as God's own possession? How about you? Do you deserve this privilege? No. Every person who has ever lived has rebelled against God and gone his own way. If anything, all of us deserve to be tossed out, not loved as God's treasure.

But when God chooses someone, he does something more—he gives him a new name. God gave Jacob the new name, Israel, which means "prince." When God chooses us to be his possession, he renames us too. We are called children of the king—the King of the universe! With this new identity, our lives begin to change and take on new purpose. We are valuable. We are God's special treasure.

October 4

Smile Train

The Lord bless you, and keep you;
The Lord make His face shine on you, and be gracious to you;
The Lord lift up His countenance on you, and give you peace.
Numbers 6:24-26 (NASB)

For more than twenty years, an organization named Smile Train has cared for over 1.5 million children worldwide who are born with a cleft lip or cleft palate. One in seven hundred babies are born with this abnormality every year, globally. Clefts cause difficulties in eating, breathing, hearing, and speaking. This charity provides free corrective surgery in eighty-seven countries and also trains local doctors. The most incredible blessing is that each one of these children is given the gift of a smile! In this passage in Numbers, we learn some exciting things about God's smile and the blessings it brings.

Imagine God's face shining on you! His loving countenance is blessing you; it's keeping you; it's being gracious to you; it's giving you peace. This is exactly why Jesus came to the earth. Through his life and death for our sins, we are offered grace and peace with God. When we accept his gift of salvation, God's blessings are bestowed upon us. His shining face is a ray of light, focused on us. It is a signal of his favor and acceptance. Our sins are forgiven and his blessings are ours!

October 5

Fads

As for me, I shall behold Your face in righteousness;
I will be satisfied with Your likeness when I awake.
Psalm 17:15 (NASB)

They will see His face, and His name will be on their foreheads.
Revelation 22:4 (NASB)

What do scrap cooking, fidget spinners, and parachute pants have in common? They are fads. They have a shelf life. They're here today, gone tomorrow. Let's face it, fads fade. That's one reason people struggle to be content. They are always looking for the next new thing to make them happy. But getting wrapped up in the latest fad is a recipe for disappointment.

The writers of today's verses had a different way of looking at life. They didn't focus on the latest fad. They had an eternal perspective. They knew that a relationship with God would fill their hearts with lasting joy. A relationship with God never fades; it only gets stronger, brighter, and more satisfying over time! We behold Jesus' face when we read his words in the Bible and when we see how much he loved his Father and treated people with compassion and dignity. We behold his face when we think about him and are guided by his example, when we pray, and when we receive his peace. I don't know about you, but I am tired of chasing after the latest fad. It's a waste of time. I'm going to concentrate on my relationship with God, the everlasting Father, and Jesus, the Prince of Peace.

October 6

Choosing an Aroma?

For we are a fragrance of Christ to God among those who are being saved and among those who are perishing; to the one an aroma from death to death, to the other an aroma from life to life.
2 Corinthians 2:15-16 (NASB)

Recent studies on the human sense of smell reveal that scent signals travel to the brain regions that process emotions and memory even faster than they travel to the nose. But this doesn't mean that our powerful smell potential is deficient at all. Research has found that we can distinguish at least one trillion different odors, which is up from the previous estimates of 10,000. We also know now that every person has a unique scent, which is just like a fingerprint.

"The fragrance of Christ" in our verse for today is a figure of speech. It gives us words to explain the atmosphere that flows from people who know Jesus Christ as their Savior and are enjoying God's grace. Each person has a physical scent that is unique to him. But the "fragrance of Christ" is something different. It is a sense of love, peace, joy, and goodness—qualities that are hard to describe, but surprisingly genuine. Not everyone who claims to be a Christian will demonstrate the "fragrance of Christ," but a true Christian who is walking with his Savior will exude Christ's aroma. Some people will experience this fragrance but reject Christ. They will perish. Others will experience this fragrance and receive Christ. They will be saved. The right choice is yours to make.

October 7

Keep Your Eyes on the Ball

Rest in the Lord and wait patiently for Him;
Do not fret because of him who prospers in his way,
Because of the man who carries out wicked schemes.
Psalm 37:7 (NASB)

I like to play golf, but I am not very good at it. I tend to take my eyes off the ball when I swing. I always look up so I can see where the ball is going. And you know what happens? My lack of focus gets me into trouble. The ball goes either left or right, and sometimes I miss it completely. It always amazes me that when I keep my head down and my eyes are focused on this little ball only 1.68 inches in diameter, it will most likely go straight and travel a greater distance. Focus is the key to this game. Distractions only bring trouble. This simple truth is the key to understanding the verse for today.

God is advising us to keep our focus on him. *Fret* in the Hebrew language means "to burn or be kindled with anger or distress." In English, it means "to fume, fuss, or agonize" over a situation. When we fret over people's bad behavior or even over their good successes, we are taking our eyes off the ball. God doesn't want his beloved children to fuss and fume. He wants them to rest in him and wait patiently for him. How much energy have you and I expended agonizing over things that are outside our control? The trouble is that fretting just makes us angry, depressed, and hard to live with! The rules of the world for success and prosperity will always be different from the rules for God's people. Believe me, I know how difficult this is.

But the first part of this verse is what I want you to remember. God always gives the best advice. He wants his people to rest and be patient. He is a straight shooter. He knows what he's doing. His purpose for you might be different from what you expected, but it will always be just right for your spiritual growth and his glory. He always wants the best for you because he loves you. If you keep your eyes on him, you will find rest, peace, joy, and love. You will never have to look back with regret because you will be in the center of his will. I don't know if I will ever shoot under 100 in my golf score, but I do know that if I keep my eyes on Jesus, I will go straight on his path for my life and straight to heaven when he calls me home.

October 8

Stirring the Nest

He found him in a desert land, and in the howling waste of a wilderness; He encircled him, He cared for him, He guarded him as the pupil of His eye. Like an eagle that stirs up its nest, that hovers over its young, He spread His wings and caught them, He carried them on His pinions.
Deuteronomy 32:10-11 (NASB)

When the mother eagle is expecting her young, she will prepare a large nest on a high cliff. She will make the nest out of large branches and sharp thorns. The mother will pad the inside of the nest with comfortable feathers and wool. Both loving parents will provide all of their eaglets with food, warmth, and protection. As they grow, the mother will start preparing them little by little for their departure. She does this by slowly removing all of the soft feathers and wool and stirring the nest. When she does this, the nest starts getting uncomfortable for the eaglets. The youngsters will soon start flapping their wings and their lessons in flight will begin. While they practice flying, the parents are never too far away. They are there to spread their wings and catch their eaglets if they get into trouble. This example of an eagle stirring up the nest was Moses' last song near the end of his life.

This beautiful illustration teaches us a lot about God and his children. God provides for us, hovers over us, and rescues us in our troubles. He does this because he is our Father, and we are a delight to him. At some point, he will stir up the nest. Even though it may be uncomfortable, God is preparing us to soar on wings like eagles. So remember, when there is no more comfort in your nest, start flapping your little wings of faith and our loving Father will catch you.

October 9

Violin Lessons

*But do not overlook this one fact, beloved,
that with the Lord one day is as a thousand years,
and a thousand years as one day.
The Lord is not slow to fulfill his promise as some count slowness,
but is patient toward you, not wishing that any should perish,
but that all should reach repentance.*
2 Peter 3:8-9 (ESV)

Several years ago I started taking violin lessons. I always loved hearing the violin in concerts and considered it very enjoyable and relaxing. I played the trumpet in my high school band and I was pretty good, so how hard could it be to play the violin? Guess what? Playing the violin was much harder than I could have ever imagined. Holding the violin correctly, gripping the bow, learning the fingerings, and shifting positions all must be precise, consistent, and steady to produce a beautiful sound. Fortunately, my teacher encouraged me to have patience. She knew how long it would take before my squeaky noises would start to sound better. Her compassion as a teacher and her wisdom about the time required to learn this instrument were a great encouragement to me. But above everything else, she was patient with me and taught me to be patient too. "It will happen," she said, "and when it does, it will bring you so much joy!" These verses in 2 Peter tell us about God's patience and encourage us to be patient too.

God looks at time much differently than we do. We tend to want everything right now. Let's go! Hurry up! But God sees one day as a thousand years and a thousand years as one day. In other words, God sees time from an eternal perspective. And because he is eternal, he sees the far-reaching outcomes of our actions. We may think that God is slow, but actually, he is waiting patiently for us to come to our senses. For instance, a person's temporary decision to reject the Lord Jesus Christ and his forgiveness is a choice that has eternal consequences. Don't forget, every person will one day stand before God and give an account for his or her actions. Jesus Christ has offered himself as a sacrifice for us, and if we accept his offer of mercy, God promises to give us eternal life. If you haven't repented of your sins and accepted God's offer yet (and you are still alive), you can be mighty thankful for God's patience. God wishes that no one would perish. He wishes everyone would repent and become part of his family. Be very thankful for his patience, but don't wait too long! Someday, it will be too late.

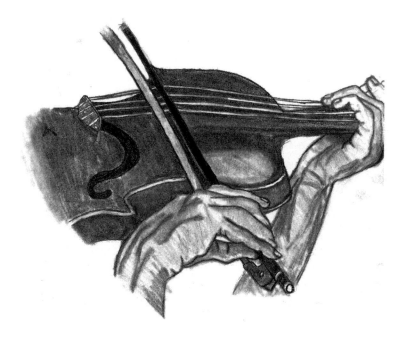

October 10

Heart of the Matter

*My flesh and my heart may fail,
But God is the strength of my heart and my portion forever.*
Psalm 73:26 (NASB)

The common phrase "heart of the matter" is used to refer to something that is most important or essential. Since the heart is the most vital part of our body and soul, this phrase is a good way to illustrate a truth we find in Psalm 73.

This verse starts out with an observation from the psalmist. It is a truth we all know about ourselves. The longer we live, the more our bodies and strength fail us. Our sins outnumber our good deeds. Our heart tells us we are not good enough to earn eternal life. The heart of the matter is that we are sinners who need forgiveness. We need a Savior. By embracing Jesus, I claim his strength for my heart. If I have a relationship with him, I have an inheritance from him because I am part of God's family. Even if I fail, I have a Savior who loves me, died to pay for my sins, and promises forgiveness and eternal life. In the end, this is all that matters.

October 11

Self-Talk

*Praise the Lord, O my soul, and forget not all his benefits—
who forgives all your sins and heals all your diseases,
who redeems your life from the pit and crowns you with love and
compassion, who satisfies your desires with good things
so that your youth is renewed like the eagle's.*
Psalm 103:2-5 (NIV)

Have you ever talked to yourself? I have, and I bet you have too! And we're not crazy! Several research studies show that talking to yourself is perfectly normal and quite healthy. Why do we do this? For me, it is usually a reminder not to forget something. Sometimes I'm just giving myself a pep talk. No matter what the reason is, talking to yourself seems to help. When I read this passage from Psalms, it sounds to me like David was giving himself a pep talk, reminding himself of all the benefits of being his child. Read the passage again. It's a good one!

We get so caught up in the details of everyday life that we forget what is really important. The devil wants us to worry about how we are going to take care of our kids, pay the bills, and manage our future. He robs us of our confidence and tells us that living in this world is lonely and depressing. When this happens, we need to engage in some serious self-talk.

We have to say to ourselves, "Praise the Lord, O my soul, and forget not all his benefits." What are his benefits? Well, here are a few: He forgives all my sins, so I can always come to him, confess my sins, and receive his help. He heals all my diseases and will someday take me to heaven where I will never be sick again. He redeems my life from the pit of hell and crowns me with love and compassion. He satisfies my desires with good things so that my youth is renewed like the eagle's. What more could we ask for?

Like we said, self-talk is normal and quite healthy, but only if we tell ourselves the truth!

Always remember to encourage yourself with the awesome benefits of being a child of God.

October 12

Why Horror Movies?

Come, behold the works of the Lord, who has wrought desolations in the earth. He makes wars to cease to the end of the earth; He breaks the bow and cuts the spear in two;
He burns the chariots with fire.
Psalm 46:8-9 (NASB)

The most obvious reason for the success of horror movies is rooted in Hollywood economics. These movies make money! But why would you watch them? Why do people love to be scared? I think there are many reasons for this. When we view any strong emotion like fear, anger, hatred, or love, we are actually put in touch with the emotion. We might be terrified, but we are safe. We can deal with our fear because we can experience it from a distance. I think these types of movies are like the verse in Psalm 46 because they make us behold desolations.

Why would God want us to see the desolations or what I call the "train wreck"? Is there something to learn from this? Yes, there is. God wants us to take a look at our struggling and striving and remember that he is God. God is sovereign and in control. All our wars and struggles are useless. Why do we fight against God? We want control of our life; we want to be independent. Just like wars, God will end them all. He will break the bows and burn the chariots when all is done. Our fight for independence will end when we embrace the King who only wants the best for us. When we lay down our arms, we are safe!

October 13

No Words!

*Then all men will fear, and they will declare the work of God,
And will consider what He has done.*
Psalm 64:9 (NASB)

There are simply no words to describe the city of Hiroshima, Japan on August 6, 1945. It is unbelievable! What words could ever adequately describe this city after being totally destroyed by a nuclear bomb? Do words like *devastating, catastrophic,* or *overwhelming* really give you the true sense of what happened there? Is it possible to capture the feelings of those survivors who lost 100,000 loved ones, neighbors, and friends? Events like this stun the world and capture everyone's attention. Today's verse does the same thing for me.

One day, all mankind will be filled with fear. That is the day when every person will stand before the judgment seat of God. Every human being who has ever lived will have to give a detailed account of what he did with the life God gave him. The story of God's mighty works of creation and his loving work of redemption will be the focus. No one will be able to debate God's power and his righteousness. No one will dispute his right to judge. Can you imagine what you will be feeling on that day?

When will this happen? We don't know the precise date, but according to the Bible, we know that each person will be held accountable for his deeds. We also know that a person who has received Jesus Christ as his Savior will be covered by his sacrificial blood, completely pardoned, and welcomed into heaven. When I think about the judgment seat of God and my pardon, I am filled with joy and gratitude instead of fear. No words could ever describe my indebtedness to him or my praise for what he has done for me!

October 14

Stuck in Mud

*I waited patiently for the Lord; he turned to me and heard my cry.
He lifted me out of the slimy pit, out of the mud and mire;
he set my feet on a rock and gave me a firm place to stand.*
Psalm 40:1-2 (NIV)

Many years ago, my car got stuck in mud. At first I thought that I could just back it up and get it out. How hard could this be anyway? The more I did this, the more it sunk down into this awful mud and mire. So I tried to go forward and speed up, but that didn't work either. By now it was getting me frustrated. My patience was being sorely tested. I even tried other options, but nothing worked. I was absolutely convinced that I could free myself. But in the end, I gave up and called for help. "Please pull me out of this mud!" I said. I think the psalmist may have felt the same way when he wrote these verses in Psalm 40.

When you are stuck in mud, your life quickly becomes messy. Things aren't happening the way you planned. What mud are you stuck in? A physical problem, a financial issue, or a relationship problem? Maybe you need to forgive someone, or he needs to forgive you. When you are in a situation like this, you are in a slimy pit and you need someone to lift you out. At some point in life, everyone needs help. Everyone needs a Savior to deliver him from troubles he has created for himself. Once you recognize that, the only thing you can do is cry out to the Lord and wait patiently for his help. When you wait for the Lord, you are trusting in his promises. You are waiting for the Savior to rescue you. You are waiting for the one who can deliver you from impossible situations.

Let me share something with you about getting out of mud. If you cry out to the Lord and wait patiently, he is going to hear your cry and come to you. He is going to bring you out of the mud and mire, set your feet on a rock, and give you a firm place to stand. The Rock we're talking about is the Lord Jesus Christ himself. So the next time you are stuck in mud, try calling out to Jesus. He is the only one who can get you out of your mess!

October 15

Fanny Crosby

*The people who walk in darkness will see a great light;
Those who live in a dark land, the light will shine on them.*
Isaiah 9:2 (NASB)

Fanny Crosby wrote more than 9,000 hymns. They are sung by worshipers in every Christian denomination. When she was just six weeks old, a quack doctor treated her eyes incorrectly. This left her permanently blind. Despite her handicap, Fanny loved poetry and zealously memorized the Bible. She memorized five chapters each week and could recite all four gospels, Proverbs, and many psalms. When she was fifteen years old, she enrolled in a school for the blind in New York. After graduating, she taught other blind students. When she was thirty-eight years old, she married one of New York's most renowned organists. Over her career as a hymn writer, she became personal friends with every single United States president. She also learned to play the harp, the piano, and the guitar. And she continued writing poetry right up until the time of her death, a month shy of her ninety-fifth birthday. Her last line of poetry was "You will reach the river brink, some sweet day, by and by." Even though Fanny's blindness kept her in physical darkness, God's light was shining on her, making her a person who has blessed millions of people with his great light.

In the verses for today, Isaiah spoke of a coming Messiah. Jesus would be the Light of the World. He would give light to every man shackled in spiritual darkness, sin, and despair. Jesus offers hope, gives truth, and provides sight for all those who are spiritually blind. What I find truly impressive is that he will find you and shine his light on you. The gift of sight can be yours when you seek Jesus and trust in him. I'm looking forward to us both reaching that "river brink, some sweet day, by and by" where we will be able to see everything—perfectly!

October 16

Hunger

Jesus said to them, "I am the bread of life; he who comes to Me will not hunger, and he who believes in Me will never thirst."
John 6:35 (NASB)

Approximately 805 million of the world's population are undernourished or hungry every day. This means these people go to bed on an empty stomach each night. Each day 25,000 people, including more than 10,000 children, die from hunger and related causes. Although this is a significant crisis, the spiritual hunger found in the book of John is of even greater importance.

In this verse Jesus makes a strong claim and then gives a promise. His claim is "I am the bread of life." He is equating himself with bread. He is essential for life. This is not physical life, but spiritual life. Jesus is claiming that he is God. "I am" is the covenant name of God or Yahweh.

The words *come* and *believe* are an invitation to trust in Jesus as our life-giver. This is a choice given to each of us. His promise is that he will satisfy our hunger and thirst for righteousness. This basic human desire that God created in each of us is eternal. If we follow him and believe in his promise, our hunger and thirst will be completely satisfied forever. What an incredible promise to know that our hunger can end when we come to Jesus.

October 17

Amex Card

*Have I not commanded you? Be strong and courageous!
Do not tremble or be dismayed,
for the Lord your God is with you wherever you go.*
Joshua 1:9 (NASB)

In 1975, American Express came up with the tagline "Don't Leave Home without Them!" This ad became synonymous with American Express travelers cheques from the mid-seventies through the late nineties, making it one of the most successful marketing campaigns of all time. Today the Amex card has changed its focus, but the Amex ad still continues with the underlying message, "Don't Leave Home without It!" This is the same message that Joshua received when entering the promised land in Israel.

Although Joshua's mission was different from ours today, God's command and promise to us are still relevant. Be strong and courageous! God is with you wherever you go. His presence with us is made possible because of what Christ did for us on the cross. When we trust in his promise, we can live a life of courage instead of fear. So let me suggest to you that the next time you leave home, don't forget your Amex card in your wallet, and never, ever forget about Jesus in your heart.

October 18

Class Reunions

The upright will behold His face.
Psalm 11:7 (NASB)

Class reunions are either anticipated or avoided altogether. There is usually no middle ground. I have personally enjoyed them because it is a great way to renew old friendships and share memories. Things like music, movies, sports teams, teachers, and special events bring back memories of what our lives were like back then. When we see our classmates, we discover that old cliques are gone, all of us have aged, and most of us are pretty much in the same boat. What a blessing it is to see former classmates, not as they were years ago, but as they are today as a result of life's experience. Today's verse tells us about another reunion, a future one that will be even more rewarding than any class reunion we have had the privilege to attend.

God has graciously extended an invitation to this reunion of a special group of people. This group is not based on age, culture, race, or gender, and there is no fee to join. What's the catch? To join, you must be upright. Does that mean you have to be "good enough" to go to heaven? No, none of us would make it to heaven if that were the case. Being upright means you have confessed your sin and trusted in Jesus Christ to save you. When you do that, even though you are not perfect, you will be accepted as God's child. As a member of his family, you are invited to the greatest reunion of all time, where you will meet Jesus face to face and spend eternity in his presence. There we will share our memories and enjoy his company.

When I encourage you to come to Christ, I am also inviting you to that heavenly reunion. Jesus is preparing everything for us right now. This forever reunion will be awesome!

October 19

Samwise Gamgee

For the Lord will be your confidence and will keep your foot from being snared.
Proverbs 3:26 (NIV)

When I think of a great sidekick, my mind goes directly to Samwise Gamgee in the book *The Lord of the Rings*. Sam is the faithful follower and close friend of Frodo Baggins. Both of these characters are hobbits who live in Middle-earth. Most people think that Frodo is the true hero of *The Lord of the Rings* because much of the focus is centered on him. However, there are also people who believe that the real hero is Sam. Sam starts as a simple gardener and transforms into a major character in all three books. It is lowly Sam who consistently and courageously defends and rescues Frodo. He even fights Frodo's enemies himself. He is willing to sacrifice everything for his friend. At the end, when Frodo seems unable to throw the ring into the fires of Mount Doom and defeat Sauron, it is Sam's words that keep him steadfast to do the right thing. As it turns out, Sam, who is usually relegated to a subordinate status, turns out to be the hero.

Just like we see in Tolkien's novel, we also have a true hero who accompanies us on our journey. We get so caught up in our own story that we forget that there is someone much more important. Take a look at this verse and be encouraged.

This verse is directed to God's people who are part of God's epic story. "For the Lord will be your confidence" (your security, your support). Jesus Christ is your closest companion. He is the one who fights to protect you, the one who sacrificed everything to be your friend. He will "keep your foot from being snared." It is Jesus' Spirit who whispers encouragement to you. This revelation might not be evident in the beginning of your own story because all of us too often focus on ourselves. But, little by little, as the truth is revealed to us, we understand this reality—Jesus Christ is actually the hero of our story. The world looks on and thinks Jesus plays a minor role, but actually, he is the major character. He was there at the beginning, he is with you right now, and if you trust in him, he will be with you forever, saving your life, and helping you do the right thing.

October 20

Protecting Your Assets

For in the day of trouble He will conceal me in His tabernacle;
In the secret place of His tent He will hide me;
He will lift me up on a rock.
Psalm 27:5 (NASB)

Protecting our assets can become a continuous financial goal. We want protection from any disaster that may happen. So we make sure our will is updated. We buy life insurance to replace income to protect those we love. We diversify investments, not putting all our eggs in one basket. We review our property and car insurance every year to ensure we have enough to cover any loss. We may even purchase an umbrella policy to cover the most dramatic catastrophes. Why? To protect us in the day of trouble. In this passage, the psalmist tells of the surest form of protection when we encounter days of trouble.

We all find ourselves in days of trouble. How are we going to respond? If you know this verse, you know God has given you an encouraging promise. He will conceal you or hide you in his tent. He will lift you up on a rock. In other words, God is going to give you protection and security. By lifting you up on a Rock (that is Jesus Christ), your footsteps are made firm. God's promise doesn't say that our lives will be without any trouble, but he did promise wisdom and guidance when we find ourselves in days of trouble. And he did promise eternal security and protection for our souls when we trust in him. I would submit to you that the best way to encourage and protect yourself is to find Jesus and ask him to put your feet on the solid Rock and conceal you in the secret place of his tent.

October 21

Distractions

But the Lord is in His holy temple.
Let all the earth be silent before Him.
Habakkuk 2:20 (NASB)

To me, distractions are like noise. They divert our attention from the most important things in life. Distractions could be entertainment, Facebook, the latest Netflix series, or even your list of chores. All of these activities demand your time and focus. Living a focused life free of distractions is a conflict we experience every day. I think the prophet Habakkuk clearly understood this conflict when God proclaimed himself in the verse for today. "Let all the earth be silent before him."

Every time I try to imagine myself standing in the presence of God, my mind is overcome with feelings of awe, dread, and expectation. God is holy, and when I come to his throne, I am face to face with the one who rules the universe and knows everything in my heart. I can't fake it. He knows my history—all the ways I have failed in the past and still fail today. This is mind-blowing. There is no way to justify myself. However, I have someone who will represent me and plead my case. It is Jesus whose blood cleanses me from my guilty conscience. He paid the debt for my sins; the conflict is over. I might sometimes get distracted, but I can draw near to God in full confidence because Jesus' promises are sure, and he is faithful.

October 22

Guard Duty

But the path of the righteous is like the light of dawn,
That shines brighter and brighter until the full day.
The way of the wicked is like darkness;
They do not know over what they stumble.
Proverbs 4:18-19 (NASB)

As a young soldier, I frequently had to pull guard duty overnight. I can still remember how dark and cold it was at 4:30 in the morning. All you look forward to is the first light of dawn. The long night is almost over, and a new day is dawning. As the sun rises, you start feeling the warmth on your face. Yes, the sun is coming up and the light tells me that my shift will be ending soon. What a great feeling it was to know that my duty was over and I could relax and enjoy a hearty breakfast with a warm cup of coffee. My story touches on light and darkness in the passage I am considering today.

The book of Proverbs is filled with comparisons. Comparing the righteous to the wicked is an important one. The proverb for today says, "The path of the righteous is like the light of dawn." In other words, the path of righteous people shows the faithfulness of God and the warmth of his love. Little by little, our lives shine brighter and brighter, culminating in the dazzling light of heaven. On the flip side, we have the wicked. A wicked person does not trust in God's faithfulness or bask in the warmth of his love. The way he chooses to go leads to danger, darkness, and destruction. Wicked people stumble over God's truths because they cannot see in the darkness.

Both righteous and wicked people make choices every day. What choices will you make? Will you follow Jesus and his path or trust in yourself and stumble around in the dark? I've made my choice. My long night is over and there's a new day dawning. I love the Light, the warmth, and a good cup of coffee—with my Savior, Jesus Christ.

October 23

Stain Remover

Be gracious to me, O God, according to Your lovingkindness; According to the greatness of Your compassion blot out my transgressions. Wash me thoroughly from my iniquity and cleanse me from my sin.
Psalm 51:1-2 (NASB)

If you have ever spilled a cup of coffee on your carpet, you will quickly learn the basics of how stain removers work. Blotting is the key. Soak up the liquid as much as you can right away. Never scrub or rub the carpet fibers. Mix together warm water with dish soap using a white cloth to blot the stain. Then use a little clean water one more time to cleanse away your spill. I wish that this simple formula would be that easy when it comes to our sins.

Sin stains our hearts. That stain puts us at odds with God. But when God convicts us of a sin, what do we often tend to do? We hide it. We justify it. We make excuses for ourselves. What we need to do is own it and turn to God for forgiveness. David understood the stain of his sins, and he knew exactly where to go to have those stains blotted out. He came in humility, pleading for God's grace and lovingkindness. He knew only God could wash away his sins and make his heart clean.

God doesn't look the other way when we sin. He is a just God, and justice demands that sinners be punished. Even if we try to "clean up our act" and promise "not to do it again," the stain of sin remains on our hearts. How can God be just and, at the same time, treat us as though we are not guilty? He can do this because Jesus Christ paid for our guilt when he died on the cross.

Now, God is offering you his grace and lovingkindness. Because Jesus shed his blood, God will "wash" you thoroughly from your iniquities and "cleanse" you from your sins. He will blot out your transgressions and declare you "not guilty." You don't have to live under the guilt of your sin. Your stains can be removed, and you can be cleansed. Just pray the prayer that David prayed, and mean it with all your heart. Really now, how can you pass up an offer like that?

October 24

Baby Monitor

For a man's ways are before the eyes of the Lord, and he ponders all his paths.
Proverbs 5:21 (ESV)

We never owned a baby monitor. We had to actually go into our child's room to see if everything was okay. My grandchildren, however, are always under the watching eye of this new technology. At first, monitors could only transmit the cries of a baby. Then a video camera made it possible to see everything the baby was doing. Today baby monitors provide a complete picture of your baby's well-being. Two-way audio provides midnight lullabies and even a reassuring hello in the morning. Overhead HD video sees every corner of the crib, and temperature and humidity are tracked. And to give parents even more peace of mind, detailed sleep reports are provided every morning that measure your child's sleep patterns, offering sleep tips,

tracking every milestone, and even offering a digital scrapbook for posterity. What do you think about that? I never realized what I was missing.

This verse in Proverbs tells us about our Father in heaven who outperforms any earthly baby monitor. Solomon was cautioning his son against sexual sin. God sees everything a person does. We may think our sexual sins are hidden, but everything is exposed to the eyes of the all-knowing God. He sees every one of our thoughts, words, and deeds. Everything is in full view no matter how careful we are to hide our sin. He knows every step we take, every move we make, every beat of our heart, and he ponders it all.

We must always remember two things about God: He is a righteous judge. He is also a compassionate Father. Even though he knows everything about you, he will still accept you if you admit your sin and trust him to forgive you. He doesn't keep a record of your sins. When you confess them, he removes them "as far as the east is from the west" (Psalm 103:12 ESV). When you turn from your sin and receive God's forgiveness, you will also receive total peace of mind, knowing your heavenly Father is always watching over you. In fact, you can sleep like a baby because he sees every corner of your crib!

October 25

Job Well Done!

His master replied, "Well done, good and faithful servant!
You have been faithful with a few things;
I will put you in charge of many things.
Come and share your master's happiness!"
Matthew 25:21 (NIV)

"Job well done!" These three little words mean a lot to most of us. We work hard and are grateful when our job is recognized and appreciated. It makes us feel like our effort was worth it after all. When we read Matthew 25:21, we get a little flash of hope. Will Jesus say these words to us when we stand before him someday?

Jesus' life was our example of a job well done. He lived to please his Father, and he died to save you and me! In the end, he could honestly say, "It is finished!" He knew he had accomplished the job God gave him to do. And he knew all his suffering was worth it! His life and death paid for his people's sins and made it possible for us to do our job too.

Have you ever thought about the work God is calling you to do? He didn't save us to sit around and live for ourselves. He called us to use our gifts to serve him and the people he brings our way. What do you want to hear when you see Jesus? I think I would like to hear these words first: "Job well done!"

October 26

Anchors

We have this hope as an anchor for the soul, firm and secure.
Hebrews 6:19 (NIV)

If you have ever owned a boat, you will understand the importance of an anchor. This device secures a boat firmly to the bed of a body of water to prevent it from drifting in the wind or a current. Anchors come in many sizes and shapes. If your anchor is too small or not used properly, it will fail, and your boat will go adrift. The bottom line is that if your anchor is good, your boat will stay firm and secure. This is the image we see in our Bible verse for today.

What "hope" is the author writing about? Our hope is the promise God has given us in Christ. A person who has Christ as his Savior has hope that his sins are forgiven and that Jesus has secured a place for him in heaven. He has the assurance that God is close to him through thick and thin and that the Holy Spirit will empower him to live a life that pleases God. There are hundreds of promises in the Bible for God's people, but it's easy to drift away in the winds of our emotions or the power of current thought. Rest in God's anchor. His promises will make you stable and secure.

What anchors your soul? Is it financial independence, a nice house, good health, or that job you always wanted? Is anything besides God really "firm and secure"? What are you going to hold on to when life gets turbulent and uncertain? I'm holding on to God's promises. He proved to be my anchor when he rose from the dead, left the tomb empty, and appeared alive to over 500 witnesses. He gave me every reason to put my trust in him.

October 27

Mistaken Identity

You alone are the Lord. You have made the heavens, the heaven of heavens with all their host, The earth and all that is on it, the seas and all that is in them. You give life to all of them and the heavenly host bows down before You.
Nehemiah 9:6 (NASB)

I have been told numerous times that I look like George Bush. This mistaken identity, however, changes quickly when you consider Bush's mannerisms, the way he talks, and what he has accomplished. If you still don't know for sure, you would eventually realize there are no Secret Service agents around. In the book of Nehemiah, the Hebrews had no problem at all identifying who the Lord was.

God's identity can be clearly seen in his handiwork in creation. It is evident in the heavens above with the stars and planets. And when you look at the earth and seas below, you can see the incredible complexity of his work! This Creator made the universe and gave life to everything. All creation belongs to him, and even the heavenly host bows down before him. There is no mistaken identity here. He alone deserves our praise!

October 28

Compatibility

Good and upright is the Lord.
Psalm 25:8 (ESV)

The word *compatibility* brings several things to mind. For computer geeks, it is the capacity for two computer systems to work together without having to be altered. For food connoisseurs, it means having the right food combinations for health and digestion. In relationships, it's talking about a lifetime friendship or a happily married couple. The bottom line is that compatibility is the ability to work together in harmony. Today I would like for you to consider this word *compatibility* in reference to the character of God.

This verse tells us that God is both good and upright. These two characteristics aren't as different as they seem. In fact, they are compatible. "God is good" means God is kind, patient, and loving. It also means that he is morally perfect and will, without hesitation, call out evil when he sees it. "God is upright" means that he never does anything evil, that he will never lower his perfect standards, and that in the end he will punish evildoers. Both these characteristics, his goodness and his uprightness, are compatible because above all else, God is holy. He is superior and sacred in every way and more powerful than anyone else in the universe.

The author of our verse for today wanted to worship this holy God. But he knew that he was sinful and needed a Savior to make him acceptable to a God like that. Jesus' sacrifice for our sin made it possible for us to be pardoned and to live in harmony with God. When we accept his free gift of salvation, we become compatible with God and will live in harmony with him forever.

October 29

Tsunami

Then Job answered the Lord and said, "I know that You can do all things, And that no purpose of Yours can be thwarted."
Job 42:1-2 (NASB)

A tsunami is a series of waves in a large body of water, like an ocean or big lake, caused by the displacement of a large volume of water. Earthquakes, volcanoes, or other explosions above or below the water can generate a tsunami. There can be minutes or hours between one wave and the next. Most of the destruction is in coastal areas. The 2004 Indian Ocean tsunami was the deadliest natural disaster in human history with over 230,000 people killed or missing in fourteen countries. When I realize the power of this natural force, it reminds me of the last chapters of the book of Job in the Bible.

Job's three friends could not convince him that he was at fault, that *he* was the cause of his own suffering, so their conversation came to a standstill. Nothing was resolved. But that's when God stepped in with a series of questions and comments that put everyone in his place. You can read them in Job 38-40. It starts with, "Who laid the

foundation of the earth? Who determined its measurements?" and ends with "Shall a faultfinder contend with the Almighty? Let him who argues with God, answer him." Everything God says in these chapters is enough to shatter anyone's pride. Job got the point. God does all things out of his own goodness and for his own glory. No purpose of his can be thwarted. When God wanted to remove Job's suffering, he did. *Everything* Job lost, God restored—*many times over!* We struggle to believe this at times.

Does God see my situation? Does he even care? Well, read the Bible and you will see he does. But he reserves the right to call the shots. He *is* God, after all! We never have to worry about what God is going to do, because God is good and takes good care of his children. Even when we suffer, we can trust God, who "can do all things." No plan of his can be thwarted, and as Christians, we are a *huge* part of his plans! When all is said and done, the tsunami of God's love toward us is going to have an impact much greater than we could ever imagine. Indeed! We will be talking about it—forever!

October 30

Seeking Approval

*And without faith it is impossible to please Him,
for he who comes to God must believe that He is
and that He is a rewarder of those who seek Him.*
Hebrews 11:6 (NASB)

If we are honest, seeking approval is a natural craving for most of us. When we are growing up, we want our parents' approval. Later on, it's our friends or boss we want to impress. We want to be accepted by everyone. It feels good to know others admire us. But this verse presents a conundrum for believers in Christ. How can we please the world *and God* in our journey of faith?

We can't. First, we'll never do enough to please "the world." We probably wouldn't even want to! But it is possible to please God. What pleases God is when we come to him, believing that he exists and that he rewards people who seek after him. The world may not always be pleased with you. But keep this in mind, when you seek God in faith, he will reward you with his approval—and a whole lot more! This is a big thumbs up for me!

October 31

Siege of Sarajevo

*Those who trust in the Lord Are as Mount Zion,
which cannot be moved but abides forever.
As the mountains surround Jerusalem, so the
Lord surrounds His people From this time forth and forever.*
Psalm 125:1-2 (NASB)

The siege of Sarajevo was the longest siege of a capital city in the history of modern warfare. Serbian forces in the hills of Sarajevo completely encircled the city. The siege lasted for four years, and fourteen thousand people lost their lives. Fortunately for the people of Sarajevo, the siege was not permanent.

God's people are encircled too! But God's encirclement isn't a siege. It's a circle of protection. These verses are a gem of a promise to citizens of God's kingdom. God doesn't enclose his people, restricting their freedom and killing their dreams. He puts a hedge around them that provides security for their souls. God surrounds his people with endless love that is sure, unfailing, and permanent. Our enemy, the devil, will never prevail against us. We are on the winning side!

November 1

Why Would He Do This?

*I am the good shepherd; the good shepherd lays down
His life for the sheep.*
John 10:11 (NASB)

Why would anyone give up his life for another person? I can think of a few people I would die for. My wife, children, and grandchildren are prime candidates. But how about a good friend? Maybe on a good day—possibly. But how about someone you don't know or someone who is an enemy? Definitely not! I wouldn't think of it! So back to the question. Why? The only answer I can come up with is the word *love*. Love was the motivating force behind Jesus' sacrifice.

Jesus says, "I am the good shepherd." So the question is, "What does a good shepherd do?" He tends his flock, gathers lambs in His arms, and gently leads the nursing ewes. He searches for the lost lambs, cares for them, and brings them out of danger. He even feeds them, binds up the broken ones, and strengthens the sick. When you put this all together, Jesus loves the sheep. The bottom line is that he lays down his life for the sheep.

Jesus is the good shepherd who willingly gave up his life on the cross for us. He sacrificed himself so we would have eternal life. And this offer of salvation was not just for family and friends, but even for his enemies. The good news is that Jesus became the sacrifice for us. What an offer he gives!

November 2

Connect the Dots

*In Him we have redemption through His blood,
the forgiveness of our trespasses, according to the riches of His grace
which He lavished on us.*
Ephesians 1:7-8 (NASB)

Connect the dots is a type of puzzle that contains a sequence of numbered dots. When you draw a line from one number to the next, you start to see the outline of a picture. The numbered dots can also be replaced with letters or other symbols. Little children love this activity, but it can also be used by adults to solve business problems. In this activity, many pieces of information from different places are used to show that by connecting the dots you can formulate a good business strategy. Whether the puzzle is for the young or old, both want the same thing. They want to see the "big picture." I think this passage in Ephesians does the same thing.

People want to know what this life is all about. What is the "big picture"? When you start to connect the dots, you begin with the number one. The first dot is Jesus Christ. "In Him" we have the source of every spiritual blessing. Drawing the line from Jesus to the next dot, "we have redemption through His blood." This means that Christ experienced death to bring us the gift of eternal life. When you connect the next dot, you get a pardon. All of the charges are dismissed. We will not have to pay for our rebellion and sinful behavior even though we are most definitely guilty. God forgives you of your trespasses when you admit your sin and put your trust in him. Moving on to the last dot, you discover "the riches of His grace which He lavished on us." God has saved us because of his kindness and mercy. He lavishes his incredible love on us! Now that the dots have been connected, what do you see? Do you see the big picture? Do you see what life is all about? I see Jesus embracing me and lavishing me with the riches of his grace, his companionship, his wisdom, his miracles, and his transforming power! What do you see?

November 3

Adoring Nicknames

Beloved, we are God's children now.
1 John 3:2 (ESV)

Why do we give nicknames to our kids like "Bright Eyes," "Tender Heart," and "Angel"? Adoring nicknames tell your children that they are indeed special and loved. They are unique and beloved. Their names also identify a positive characteristic or trait of who they are. And of course, only family members have the privilege of using these names. These are the people who share a common history of all of our ups and downs in life. For better or worse, these are our family members. These are the people God has ordained for us.

In our Bible verse today and, for that matter, through the entire Old and New Testament, God has specifically called those who trust in him his family members: "Beloved, we are God's children now." When you accept God's call to follow him, you are immediately adopted into his family. You are now identified as a child of God. You are now a beloved son or daughter of King Jesus. You are chosen, holy, and set apart! Did you know that?

I have no idea what type of family situation you are in, but I can tell you that we have a loving God who wants only what is best for you. We have a God who doesn't care about your history. It only matters who you are right now. Embrace Jesus. He is inviting you to be in his family, and he has a very special name for you.

November 4

Disappointing News

*Because Your lovingkindness is better than life,
my lips will praise You.*
Psalm 63:3 (NASB)

"This is disappointing news." Chicago Cubs fans heard this phrase for 107 years until they won the 2016 World Series. Baseball teams are all too familiar with bad news. Hopes and dreams for this year's team often have to be postponed to some unforeseeable future. Aren't disappointments like this a reality for all of us? Isn't this what we come to expect in life? But if you consider this verse in Psalms today, you may see life in a different way.

David concluded that God's lovingkindness is better than life. Why this comparison? I think most of us would say that life is better than the alternative. But David's question was whether God's steadfast love is better than the specific challenges we are experiencing right now. What I know about life is that it is short and filled with surprises, challenges, heartaches, hopes, and dreams. Most of all, life is unpredictable. I can't depend on anything being permanent, and disappointments are common. When you really think about it, there is no way that you can say that life is better than God's lovingkindness!

It's because of God's kindness that he offers us eternal life when we trust in him. It's his kindness that gives believers a full pardon for all of their sins. It's his lovingkindness that makes us members of his family and gives us confidence for the future. He has also given us a taste of who he really is. I do know that God has never disappointed me. I also know that he has never broken any promise he has made to me. His blessings have been so incredible that my hope in him grows stronger every day.

So when I make a comparison between God's lovingkindness and life, I think there is no contest. God's lovingkindness is the only truth that offers you any real hope in life. We have a future with Christ, who keeps every promise and wants only what is best for us. With Jesus, good news is routine. So it is your choice: you can either hope the Cubs win next year, or go with the winner in Jesus.

November 5

Jumping Together

*Now, therefore, fear the Lord and serve
Him in sincerity and truth; and put away the gods
which your fathers served beyond the River and in Egypt,
and serve the Lord.*
Joshua 24:14 (NASB)

When my wife and I were discussing if we should move into a fifty-five-plus community, I started to doubt my plans. But my faithful partner of forty-eight years strengthened my resolve with this statement: "We are not going to look back. We are going to hold hands and make the jump together!" Wow! That was a great idea. It was exactly what we needed to do! When you start over-thinking something, it becomes impossible to make a decision. God's challenge to his people, the Israelites, was three-fold. Fear the Lord. Serve the Lord sincerely. Put away the false gods your fathers served in Egypt.

God challenges us in the same ways today. Fear me. Serve me. Put away the gods of this world. Do we need more information before we can commit? Are we overthinking our decision to follow Christ? Remember, doing nothing means maintaining the status quo, worshiping this world and everything it offers. God is saying, "Don't look back! Take my hand. We will walk through life together and on into eternity." God wants your whole heart. Nothing half-hearted will do. It is an all-or-nothing offer. You choose the world, or you choose Jesus. If I can ever give you any advice in life, take Jesus' hand and jump into a whole new life together. This is exactly what you need to do!

November 6

Hideout Cities for Fugitives

Where can I go from Your Spirit? Or where can I flee from Your presence? If I ascend to heaven, You are there; If I make my bed in Sheol, behold, You are there.
Psalm 139:7-8 (NASB)

A few years ago I read an article about the top ten cities for fugitives. These are places a person can go to hide from the long arm of the law. Most of these cities don't have extradition treaties with the US, so chances are you won't be arrested. The downside is that most of these places are rife with crime, poverty, and disease. They are typically places where a person would not want to live. In case you are interested, the number one hideout is Andorra la Vella, in the little country of Andorra. In Psalm 139, we see the psalmist ask a very similar question about hideouts.

Speaking to God, the psalmist asks, "Where can I flee from your presence?" But why is a psalmist asking a question like that? Is he looking for a place to hide? Has he broken the law? Yes, of course. Everyone has broken God's law, and everyone knows he is guilty. We sin, thinking our bad decisions will make us happy. Then we run away from God to avoid our feelings of guilt. But these verses tell us that escape is impossible. God is everywhere. We can't hide from him. The odd thing is that we're running away from the person who can give us the very thing we need—forgiveness—to be legally acquitted in God's sight. We don't have to be fugitives anymore. All we need to do is stop running and admit our need for Jesus. Wherever we run, he is already there, ready to save!

November 7

Unspoken Words

*Then Esther told them to reply to Mordecai,
"Go, assemble all the Jews who are found in Susa, and fast for me; do
not eat or drink for three days, night or day.
I and my maidens also will fast in the same way.
And thus I will go in to the king, which is not according to the law;
and if I perish, I perish." So Mordecai went away
and did just as Esther had commanded him.*
Esther 4:15-17 (NASB)

Some people talk a lot but never say the words a person needs to hear. For instance, take a wife who yearns to hear her husband say, "I love you." Or how about a young lady who has been dating a young man for several years and has never heard him say, "Will you marry me?" On the positive side, love can often be demonstrated *without* words. A look, a touch, a smile, a pat on the back, or a hug can communicate affection without the need for words. This might be the case in the story of Esther.

Esther was a beautiful Jewish queen, married to Xerxes, king of Persia. Xerxes had been tricked into a plan to kill all the Jews in Persia. He had no idea that his wife, Esther, was a Jew. Esther knew she should go to Xerxes and plead for the lives of her people, but she also knew that Xerxes could kill her for entering his presence without permission. Her fear was great, but her courage was even greater. What fueled Esther's courage? All her life, she had grown up loving God. There was no need for words to express her devotion. Instead of words, she went into action. She called all the Jews to a three-day fast. Jewish fasts were always combined with prayer to God. She didn't need to explain that. Jews already knew. She also believed that God was able to deliver her people, and she was willing to sacrifice her life just to take a stand for them. You never know, she thought, "This might be the moment for which I have been created!" Did God save the Jews? Ah-h-h, no spoiler here. You'll have to read the story yourself. It's in the book of Esther in your Bible! The author of the book might not have shared all of Esther's words, but we know from her actions that she trusted her life to God, and he took care of the rest. Always be ready to do the right thing, and believing in Jesus Christ is the right thing to do.

November 8

Pass in Review

Forever, O Lord, Your word is settled in heaven.
Psalm 119:89 (NASB)

While I was a cadet, I marched in many parades. These parades always include a long-standing military tradition, dating back to the American Revolution. It is called "pass in review." Soldiers line up in each company to take part in the parade. The commander organizes the soldiers by their height. Since I was 5'8," I was usually in the last row. As each company of soldiers passes by the dignitary, they are ordered to turn their heads and eyes right. This shows honor to the VIP. Although Psalm 119 never mentions parades, the psalmist was very aware of orders given by his commander, the Lord of heaven.

The Hebrew word for *settled* is a military term that applies to arranging soldiers in a battle plan. The battle plan was the exact order in which the soldiers would be deployed. The word *settled* in this verse means "to stand firm." God's word is determined, fixed, and immovable. God's purposes, promises, and precepts to us are determined in heaven where nothing can be changed. God will keep every promise he has made. The good news here is that God's plan of salvation is a completed fact that can never be altered. Jesus Christ died for us, and nothing can change that historical event. God's promises of salvation are forever sure for everyone who puts his trust in him. What an encouragement this is when we pass in review before our Commander. God's word, Jesus' death on the cross, and our salvation are all settled in heaven! It's a done deal.

November 9

Why We Study

Great are the works of the Lord;
they are studied by all who delight in them.
Psalm 111:2 (NASB)

When we start to dig into any subject like medicine, law, art, history, or science, we quickly discover how little we really know. Take the topic of botany. Why would someone study plants? Well, plants provide us with oxygen, food, fiber, and fuel. Botanists study plants to discover their properties because knowledge of plants can lead to improvements in nutrition and production and give new sources of medicine and biofuels. Studying the works of the Lord leads to improvements in ourselves too because everything he created gives us additional knowledge about him.

For example, folks love to study the human body, the art of dancing, the science of astronomy, the events of history, the intricacies of the brain, and so many other wonderful things! As people study these works of the Lord, they are also discovering aspects of his nature: his magnificence, his beauty, his mathematical genius, his attention to detail, his infinite power, and his intervention in history. Everything we study reflects the glory of God and magnifies our knowledge of his character. This is the reason people are delighted when they study the works of the Lord. It is such a pleasure to know God better. Of course, the best way to learn about God is to read the Bible. God's deeds in history, his judgment of sin, his gift of Jesus, his wonderful promises, and his transforming power are food for our souls and a pleasure to know. The bottom line is that when we study the works of the Lord, we can also discover the person of God and become believers in his Son, Jesus Christ!

November 10

Masterpiece

*For we are His workmanship, created in
Christ Jesus for good works, which God prepared beforehand
so that we would walk in them.*
Ephesians 2:10 (NASB)

My Dad was a carpenter when I was growing up—not just any kind of carpenter, but a finish carpenter. The difference between rough and finish carpentry is big. Rough carpenters focus on the basics of framing and are called framers. They construct walls, roofs, windows, and floors. Their focus is very practical as they precisely measure, cut, and shape the wood products. Finish carpenters are more concerned with aesthetics. All of their work is done inside the house after all the framers are done. Their focus is on all the intricate details like crown molding, baseboards, custom cabinets, trim, interior doors, wainscoting, and hardwood floors. All these tasks are the final steps in producing a new home. Finish carpenters like my Dad are craftsmen, completely focused on the end product. It is the fine details that make the home a unique masterpiece.

When I was studying this verse in Ephesians, the word *workmanship* stood out to me. The word *workmanship* in the Greek language is *poiema*. This word sounds like the word *poem* in English, and that is exactly what it means. A *poiema* is a masterful work of creativity.

This verse tells us that you and I are God's workmanship, his masterful work of creativity. The Bible says that God "knit you together in your mother's womb." He created everything about you: your eye color, your height, your unique personality, and your talents. Why? Because he had a special purpose for your life. He made you to be part of his grand design for the world. He created you "for good works" and equipped you to do good things. You and I are under construction right now. God will work with us until his masterpieces are complete. When we are complete, he will transport us to our heavenly home. We'll have work to do there too, but we will be finished products there, unique masterpieces without a single flaw. God's work in you is an important part of the good news we have in Jesus.

November 11

Good to Great

For this reason You are great, O Lord God;
for there is none like You, and there is no God besides You,
according to all that we have heard with our ears.
2 Samuel 7:22 (NASB)

In 2001, Jim Collins wrote a business book on how companies transition from being a good company to a great one. He defines "greatness" as a company that "achieves financial performance several multiples better than the market average over the long-term." He then identifies companies that have done this for more than fifteen years. In his view, this is the kind of success that makes companies great. Is this a good way to measure our own performance? If you can win more PGA Tournaments than Tiger Woods, you are considered great. Or how about Tom Brady winning the Super Bowl six times? Can anyone compare with him? Wouldn't his record define greatness? King David compares human greatness with the greatness of God and proclaims, "You are great, O Lord God; for there is no one like you!"

God shows his greatness in the incredible deeds he has done. No one else can even compare. When I think of the creation and its complexity and beauty and of humans with their moral sensibilities, their logical minds, and their sense of purpose, there is no way to doubt the ultimate greatness of our Creator God. But to me, God performed the epitome of greatness when he came to Earth himself in the person of Jesus Christ. Nothing can compare to the perfect life he lived, the miracles he performed, or the sacrifice he made for those who hated him. No one can hold a candle to him. By simply receiving Jesus' gift of salvation, we are forgiven and have eternal life. This is true greatness.

November 12

Call to Arms

Finally, be strong in the Lord and in the strength of His might. Put on the full armor of God, so that you will be able to stand firm against the schemes of the devil.
Ephesians 6:10-11 (NASB)

If you've turned on your television lately, you know that the world is in pretty bad shape. Things are falling apart. Wars are causing chaos and devastation. Murders are increasing at an alarming rate. Political fights are paralyzing nations. Social norms and moral standards are being tossed out the window. Everything seems to be turning upside down. What is happening? Who is in charge? Are the devil and the forces of darkness winning? The Bible verse we are considering today answers these questions. It is a call to arms for all believers.

It's important to know that when you accept the invitation to join God's family, you are also enlisting in the army of the Lord. Every true believer is at war with the devil and his schemes. That sounds frightening, you might say. There is no way I can fight the devil; he is too crafty and powerful! But here's the good news. Jesus is the *all*-powerful commander of *his* army, and he has already secured the victory in the war against the devil. The Bible says that Jesus came to destroy the works of the devil. He did this when he died on the cross. When he did that, he paid the debt for our sins, and that set us free from slavery to the devil, rendering him powerless! You can read about this in Hebrews 2:14-15.

Jesus overcame the devil when he died on the cross, so our final victory is assured. No matter how bad your current situation looks, it's only a matter of time and the devil will be toast (literally)! In the meantime, God is calling you to arms. There are still battles to fight, and they could be ferocious. Stand firm. Hang in there. Hold your position in the line. Put on the full armor of God. God's armor will protect you. God's Spirit will make you strong. Be assured, you are on the winning side.

November 13

Rolaids

*Then they cried out to the Lord in their trouble;
He delivered them out of their distresses.*
Psalm 107:6 (NASB)

How do you spell relief from heartburn? The answer is R-O-L-A-I-D-S, Rolaids! Common causes of heartburn are acidic foods or foods high in fat, such as tomatoes, onions, chocolate, coffee, spicy food, or large meals. In Psalm 107, God addresses the source of true heartburn and his answer for relief.

When we're talking about a person's spiritual heartburn, we're talking about trouble and distress. These are things we deal with every day, like divorce, death, job loss, illness, anxiety, anger, or guilt.

They cause storms, darkness, and brokenness in our lives. We worry and are anxious about what lies ahead. But in this verse we find the answer for relief. "Then they cried out to the Lord…He delivered them out of their distresses."

The answer to our emotional and spiritual "heartburn" is found in the person of Jesus Christ. He is the one who leads us out of darkness and hopelessness. He is the one who breaks the chains of slavery to anger and depression. He is also the one who heals our broken hearts and quiets the storm. Our relief is found in Christ alone. Rolaids can never fix our true heart issues. Jesus is the only one who can do that!

November 14

Why a Tree?

Blessed is the man who trusts in the Lord and whose trust is the Lord. For he will be like a tree planted by the water, that extends its roots by a stream And will not fear when the heat comes; but its leaves will be green, And it will not be anxious in a year of drought nor cease to yield fruit.
Jeremiah 17:7-8 (NASB)

Why do we plant trees by water? A tree needs water, so its roots seek out a stream. Water is needed to make oxygen. This process cools the leaves, exchanges oxygen and carbon dioxide, and then moves the nutrients up the tree. If there is no water in the soil, there is no cooling of the leaves, no nutrient transfer, and no photosynthesis. If you would rather have a more simplistic explanation, this is it: plant a tree by the water and you will harvest a great crop. You never need to worry about drought. This little comparison of a tree to a man who trusts in the Lord was given to us in the book of Jeremiah.

Why this analogy between a man and a tree? The man who trusts in the Lord for his salvation is relying on God alone in all of life's circumstances. He knows that the living water Christ gives sustains him even in droughts. There is no need to be anxious about our future because the Lord is continually giving us living water. Our confidence is in "what God does and not what we do." Just remember that if you plant a tree by the living water, you can expect to yield good fruit!

November 15

Big Projects

For it was fitting that he, for whom and by whom all things exist, in bringing many sons to glory, should make the founder of their salvation perfect through suffering.
Hebrews 2:10 (ESV)

I don't know about you, but whenever I plan a big project, I tend to overreach what I can do. When I plan the amount of time needed, I usually don't build in extra time for difficulties. The same thing goes with the cost. If I think it will cost a certain amount of money, the real cost is usually over my budget. So basically I am telling you that my planning for big projects often lacks realism. My plans fall short of my expectations. I like to think that I am not alone. It seems that no one is able to achieve exactly what he plans to do. But when we look at this verse in Hebrews, we discover someone who is able to complete *his* plan perfectly.

God's plan was to "bring many sons to glory." His expectations were always realistic. He possessed all the resources needed to accomplish our salvation. But his plan would be costly. Jesus Christ, his only Son, would humble himself, become a man, and come to Earth. While here, he would suffer extreme difficulties: rejection, ridicule, torture, and death. God, the Father, considered the cost, and Jesus, his Son, anticipated the difficulties. Both were so full of love for mankind, they decided to go ahead with their plan. There were no miscalculations. There were no mistakes. In his suffering, Jesus paid the price for sin and became the founder of salvation for everyone who comes to him for forgiveness and eternal life.

Are you part of God's plan? Don't miss the opportunity he is offering you. Come to him for the forgiveness he offers. This is the best news ever!

November 16

Fresh Start

*For I will be merciful toward their iniquities,
and I will remember their sins no more.*
Hebrews 8:12 (ESV)

Divorce is ugly and painful. No words can adequately describe a catastrophe like this. Lives are shattered and dreams are left unfulfilled. How can you move on when your life has been disrupted? How can you forget all the hurtful words and actions? What can you do when your life is in total chaos? Unfortunately, there are many people who experience divorce. And there's a lot of sin involved in the process. How to cope with this upheaval in life is an important question to consider. A person going through it needs a fresh start and a lot of encouragement to resume his or her life. This is exactly what this verse offers you.

This verse is about our iniquities and sins. It is about our broken promises and rebellion against God. The promise is simple. Jesus Christ offered his life to pay for all our sins. He became the perfect sacrifice so that we can start over. Now, Jesus offers pardon when you ask him for forgiveness. In spite of your messy situation, Jesus Christ "will be merciful" to you and "remember your sins no more." He wipes your record clean. He doesn't hold any grudges and never reminds you of your past. Because of Christ, you are given a fresh start. You are free to live a new life!

November 17

Out of Options

For the Lord will vindicate His people,
And will have compassion on His servants,
When He sees that their strength is gone,
And there is none remaining, bond or free.
Deuteronomy 32:36 (NASB)

When someone says, "I've run out of options," you know that everything he has done has failed. He is finished, completely out of any more ideas or plans of what he can do. An example of this might be when the doctor tells a person he has an untreatable disease. What can that person do? Where can that person turn for help? This wonderful verse answers these important questions.

There are times when our strength is gone. We've tried everything, and no one we turn to can help us. Even in times like these, we do not need to despair. Why? Because as this verse says, God sees when our strength is gone and has compassion. Compassion doesn't just mean that God feels sorry for us. No! God's compassion moves him to action. When your strength is gone, God empowers you with *his* strength. God's strength comes in different forms. His strength may make you resilient and patient. It may give you hope and the fortitude to endure. In his compassion, God might send someone to you who has a solution you never thought of. Or God might intervene with a miracle and turn the whole situation around. Whichever action he chooses, we know he sees and hears our cries for help and acts. He will have compassion on you. He will empower you. He will never abandon you in a crisis. And so we can say that a person who trusts in the Lord *never* runs out of options.

November 18

Star Wars

*The Light shines in the darkness,
and the darkness did not comprehend it.*
John 1:5 (NASB)

George Lucas, who created and directed the movie *Star Wars*, did an excellent job portraying the conflict between good and evil. Names like Darth Vader and Luke Skywalker, attire with black and white colors, and music with striking contrast bring that conflict to life. The theme of good and evil is not new. The Bible told us about it long before any movies were created. This verse in John 1 is a simple fact about God.

Light is the Messiah who makes the truth visible for all to see. We love darkness because we can hide and cover up the evil we have done. The conflict between light and darkness was most striking in the event of Christ's death on the cross. What he did was a victory of light over darkness. This is the good news of Christ. Jesus overcame death. His power is greater than any darkness. There are no sins that God's love and mercy cannot forgive. This truth about Jesus is what gives us hope, joy, and life everlasting in a world that is filled with pessimism, hatred, and anger. God's victory over darkness is the gospel.

November 19

Burden to Blessing

*Praise be to the Lord, to God our Savior,
who daily bears our burdens.*
Psalm 68:19 (NIV)

At the end of Sir Winston Churchill's life, he said, "When I look back on all these worries, I remember the story of the old man who said on his deathbed that he had a lot of trouble in his life, most of which had never happened!" How many of us carry a heavy load filled up with anxious thoughts, stress, uncertainties in life, and what-if situations? The verse for today is a special promise for those who have a heavy burden to carry.

God has promised you that he will take all of your troubles and worries and carry them. It doesn't matter how difficult the situation is. As the Creator, he has no problem at all with both running all of the major functions of the earth and knowing about what is troubling you. So when he promises to daily bear your burdens, he must really care about you. And for God to know exactly what is happening to you every hour of the day is simply unbelievable. But this is the promise he gives to those who trust in him.

If Christ can carry your heavy load of sins to the cross, can he not carry your burden daily? If Christ was raised from the dead, can he not raise your head above these worries? I don't know what burden you are carrying today, but I do know that we have a big God who can handle any situation you will ever face in your life. Every day, this Savior promises to take your burden and turn it into a blessing!

November 20

ADT Protection

Be anxious for nothing, but in everything by prayer and supplication with thanksgiving let your requests be made known to God. And the peace of God, which surpasses all comprehension, will guard your hearts and your minds in Christ Jesus.
Philippians 4:6-7 (NASB)

If you take a walk around your neighborhood, you will probably see little signs in front yards that say ADT. This, of course, is a home security system. The advertisement says that ADT is for "Protection & Peace of Mind, 24/7, 365. Sound asleep or away from home, we're always working to help you protect what matters most." Are you ready to purchase this protection? I hear that with all of the cameras, listening devices, and technology, it is possible to know about everything that enters and exits your home. This knowledge protects you and your possessions. It seems almost too good to be true. And it is! The Bible challenges this claim of full protection in our passage for today.

The very first statement says, "Do not be anxious about anything." What are some things that make us anxious? COVID? Finances? Job? Marriage? All the things you cannot possibly control in your future? Pray to God and let him know your concerns. Give all of these things you are fretting about to God. Let him deal with these things. This is a decision we make. We trust him because we realize we need a Savior. When we make our requests known to God, he promises to guard our hearts and minds. He gives us a peace that far surpasses anything we can comprehend. This is called *full* protection—with a promise!

But, you might say, these anxieties are stubborn things that never seem to leave my mind no matter how hard I pray. How do I stop worrying? The short answer is to dwell on ways that God has answered your prayers in the past. Thank him! Then, fill up your mind with the truths of God's word. Replace your anxieties with the good news of Christ. These are important decisions to make every day. What happens over time is that God replaces your worries with peace that quiets your heart and mind. This is protection that only Jesus can give. It will help you sleep soundly.

November 21

Leading by Example

*For this reason he had to be made like his brothers in every way,
in order that he might become a merciful and faithful high priest
in service to God, and that he might make atonement
for the sins of the people.*
Hebrews 2:17 (NIV)

When I was an officer in the infantry, I learned that the best way to inspire young soldiers was to lead by example. If a soldier sees his superior getting his hands dirty, he will follow his lead. The officer's *behavior* sets the example; no words need to be said. Whether it is training on a rifle range, running five miles in combat boots, or suffering the same hardships as an enlisted soldier, an officer's actions speak louder than words. The ultimate reason he provides this kind of leadership is so he can understand the suffering of his soldiers and show them mercy, at the same time modeling faithfulness to his military service. Someday he might be called to make the supreme sacrifice for his brothers in arms. Someday *they* might have to sacrifice their lives for each other. Inspiring sacrifice such as this can only be done by one's actions. This was the kind of leadership modeled by Christ, as we see in our verse for today.

Jesus "had to be made like his brothers in every way." He had to go through all the same things we suffer, like hunger, thirst, dismissal, humiliation, and even the temptation to sin. He experienced everything we experience, so he could be our "faithful and merciful high priest." He showed ultimate leadership when he made atonement for the sins of his people, giving his life as an example of sacrificial love in service to God. Jesus led by example. Now because of his actions, we are offered eternal life. He also leads *us* to be merciful to each other and to give *our* lives in service to God. His leadership and his love are breathtaking!

November 22

A Clean Slate

If we confess our sins, he is faithful and just to forgive us our sins and to cleanse us from all unrighteousness.
1 John 1:9 (ESV)

Slate is a fine-grained metamorphic rock that for years was primarily utilized as a roofing tile. Later, it would serve as a writing tablet—a small, smooth piece of the rock would be framed in wood and used with chalk as a notepad for recording charges in pubs and inns, then for blackboards in 18th- and 19th-century schools. A clean slate meant that you wiped the board clean and started over. It was a fresh start. Today it means to receive forgiveness from a past financial debt or a criminal offense. Isn't a clean slate what many of us want today? To be set free from our past? Look at this verse in 1 John and be encouraged.

God has promised that "If we confess our sins," he will forgive us. When you confess your sins, you are acknowledging and declaring that some of your thinking, words, or actions are wrong. You are admitting that you are guilty before God. You are not giving any excuses but merely asking for God's mercy. In fact, he cleanses us from all our sins when we genuinely confess the sins we know.

When we do this, what do you think God does? Believe it or not, God is faithful and just. He will forgive your sins. Since he knows your heart, he knows what you have done. It is not a surprise. And the promise he gives to you is that he will forgive you and give you a clean slate. He will cleanse you "from all unrighteousness." This means that he is going to clean you up and give you a fresh start. What a wonderful promise! Why not check it out? I promise that you will forever be changed for the better!

November 23

Garbage Dumps and Ash Heaps

*He raises the poor from the dust and lifts the needy
from the ash heap, To make them sit with princes,
with the princes of His people.*
Psalm 113:7-8 (NASB)

I have visited garbage dumps in Nairobi, Mexico City, and Port-au-Prince, and I can tell you, these places would turn your stomach and break your heart. The sights and smells are repulsive. Little children looking for items of value or food in tin cans. Stinking fires raging here and there throughout the rubbish. Cesspools of liquid waste giving off the stench of death. This is one of the most distressing sights I have ever experienced, but it provides a powerful visual for what we read in Psalm 113.

God is not a respecter of people. He doesn't bless one nation, one race, one class, or one income level of people and ignore everyone else.

He is the Creator of all nations and all people, and he values every person, every race, and every class of people, rich or poor. So when he sees and hears the poor crying out to him, he helps them. When we get to heaven, we will hear millions of amazing stories of how God lifted people from their ash heap and gave them a better life. The biggest killer of happiness and success is sin. The biggest cause of sin is our rebellious hearts. What we all need to do is repent, turn to God for help, walk away from our sin, and stop sitting in the ash heap of hopelessness. We need to ask God to forgive us, transfer us to a whole new kingdom, and make us his royal children.

This is the story of God's mercy. We are poor and needy, but Jesus has given us an invitation to be part of his kingdom and to sit with princes and princesses. This is God's rescue story. This is the good news!

November 24

Unfinished Business

*Work, for I am with you, declares the Lord of hosts.
My Spirit remains in your midst. Fear not.*
Haggai 2:4-5 (ESV)

I don't know about you, but some projects just never get done. For instance, cleaning up a storage room or a garage is a chore you might tend to put off. It is a fairly easy task to do but takes time away from other really important things—like playing golf! You put it on a mental shelf and hope it will magically go away. But it never does. It continues to haunt you, and every time you think about it you feel discouraged. It is your "unfinished business." In the book of Haggai you see a similar situation concerning the rebuilding of the temple in Jerusalem. These folks had so many excuses for why this project could not be done—at least not right away! Isn't this just like us? We do what we are interested in and put off the things that we consider drudgery. This passage in Haggai gives you a promise that should encourage you to complete your unfinished business.

The promise given by the Lord is "I am with you" and "my Spirit remains in your midst." This promise was not only for the people in Haggai's time; it is for us as well. God's presence with us is permanent. We never need to doubt it. Jesus' work on the cross is complete. His work to save us is finished. Now his promise is to remain with us, to be by our side. He will give you strength to do the thing you have been avoiding, the thing that is really hard or that seems impossible to complete. Did you know that when you give your life to Christ, his Holy Spirit comes to live in you to empower you to do hard things? You don't need to feel overwhelmed. Tackle that project, for the Lord is with you!

November 25

Supreme Court Justice

*Therefore having overlooked the times of ignorance,
God is now declaring to men that all people everywhere should
repent, because He has fixed a day in which He will judge the world
in righteousness through a Man whom He has appointed, having
furnished proof to all men by raising Him from the dead.*
Acts 17:30-31 (NASB)

The Constitution of the United States includes the Supreme Court, the highest and final court in our country. The Supreme Court is comprised of nine judges. Each judge must be appointed by the President and confirmed by the Senate. This honor and duty is a life-long appointment. The duties of a Supreme Court justice are significant, so choosing a judge demands special scrutiny. The judge must be a person with an excellent knowledge of the law, a record of the highest standards of judicial wisdom, and a record of integrity.

Our verse today tells us that God appointed his Son, Jesus, to be the supreme judge of his divine kingdom. Jesus was perfect for the job. He had firsthand knowledge of the law of God, the highest standards of judicial wisdom, and a record of the utmost integrity. With God's appointment and his flawless resume, Jesus didn't need any human confirmation! Because of God's appointment, he stands *forever* as the final judge of what is right and what is wrong, who is good and who is evil.

The most important question we can ask ourselves is, "Where do *I* stand?" The Bible says that every person will stand before the judgment seat of God. We are all guilty sinners. Will you have an advocate to plead your case? Jesus has been appointed as the supreme judge, but he also offers to be our advocate. He died for sinners and rose again to plead our case. The fact is, our innocence cannot be assumed. His mercy is not automatic. God's mercy comes to those who repent of their sin, surrender themselves to the authority of Christ, and throw themselves on his mercy. Where do you stand?

November 26

"Houston, we've had a problem here."

For my iniquities have gone over my head; like a heavy burden, they are too heavy for me. I confess my iniquity; I am sorry for my sin. But for you, O Lord, do I wait; it is you, O Lord my God, who will answer.
Psalm 38:4, 18, 15 (ESV)

"Houston, we've had a problem here." These now famous words were spoken by astronaut John Swigert on Apollo 13's third mission to the moon. He was reporting a critical problem to NASA. They had just heard a loud bang, which turned out to be an oxygen tank exploding. This was big! The loss of oxygen would not only jeopardize their mission; it would end the lives of everyone on board. From that point on, their goal was to get back to Earth alive. The spacecraft was badly damaged, but the lunar module might be used for their escape. Everyone's problem-solving skills immediately went into action. A solution was implemented, and the Apollo crew was able to arrive home safely. Big problems call for big solutions, and that is exactly where King David found himself in Psalm 38.

To give you a better idea of what was going on, you need to understand that when he wrote this psalm, David's personal life was a disaster. He was well aware of his sins and was pretty sure God was angry with him. The thought of God's anger tormented him and made him feel sick, overwhelmed, and depressed. His friends didn't know what to do with him, so they avoided him completely. His neighbors stayed away too. His enemies hated him with a passion. They were plotting to assassinate him or at least oust him from power. He was miserable and isolated. To add to his problems, the burden of his sins was too much to bear. Have you ever been there?

Then, there is only one thing for you to do—confess your sins to the Lord and receive his forgiveness.

In verses 15 and 18, David looks outside himself and implements this solution. He confesses his sins to God. "I am sorry for my iniquity," he prays. "It is you, O Lord my God, who will answer." Jesus Christ is the only one who can carry the heavy burden of your sins. His sacrifice to pay for those sins turns away God's wrath. When you confess your sins and receive God's offer of forgiveness, Jesus becomes your advocate and stands in your defense. No more pain, misery, and depression. What freedom it is to know that even in your biggest failures in life, you have an even bigger Savior in Jesus!

November 27

My Only Job

I love the Lord, because He hears My voice and my supplications.
Because He has inclined His ear to me,
Therefore I shall call upon Him as long as I live.
Psalm 116:1-2 (NASB)

I have a very special friend whom I have known for almost forty years. She is now a widow, but most of her family lives nearby. Every Thanksgiving, the family contributes to the meal by bringing a dish to share. My friend was always the one to buy and cook the turkey. But one year all of her children decided that it was time for her to retire from her duties so she could relax and enjoy the Thanksgiving meal without any work. This change of responsibility was alarming to her. All of a sudden, she felt completely unnecessary. The family assured her this was not the case, but that didn't help. She insisted on doing *something*, so the family relented and asked her to bring the paper products. Instead of solving the problem, this made her feel worse. Her feelings of insignificance were devastating, but she didn't want to make a fuss or make people feel sorry for her. Thankfully, she had another option. She could call on the Lord. Psalm 116 tells us we have a God who hears all our prayers and is sensitive to all our needs, that he listens to us and really understands how we feel. Sometimes all a person needs is a good listener, and God is *so* good at listening that the psalmist says, "I love the Lord…I shall call upon him as long as I live."

In this hectic life, it is easy to be caught up in our work, our ambitions, and our goals. We have important jobs to do, and we don't have time to waste. But sometimes we feel like we get lost in this fast-paced world. We feel overlooked and misunderstood. We don't have a prestigious job or title, and we feel like we don't matter. But in God's sight, every person is valuable and precious. So never forget that even if your only job is bringing the paper products, you are of great importance to God.

November 28

Five Kernels of Corn

*I was glad when they said to me,
let us go to the house of the Lord.*
Psalm 122:1 (NASB)

After the *Mayflower* landed on shore in Cape Cod, the Pilgrims came very close to starvation. At one point, the daily ration for each person was only five kernels of corn. They believed that God would sustain them, and he surely did!

Years ago we started a family Thanksgiving custom to thank the Lord for our blessings. It comes from an old Thanksgiving tradition. We incorporate five kernels of corn into our celebration as we remember what God has done for us. While each of the kernels is dropped into a special glass container, a family member talks about five blessings he received from God during the year. We carefully copy each blessing into our book of Thanksgiving blessings. Over the years it has been a real joy to remember what God has done and how he has worked in our lives. Psalm 122 is about one of the times that the psalmist came to Jerusalem for a holy feast. It was a lot like our Thanksgiving holiday. This pilgrimage gave him a time to remember and celebrate God's goodness.

You can sense the joy of the psalmist talking about going to the house of the Lord with his family. This was a special time and a delight to worship the Lord. The psalmist was glad for the opportunity. Anytime we share with others about what God has done, we honor God. I think Jesus smiles when he sees those kernels of corn and when he sees the gratitude in our hearts.

November 29

"Trust and Obey"

*Praise the Lord! How blessed is the man who fears the Lord,
Who greatly delights in His commandments.*
Psalm 112:1 (NASB)

"Trust and Obey" is a hymn written by John H. Sammis in 1887. This familiar gospel song has been a favorite for Sunday school classes, worship services, and many other gatherings for over one hundred years. The lyrics for the song were inspired in 1886 when Daniel B. Towner, a music leader for one of Dwight L. Moody's famous revivals, heard a young man's testimony. "I am not quite sure," the young man said, "but I am going to trust, and I am going to obey." When Towner heard this testimony, he jotted it down and sent it to Sammis, who was a Presbyterian minister. That little phrase, "trust and obey," became the theme of this beloved hymn.

These three words capture several of God's truths in Psalm 112. "The man who fears the Lord" is blessed. When you fear the Lord, you are holding him in high esteem. You are honoring and respecting his authority over you. His commandments aren't a burden. They are wonderful—a delight. That's because you trust God, and when you obey him, you are blessed. You are happier, healthier, more at peace, and more productive. And when you fail (we all do), you are in awe of the God you can trust to forgive you and to rescue you from your sins. So we study God's commands, we strive to obey them, and then we reap the benefits: we are forgiven, we are changed, and we are blessed. It all fits together for a person who is experiencing God's grace. As he fears God, God is making him into his obedient child. Only a person who has experienced God's grace can trust and obey. And this is precisely why we say, "Praise the Lord!"

November 30

Superstition vs God's Sure Promises

You who fear the Lord, trust in the Lord;
He is their help and their shield.
Psalm 115:11 (NASB)

Superstition is belief in the power of magic spells, omens, good luck charms, a lucky penny, astrology, ghosts, or numbers like thirteen. Most people are superstitious to some extent. "It's worth a try," they say. "You never know! It might just work this time. I might as well cover *all* my bases." Superstitions give fearful people the feeling they are in control of their circumstances. If we aren't careful, little superstitions can easily invade our lives, but they always lead to a dead end. That's because they are invented by human thinking, which is seriously limited and often faulty. Psalm 115 gives us a better option.

It's better to fear the Lord and it's better to trust the Lord. Why? 1. Because God is all-knowing and all-wise. 2. Because God is a real person who cares about you and actually has the power to help. 3. Because God's promises to those who trust him are sure for this present day and for eternity. One promise is that he gives eternal life to those who believe in him. Another promise is that he will be our help and our shield. When you have a God like this, you don't need superstitions. God is holding you in his hands. Underneath you are his everlasting arms. He knows what is best for you. You have solid promises you can hold on to. You can trust God completely.

December 1

The Trip to Bountiful

The righteous will surround me,
For You will deal bountifully with me.
Psalm 142:7 (NASB)

The Trip to Bountiful is a movie that tells the story of an elderly woman who wants to return to her home in a rural town named Bountiful near the Texas Gulf Coast. Her son and daughter-in-law love her and know that the town of Bountiful has long since disappeared due to the Depression, so they forbid the elderly woman to travel alone from Houston to her childhood home. The old woman, however, is determined to go and outwits them. She meets a young lady on the journey, and she shares both secrets and memories. Although it will be difficult, she wants to see an old friend and visit her home one last time before she dies. The local sheriff makes this possible, and she finally reaches her destination. However, she soon learns that her old friend has died and most of her home has been destroyed by neglect. Tearfully, she accepts the reality of her situation and begins her journey back to her loving family. *Bountiful* is a story of hope just like the psalmist's story in Psalm 142.

It is so easy to take the blessings of the present for granted and to long for the past. We feel like the love we are experiencing now doesn't compare to what we remember of "the good old times." We glorify the past and think that if we could just go back in time, we would be happy again. What we forget is that God has blessed us with a bountiful place at every season of our lives, especially if we have righteous, loving people around us. And if we can't find people like that? Then the Lord will encircle us with his love and encouragement. He will deal bountifully with us—even if we feel like we don't deserve it! Our trip to Bountiful will probably end in disappointment, but our trip back to the arms of Christ will never let us down—because that's exactly where he wants us to be!

December 2

Fishing Nets

You will pull me out of the net which they have secretly laid for me, For You are my strength.
Psalm 31:4 (NASB)

What do you think of when you see pictures of commercial fishermen in boats loaded down with nets and large buckets full of fish? I think about the fishermen and how difficult and dangerous their job can be, especially in the middle of the night when they are cold and tired and wet. But what about the fish? To be honest, I never really thought about the fish. But when I read our verse for today, the picture of a fish caught in a net got my attention. I started to think about myself. What if I were caught in a net, with no way out, destined for death? It gave me a terrible feeling!

The writer of the verse for today seems to be feeling like a fish trapped in a net. He is struggling with a lack of freedom in his life. Maybe his struggle is against physical enemies, or maybe he is experiencing the attacks of what the Bible calls "the powers of this dark world… the spiritual forces of evil in the heavenly realms" (Ephesians 6:12 NIV). In any case, enemies were seeking to ensnare him in a trap they had secretly laid for him. These powerful forces wanted to destroy him. Have you ever felt trapped by something that is robbing you of your freedom? Maybe it's the trap of fear, anxiety, or a broken heart. Maybe it's an addiction to alcohol, drugs, or pornography. How can you break free? Where can you go for help?

This verse gives the answer: "You will pull me out of the net they have secretly laid for me, for You are my strength." There is only one person who can free us from Satan's traps, and that person is Jesus Christ. He may use friends, counselors, and programs to encourage you. But in the end, it will be the power of God that will set you free. Don't believe that sheer willpower is all you need. Satan's nets are stronger than you are, and his goal is your destruction. Jesus offers freedom from captivity. He will pull you out of the net. Come to Jesus. He will deliver you!

December 3

Apron Lady

Clothe yourselves, all of you, with humility toward one another.
1 Peter 5:5 (ESV)

My wife wears aprons. She has been doing this for years. As a matter of fact, you will not catch her without one. She is usually doing something in the kitchen, so this is the reason she wears them. Friends and family have actually nicknamed her the "Apron Lady" because of her love of cooking and her service to others. Today, the verse we are considering in 1 Peter starts off with the words "clothe yourselves." This phrase refers to a slave who puts on an apron before serving. These words are an important part of the command God gives to all believers.

God wants us to put on our aprons and serve others. That is what Jesus Christ did when he came to Earth. He served us. He came to deliver us from the mess we've created with our rebellious lives. He did this by teaching us what is right, by exemplifying a life of humility, and by offering us forgiveness and eternal life. He set the example for us to follow. When I serve others, I am imitating Jesus and bringing praise to his name. By serving others, I am glorifying Jesus as I share my life with them. I am giving them encouragement and loving them through my actions. My Apron Lady gives people encouragement whenever she serves or delivers a meal. She encourages me to be a better servant as well. Our service might be the only opportunity people have to see the good news of Jesus Christ in action.

December 4

Upside-Down Life

But I call to God, and the Lord will save me.
Cast your burden on the Lord, and he will sustain you;
he will never permit the righteous to be moved.
Psalm 55:16, 22 (ESV)

Crises have a way of turning your life upside down. Your world crumbles around you. Everything seems to be changing, and it seems like nothing will ever be the same. You imagine yourself flying away to a place where you don't have to deal with the fear that is filling your heart. But that is hardly ever an option. Why do you feel so afraid, so emotionally and physically weak and helpless? Well, fear is a common problem for us all. King David struggled with fear just like you, so you are not alone. Let me suggest the solution he wrote about in Psalm 55.

David writes that he didn't fly away from fear, he ran to God instead. He had no idea how to fix his situation, so he called out to God. He chose to take these actions because he knew from experience that the Lord would save him. He knew that the sovereign God who rules the universe would see him through his darkest hour.

David's words to you are that you should "cast your burden on the Lord, and he will sustain you; he will never permit the righteous to be moved." God is strong and able to carry your burdens. This is no problem for him because he can handle anything. In fact, an upside-down life can be a good thing because it makes you run to God, talk to him, and see his mighty power in your life. Do you believe God can do this for you?

An upside-down life can actually be a blessing if you live it in the power of God.

December 5

Strikingly Different

But God, being rich in mercy, because of His great love with which He loved us, even when we were dead in our transgressions, made us alive together with Christ (by grace you have been saved), and raised us up with Him, and seated us with Him in the heavenly places in Christ Jesus.
Ephesians 2:4-6 (NASB)

When my mother-in-law died, my oldest granddaughter was born. The contrast between these two events could not have been more striking. Mourning death and celebrating new life is pictured beautifully in our passage for today, Ephesians 2:4-6.

Did you know that before we meet Christ, we are spiritually dead in our transgressions and sins? That's what these verses say! And there's nothing we can do about it. Dead people can't will themselves back to life. And people who are dead in their sins can't make themselves spiritually alive! But God is rich in mercy, and he *is* able to make us alive! This new life is granted to us because of the grace of Christ, who paid the debt for all our sins. This, then, is what God does for us! He saves our lives!

But that's not all! People who respond to God's call are raised up to a brand-new life in the presence of God, and now we are in his spiritual presence in the heavenly places. All we need to do is answer God's call, and we are raised from death to life! What could be more striking? God raises us from the dead!

December 6

Shelter-in-Place

*The Lord is a refuge for the oppressed,
a stronghold in times of trouble.*
Psalm 9:9 (NIV)

On March 16, 2020, the state of California issued a shelter-in-place warning for the residents in San Francisco and the surrounding Bay Area to slow the spread of the COVID-19 pandemic. Orders like this are rare and usually involve emergencies like an impending tornado, hurricane, nuclear power plant disaster, hazardous chemical spill, or any other serious threat that demands our immediate attention to ensure our personal safety. It is easy to understand dangerous situations for our communities, but what about when times of trouble involve you personally? What happens when your life has been turned upside down and you don't know where to go? We hope this will never happen, but the truth is that all of us will face times of trouble. The verse for today encourages anyone who is facing a situation with dire consequences. "The Lord is a refuge for the oppressed, a stronghold in times of trouble."

A refuge is a shelter, a safe place, a place where we can hide. He is the "stronghold in times of trouble." He is the King who rules over heaven and Earth. He is the one you can turn to in your crisis. He will hear your prayer and will meet you in your hour of need. He knows your heart when you cry out to him. He knows you are trusting in him. And best of all, wherever you are, you can experience the reassuring peace and presence of God. This is a promise from God. He holds us close to himself in times of trouble.

December 7

Annual Christmas Letter

*But God chose what is foolish in the world to shame the wise;
God chose what is weak in the world to shame the strong;
God chose what is low and despised in the world, even things that are
not, to bring to nothing things that are, so that no human being might
boast in the presence of God.*
I Corinthians 1:27-29 (ESV)

The annual Christmas letter is intended to update all the friends and relatives you haven't seen for a while on what is happening in your life. For most of us, the news we share is good news, news we want others to see. Bad news is hidden and will never see the light of day. Good newsletters are written in what's called the "Norman Rockwell" style. They give an idealistic or sentimentalized portrayal of our lives. This tends to put a happy face on a person's entire existence and quite often borders on boasting. This passage in Corinthians warns us against boasting and gives us special insight into the gospel.

Many people who think they are smart, strong, important, and sophisticated don't think they need God. Actually, God is the one who made them and gave them all their gifts, but they don't acknowledge God or thank him. Instead, they look down on others they see as ignorant, weak, lowly, and unimportant. They despise people like that. They boast.

To put them in their place, God turned the tables. When Jesus preached and healed and died a criminal's death on the cross, he was considered by many people to be weak, lowly, and unimportant. He was despised and rejected by the powerful people of his day. But he proved his strength when he rose from the dead and established a huge movement of lowly people who went out and changed the world! How does Jesus look now? He is the most prominent person in the history of the world! And what have his chosen people done? They have nullified human wisdom and been the world's greatest force for good! When we stand before God someday, none of us will be able to boast about ourselves. Instead, we will all bow before the God who gave us everything. Boasters will be nullified, but God's chosen ones will receive life. Are you a boaster or chosen one? Jesus, the Savior, is someone you can boast about in your next annual Christmas letter!

December 8

It's All Gravy!

*How blessed is everyone who fears the Lord,
who walks in His ways.*
Psalm 128:1 (NASB)

One of my favorite meals is roast beef and potatoes with brown gravy. Meat and potatoes for a Midwestern boy is a staple. When I moved to the East Coast I discovered that people actually eat meals with no meat and no potatoes. They eat vegetables as their main course! People who do this miss out on one of the greatest blessings in life—which is, it's all about the gravy! The psalmist was well acquainted with life's blessings when he composed Psalm 128.

People who fear the Lord are blessed. This is a promise to every person who puts his life in God's hands. You don't have to do something big or be somebody special to earn God's salvation. Salvation is a lot like meat and potatoes—standard fare for every person who fears the Lord. The condition of a person's heart, however, is revealed in his obedience to God. Blessings come when a person's heart *and* walk are in sync, when that person is walking in God's ways.

As I said, God's gift of salvation is like meat and potatoes. Blessings are the gravy that tops it all off. Blessings come to us with God's mercy and approval. Everything we receive after our salvation—is gravy! And oh, how I love gravy!

December 9

Bungee Cord

Cease striving and know that I am God; I will be exalted among the nations, I will be exalted in the earth.
Psalm 46:10 (NASB)

A bungee cord is made of one or more strands of elastic material, usually rubber, bound together by a fabric covering. It is also known as a tie-down. Bungee cords are very helpful when it comes to securing objects to a vehicle or absorbing any shock. When bungees are stretched out, a natural tension occurs that makes it difficult to free the object being secured. The harder you struggle with the cord, the harder it is to release the object. This common multi-purpose cord has so many uses around the home that a person can easily forget its original purpose. The bottom line is that it secures objects by creating tension. This makes it a very good object lesson for the psalm being considered today.

God wants us to "cease striving." What am I saying when I strive or struggle with my circumstances or even with God? "I want control of my life. I want to be independent. I want to call the shots. After all, I don't owe anybody anything." Whoa! Wait a minute! You don't owe anyone anything? Let's think about that! First of all, you wouldn't even be alive if God hadn't created you. Seems to me, you owe him your life! Second, lots of people, even people you don't know, have sacrificed so you can live and make something good of your life. The prideful statement, "It's my life, and I'm going to make my own decisions," doesn't hold up very well, if you consider the facts. A life based on selfishness just creates tension between families, co-workers, neighbors, and, most importantly, between you and God. Our personal goals and God's goals seldom work together. Do you know why? Because God is all-knowing and all-wise—and we aren't! We are limited, sinful, and often don't have a clue about what is good for us. God is also sovereign.

He is the one in charge! He declares, "I *will* be exalted among the nations, I *will* be exalted in the earth."

Do you see the conflict? Your struggle for independence creates more tension. Struggling for independence will only give you anxiety, heartburn, and sleepless nights. None of us will ever win a war against a holy God.

So what are you going to do my friend? God can give you rest. He can give you peace in this hectic world of ours. He is offering you safety and provisions for your journey. He is offering himself and a personal relationship with him forever. He loves you and wants what is best for you. You don't have to strive anymore. You can be at peace, secure in the midst of tension. Instead of holding on to your own independence, and struggling against God, you can attach yourself to him, relax, and enjoy the safety of your journey. A journey in which Jesus is holding on to you tightly and nothing can make him let you go!

December 10

High School Prom

And no creature is hidden from his sight, but all are naked and exposed to the eyes of him to whom we must give account.
Hebrews 4:13 (ESV)

Who could ever forget going to a high school prom? The boys rent tuxedos and the girls buy fancy dresses to impress their dates. Hide your flaws, zits, and bad manners. Look your best and everyone will think you're cool. The truth is that no matter how hard we try to make ourselves look good, our sins tell a different story. Today's verse tells the naked truth about our standing before God. Hiding from God is impossible. Everything is laid bare before him, even the sins we've hidden deep inside where no one else can see.

Exactly what does that mean? It means we're in trouble! Standing before God and giving an account for the thousands of sins we have committed in our lifetime will be terrifying. The penalty for sin, after all, is death. But, as we have said so many times before, God sent his Son, Jesus, to rescue us from the judgment we deserve. The Bible tells us that when we turn to God and receive his free gift of salvation, he clothes us with the righteousness of Christ. We don't have to dress ourselves up to look good for God. Jesus did that for us! No need to fake it; no need to look cool. When God looks at us, he only sees Christ's perfection. This is the best gift ever, and lasts for eternity!

December 11

The Mystery of Tapestry

*All Scripture is breathed out by God
and profitable for teaching, for reproof, for correction,
and for training in righteousness.*
2 Timothy 3:16 (ESV)

Tapestry is textile art that it is woven by hand on a loom. It is very difficult to make and requires a huge investment of time to complete. A good weaver can only produce a square yard of tapestry in a month. Tapestries have been around for thousands of years. Egyptians and Incas used woven tapestries as shrouds to bury the dead. The Greeks and Romans used them as wall-coverings for buildings and temples like the Pantheon. Today they are used primarily to cover walls or furniture. If you look at a piece of tapestry, you will discover something that will surprise you. I call it the mystery of tapestry. When you look at the front side, you will see a beautiful pattern. But turn it over, and you see a messy jumble of threads all tangled up with no apparent pattern at all. Tapestries are a good illustration of our lives with God.

Read today's verse again. It tells us that all Scripture is breathed out by God. The Scriptures are the writings of human authors who were inspired to write the very words of God. The combination of all sixty-six books reveals the gospel message that leads to salvation through faith in Jesus Christ. Scripture is "profitable for teaching, for reproof, for correction, and for training in righteousness." I like to compare the Bible to a tapestry. When you study the words of God, you will find them to be perfect and delightful. In fact, nothing can compare to the beauty of God's revelation.

But when we look at our lives in comparison, we see messes and tangles, strings and loose ends. God's message is perfect; we are not. That's why God sent his Son, Jesus. He delivers us from our sins when we look to him in the pages of the Bible. He will teach us, reprove us, correct us, and train us to straighten out those tangles, those messes we've made, those loose ends we need to tie back together again. Our side of the tapestry will never be perfect, but God's work up front is beautiful! It's a picture of you with Jesus—and it is a brilliant work of art!

December 12

Paying Off the Mortgage

In this is love, not that we loved God, but that He loved us and sent His Son to be the propitiation for our sins.
1 John 4:10 (NASB)

The biggest debt for most of us is our mortgage. Many of us will spend at least thirty years paying it off. What a relief that will be! It will give a sense of freedom. Finally, you will have nothing hanging over your head. Now imagine that a bank loan manager notified you that an anonymous donor has paid off your mortgage. What an incredible gift! This is a little picture of what God did for us.

We have rebelled against God and betrayed him by our sinful deeds. And because God is holy and just, we are in big trouble! Here's the problem. If God overlooks our sin, he wouldn't be holy. If he doesn't punish our sins, he wouldn't be just. But God is also personal and loving, so he solved the problem by sending Jesus to take our punishment and pay off our debt. Jesus is our propitiation, our donor. He assumes our obligations to God. He pays off our debt. Of course, he isn't an anonymous donor. He's Jesus, the Savior, and he's known around the world for his generosity! No more debt, only Jesus.

December 13

Annual Physical Exam

*And hearing this, Jesus said to them,
"It is not those who are healthy who need a physician, but those who
are sick; I did not come to call the righteous, but sinners."*
Mark 2:17 (NASB)

Every year I am scheduled for an annual physical exam, and every year I hate it. Will the blood work be okay? Did the physician see or hear anything suspicious? Unfortunately for many of us, it takes a sudden event like a heart attack to wake us up. Physicians are good at pinpointing problems. They will let you know what you need to do to stay physically healthy. Lose some weight, exercise four to five times a week, and by all means, watch your diet. As I consider my doctor's recommendations, I am reminded of 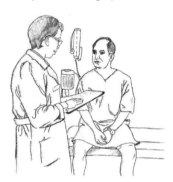 another physician who lived two thousand years ago. Jesus not only healed people's physical problems, but he also taught us all how to become spiritually healthy.

One day, as Jesus was teaching a crowd of people, he noticed Levi sitting at a tax collector's booth. Most Jewish people hated tax collectors. Tax collectors not only worked for the Roman government, they also overcharged people, taking the extra money for themselves. Everyone knew tax collectors were "sinners"! But Jesus didn't hate Levi. Instead, he told Levi to follow him. And Levi did! That night Levi invited Jesus and his disciples over to have dinner with him and his tax collector friends.

But when the Pharisees saw Jesus eating and drinking with "sinners," they went right over to his disciples and asked, "Why does he eat with tax collectors and sinners?" They, of course, were insinuating that Jesus was doing something wrong, that he shouldn't be associating with "those people." Jesus heard them talking, and this is how he answered: "It is not those who are healthy who need a physician, but those who are sick; I did not come to call the righteous, but sinners." Jesus was saying that he was the physician everybody needs, that the reason he came to Earth was to heal sinful people and make them spiritually healthy. And you know what? He's still doing that today! I don't know anyone who has it all together spiritually. Do you? But Jesus tells us to follow him. He will heal our sin sickness and give us spiritual health that will last forever. This is exciting news. By trusting in Christ, I will never need to schedule an annual *spiritual* exam. Jesus' blood work was good enough to heal me and keep me spiritually healthy forever! No more bad news to fear. Just a clean bill of health and eternal life in heaven!

December 14

No Strings Attached

*The sons of Israel said to the Lord,
"We have sinned, do to us whatever seems good to You;
only please deliver us this day." So they put away the foreign gods from
among them and served the Lord; and He could bear the misery of
Israel no longer.*
Judges 10:15-16 (NASB)

The origin of this phrase, "no strings attached," comes from the cloth industry where a small flaw in a fabric would be marked by a string so it could be easily spotted. This is where we get the phrase, "without flaws." Today, the meaning of "no strings attached" is a little different. It means without obligations. It is also used to show that an offer or opportunity carries no special conditions or restrictions. This phrase is a good example of God's willingness to forgive us when we come to him in repentance.

In the book of Judges the cycle of sinning, rebelling, repenting, and finally, God's deliverance is a never-ending story. Thank God, his grace and mercy run throughout the whole history of Israel. These verses in the book of Judges teach us a lot about what true repentance looks like. First, there is the acknowledgment of a sinful thought or deed. The Israelites did not try to cover up their sins or make excuses for themselves. They admitted they were wrong and surrendered themselves to God for his judgment. But they did more than just admit their sin. True repentance includes turning away from your sin. The Israelites showed true repentance by putting away their foreign gods and turning back to serve the Lord. Their confession of sin was coupled with words and actions. This demonstrated what was truly in their hearts. When God saw their repentance, he forgave them. "He could bear the misery of Israel no longer." Sin makes a person miserable. Repentance takes away our load of guilt and replaces it with God's gift of forgiveness—no strings attached!

December 15

The Selah Moment

Behold, God is my helper; The Lord is the sustainer of my soul.
Psalm 54:4 (NASB)

The Hebrew word *selah* means "to lift up or exalt." This word is used seventy-four times in the book of Psalms. We are not actually certain of the meaning of this word, but most people believe it was a musical interlude. This was a pause or a crescendo in the song being sung. So when this word is inserted at the end of the sentence, it means "this is really important" or "take a moment to think about this." The word *selah* was inserted right before this verse in Psalm 54, so let's take a moment to think about it!

The psalmist was facing a very serious crisis in his life, so he cried out to God to save him. He was in big trouble that only God could handle. So what did he do? He looked to God and took a "selah moment." I think this is exactly what God wants each of us to do, especially when facing an overwhelming problem. He wants us to turn to him, take a breath, and think about what he might want us to do. You can be sure that he has an interest and a preference in regard to our courses of action.

When the psalmist took a moment, what do you think he discovered? He discovered that God was his helper, the Lord was the Sustainer of his soul. If you have accepted Jesus Christ as your Savior, you, too, have a helper who will counsel you, sustain you, and deliver you from trouble. I don't know what problem you are dealing with today, but I do know that you can find help in Jesus. Why not take a "selah moment" and consider what Jesus is urging you to do? He might surprise you with an alternative course of action, an action that will honor him and be a blessing to others!

December 16

Down Payment

Now He who establishes us with you in Christ and anointed us is God, who also sealed us and gave us the Spirit in our hearts as a pledge.
2 Corinthians 1:21-22 (NASB)

A down payment is an initial partial payment to purchase an expensive item like a home, car, boat, or jewelry. It usually requires cash to make the transaction possible. The buyer makes a pledge to pay off the remainder of the loan before taking possession of the item. In Paul's letter to the Corinthians, he wanted believers to be encouraged in their faith, so he reminds us of God's pledge.

For most of us, our most expensive purchase will be our home. In the case of Jesus, spiritual matters were his top priority, so his most expensive purchase was the souls of men. He had to pay the price of his own life to pay for my sins. So at the time that I accept the gift of salvation, Jesus makes a down payment. He puts the Holy Spirit in my heart. That means that God's own Spirit comes into me to rule, guide, and comfort my soul. The Holy Spirit is God's promise that he will complete the deal. The believer is branded as God's property. God starts there and continues to build and strengthen the believer in his faith and gradual transformation. And when our life is over, Jesus makes good on his promise. He delivers us to our heavenly home!

December 17

Mixers

*Jesus was going throughout all Galilee, teaching in their synagogues and proclaiming the gospel of the kingdom, and healing every kind of disease and
every kind of sickness among the people.*
Matthew 4:23 (NASB)

I attended West Point, which was all male at the time. Because of this, "mixers" were a good way to meet young ladies and develop enjoyable relationships. When I entered the business world, I was introduced to business mixers, also known as "networking events." These social events were a good way to meet people, develop business contacts, and socialize with like-minded people over good food, drinks, and entertainment. Events like these are friendly, non-threatening, and usually quite delightful. When I looked at the verse for today, I immediately thought about mixers. Jesus spent his entire life mixing with people. As this verse says, he was "among the people."

Jesus was going "throughout all Galilee." He didn't stay put; he went to where the people were living. He taught in the synagogues, so the people could understand who God is. He proclaimed "the gospel of the kingdom" so they would hear the good news of salvation. Jesus wanted all the people to hear his message for themselves. But he didn't stop with speaking engagements. He also healed "every kind of disease and every kind of sickness among the people." He was never afraid to touch people. It didn't matter what disease they had. He could heal them all.

Jesus was seeking people because he wanted to communicate with them. He wanted to touch their hearts. He understood their deepest needs and knew that saving them would require his own suffering and death on the cross. Jesus chose to be among the people so they could see his compassion, his power to heal, and his passion for truth. He could also warn them of the judgment to come and could offer them the gift of salvation. As he lived his life of sacrifice, he encountered temptations to sin in all the ways we are tempted to sin—but he never gave in. Because of this fact, he is able to sympathize with our weaknesses. Because he sympathizes with us, we can come to him with confidence, asking for his forgiveness and receiving power to live the Christian life. It is a great blessing that Jesus was willing to be "among the people." It is a great blessing that he is still willing to walk this life with all of us!

December 18

Humpty Dumpty

*You are to be holy to me because I, the Lord, am holy,
and I have set you apart from the nations to be my own.*
Leviticus 20:26 (NIV)

Humpty Dumpty is a character in a popular English nursery rhyme. His origins remain a mystery. Some people believe that Humpty Dumpty was the nickname for a large and heavy cannon strategically placed atop a wall in a church tower in Colchester, England. When the wall was hit by an enemy attack, the cannon fell to the ground and shattered. It could never be put back together again. Another version portrays Humpty as an egg, or an overweight boy who always muddled things up. He was clumsy and insecure, and when he fell, he broke into so many pieces, no one could put *him* back together again. This children's rhyme actually speaks to a truth all of us should consider.

Humpty is a lot like us. We are fragile creatures who can easily be broken. We like to think that we have it all together in life, that we can handle and solve all our problems. But if we are honest, we know this isn't true. We are sinners. We are broken. We need to be repaired!

God wants us to be holy like he is holy. My first impression of the word *holy* is a bit negative. I sure don't want to be a "holier than thou" person! But the word for *holy* in the Bible has a different meaning. It means "whole" or "complete." God is perfectly whole and complete, and he wants to take us, hopelessly broken and beyond repair, and put us back together again. When you accept Christ's offer to trust in him, God "sets you apart," and begins this process. He picks up the pieces and makes you whole and complete—a person who truly loves God and loves your neighbors. This truth is a life-changer! You were never meant to be a Humpty Dumpty, relegated to the trash heap. God has high expectations for you, and he's the best "fixer-upper" ever!

December 19

Les Miserables

*For the Law was given through Moses;
grace and truth were realized through Jesus Christ.*
John 1:17 (NASB)

Les Miserables is a French historical novel written in 1862 by Victor Hugo. It is considered one of the greatest novels of the 19th century. Hugo unveils the history of France during this time by looking at politics, moral philosophy, justice, religion, and family love. The centerpiece is an examination of the nature of law and grace, and this contrast is precisely what John writes about in his gospel.

Moses was God's representative to deliver God's law to mankind. The Ten Commandments are God's standard of righteousness. They summarize God's moral requirements for humanity. God's law is good, but it is impossible for anyone to obey perfectly. Impossible for anyone—but Christ! Jesus obeyed God's law perfectly, so he was able to pay the price for our disobedience. His sacrificial death provides us with forgiveness when we turn away from our sins, receive his free gift of grace, and trust in him as our Lord and Savior.

Les Miserables is a spiritual struggle we all face in life. The law reminds us that we are unable to keep all of God's commands. Grace reminds us of the forgiveness Christ earned for us on the cross. Our struggle to be perfect keeps us enslaved. Jesus comes along, gives us forgiveness from our past failings, and offers us freedom from guilt. Our struggle ends when we admit our sins and embrace the truth of Jesus. Remember to do this every day!

December 20

Hidden Treasure

*Oh, the depth of the riches both of the wisdom and knowledge of God!
How unsearchable are His judgments
and unfathomable His ways!*
Romans 11:33 (NASB)

In 2010, Forrest Fenn hid a treasure chest in the Rocky Mountains. It was filled with gold and gems valued at around two million dollars. Forrest is a wealthy art dealer who published a book called *The Thrill of the Chase*. In his book, he gave clues and a map to look for his treasure chest. In 2020, after more than 250,000 treasure-seekers failed, and at least four people died, the treasure was found. How sad it is to think that so many people would look for a hidden treasure, only to come up empty in the end. Fortunately, the Bible never hides God's clues for finding the most important treasure of all!

When Jesus died on the cross, he purchased salvation for us. He paid the full price for all of our sins. Today he offers us a true treasure. All we need to do is accept it. This treasure is Jesus Christ himself. His wisdom, knowledge, judgments, and ways are all part of the depth of his riches. Our search in life will end with success when we meet our priceless treasure, Jesus Christ.

December 21

Encyclopedia Britannica

For the Lord gives wisdom;
From His mouth come knowledge and understanding.
Proverbs 2:6 (NASB)

When I was growing up, I thought that there was only one reliable source to go to if you wanted to know anything at all. I would go the bookcase and find twelve volumes labeled A to Z. Any topic you were interested in was right there inviting you to learn. It was fun and made my homework assignments a snap. My source was the famous *Encyclopedia Britannica.* This series of books was first published in 1768 and is still in existence today. Although the printed version ended in 2010, the online version is still available. The last printed version spanned thirty-two volumes and had 32,640 pages. That final version required 100 full-time editors and more than 4,000 contributors. Today the online Britannica includes 228,274 topics, 40 million words, and 24,000 images. This source of knowledge is incredible if you need information! But even the *Encyclopedia Brittanica* is limited in the information it can provide.

There is only one source of unvarnished and unlimited information. That source is God. Humans have limited knowledge, but God is all-knowing. He's never wrong or misinformed, and he has gifted his people with the knowledge we need to be a blessing to the world. Knowledge is important. But God wants to give us another gift, the gift of understanding. A person with understanding knows how to interpret the facts and make changes that benefit the human race. Understanding, under God's influence and direction, produces wisdom. Wisdom is the proper application of information and understanding. Wisdom gives people the ability to discern what is true and what is false; what is good and what is evil. A wise person will choose what is good. That person is virtuous.

God is willing to share these three amazing gifts with people who read his Word, fear him, and obey him. If you receive these gifts from him, you will become part of the solution to the problems people face today. God, through his Word and the power of the Holy Spirit, will make you a valuable member of your family, your community, and the whole world!

December 22

Rivers Bring Life

There is a river whose streams make glad the city of God,
The holy dwelling places of the Most High.
God is in the midst of her, she will not be moved;
God will help her when morning dawns.
Psalm 46:4-5 (NASB)

Rivers hold less than one percent of all the world's water, yet they are one of the most vital sources of *fresh* water. They provide excellent habitats for plants, animals, and many of the earth's organisms. Rivers helped to shape early agriculture in our country with irrigation playing a key role in our history. Rivers bring life wherever they are found. This observation was noted in Psalm 46 as well.

The river found in Psalm 46 is divine grace. It brings life-giving water. It is a never-ending supply providing for all of our spiritual needs. It is clear, fresh, and abundant. It gladdens our hearts. And this river isn't a tiny stream; it is a powerful, rushing river. The river of life represents God's presence. This is where the Most High lives with his children. Right in the middle of everything! And this living water is offered to us. This is good news that will gladden any heart.

December 23

Puppets & Kings

*For not from the east, nor from the west, nor from the desert comes
exaltation; But God is the Judge;
He puts down one and exalts another.*
Psalm 75:6-7 (NASB)

Everybody loves puppets, especially children. Puppets can't talk, walk, or do anything. They just sit there. They are completely dependent on the puppeteer. He decides how they move, what they say, and the role they play. He is the one who has all the answers. But despite this dependency, children are completely intrigued by the puppets. Just as these puppets have a very rare power, the passage from today gives you a complete perspective of just how powerful this holy God really is.

Let me ask you to think about where exaltation comes from. The word itself means "promotion, lofty, uplifted, or haughty." The question of where advancement comes from is one for you to consider. Do you think that your promotion comes from what you did? Do you think that your hard work and creative genius have anything to do with your position of power? The Bible tells us that exaltation does not come from the east, west, or the desert. Advancement does not happen by chance. God appoints kings and leaders. He is the one who puts one down and exalts another. God makes all of the decisions. He is at work behind every action in this universe. God is judging all the time, and his throne in heaven is never vacant.

Do you know what this really means? Kings are like puppets in God's hands. Nations rise and fall at his bidding. "It is God who executes judgment, putting down one and lifting up another." He doesn't need our help. All of us are dependent on Christ for our salvation and deliverance. Jesus did all the work on the cross and gets all the credit. Any heavenly promotion you get is a gift from the God who loves you! Believe in God's greatest gift of all—receive Jesus.

December 24

Mary's Surprise

*Now in the sixth month the angel Gabriel was sent from
God to a city in Galilee called Nazareth, to a virgin engaged to
a man whose name was Joseph, of the descendants of David;
and the virgin's name was Mary.
Mary said to the angel, "How can this be, since I am a virgin?"
The angel answered and said to her, "The Holy Spirit will come upon
you, and the power of the Most High will overshadow you; and for that
reason the holy Child shall be called the Son of God."
And Mary said, "Behold, the bondslave of the Lord; may it be done to
me according to your word."*
Luke 1:26-27, 34-35, 38 (NASB)

I'm amazed by this incredible story. God sent an angel to Earth to deliver a special message to a young lady named Mary. She was a virgin and engaged to a man named Joseph. The angel told her that she was pregnant and would give birth to a son.

Can you even begin to think what this must have been like for her? And she had only one question? "How can this be, since I am a virgin?" For most of us, it would generate many more questions. How do I tell others I am pregnant? What do I tell my fiancé? So many unanswered questions. Yet Mary's response was one of simple obedience to God. She didn't have all of the answers, but she completely trusted in God: what a role model she is for all of us.

Gabriel's message was more than a baby announcement. It proclaimed that God was delivering a Savior for us. He is sending his Son as a baby. The little boy will grow up to manhood and then carry out his mission. He will preach the gospel to the poor, proclaim release to the captives and recovery of sight to the blind, and set free those who are oppressed. Jesus fulfilled this proclamation when he sacrificed his life on the cross to provide for the forgiveness of all of our sins. Today each of us is offered a pardon, and all we have to do is believe and trust him. Mary's surprise is now our good news!

December 25

The Baby That Changed the World

In the same region there were some shepherds staying out in the fields and keeping watch over their flock by night. And an angel of the Lord suddenly stood before them, and the glory of the Lord shone around them; and they were terribly frightened. But the angel said to them, "Do not be afraid; for behold, I bring you good news of great joy which will be for all the people; for today in the city of David there has been born for you a Savior, who is Christ the Lord."
Luke 2:8-11 (NASB)

Soon after Mary's surprise, Caesar Augustus sent out an order to have a census taken. That meant Mary and Joseph would have to travel to Bethlehem to register even though she was due to deliver her baby anytime. By the time they arrived in Bethlehem, there were no vacancies in the local inns. Mary ended up delivering her baby in a stable. This is where the story begins for the shepherds.

Local shepherds who were tending their sheep were frightened when a bright, shining angel suddenly appeared before them. I can imagine the fear they must have felt. This heavenly messenger was sent to bring good news of great joy for all of the people. What news did the angel give to these shepherds? What could be that important? A baby boy had just been born in Bethlehem. This baby is named Jesus, and he is the long-awaited Messiah. The angel then told the men they would find a baby wrapped in cloths and lying in a manger. With that news, a multitude of the heavenly host praised God and said, "Glory to God in the highest, and on earth peace among men with whom He is pleased" (Luke 2:14 NASB).

I wonder if these sheepherders understood what had just happened. I do know that when the angel departed, they left in a hurry and found their way to Mary and Joseph and the baby. This must have been some incredible meeting, talking to these new parents and seeing the newborn. I am sure that this baby's birth was one they talked about for a long time.

Why was the birth of this baby so important? Why would God send an angel down to Earth to deliver this news to some shepherds? And what does it mean for us now? The good news is that this baby was sent to Earth to save a world lost in sin and despair. He was the Messiah that the prophets of old had talked about. This baby was the King who would give hope to all of mankind. Because of this baby, you and I are offered eternal life. By believing in him, you will be changed forever.

December 26

God's Promise to Simeon

And there was a man in Jerusalem whose name was Simeon; and this man was righteous and devout, looking for the consolation of Israel; and the Holy Spirit was upon him. And it had been revealed to him by the Holy Spirit that he would not see death before he had seen the Lord's Christ. And he came in the Spirit into the temple; and when the parents brought in the child Jesus, to carry out for Him the custom of the Law, then he took Him into his arms, and blessed God, and said, "Now Lord, You are releasing Your bond-servant to depart in peace, according to Your word; for my eyes have seen Your salvation, which You have prepared in the presence of all peoples, a light of revelation to the Gentiles, and the glory of Your people Israel."
Luke 2:25-32 (NASB)

Soon after Jesus was born and circumcised, Mary and Joseph took their son to Jerusalem to present him to the Lord. The law of the Old Testament required that every firstborn male had to be consecrated to the Lord. In compliance, they went to the Jewish leaders and offered a sacrifice to the Lord. This is where the story begins for Simeon.

Simeon lived in Jerusalem. He was a priest serving in the temple. He was a righteous and devout man who lived his life with integrity. We know that he was looking and waiting for Israel's deliverance in God's Messiah. God had given Simeon the promise that he would not die before he saw God's salvation (which was the arrival of the Messiah).

When Mary and Joseph brought Jesus to the temple for the dedication ceremony, it was Simeon who was in charge of the service that day. Simeon held Jesus in his arms and looked into his face. Simeon knew immediately that God's promise had been fulfilled. He knew that Jesus was the Messiah. Simeon's blessing on Jesus revealed that he understood that God's promise of salvation was being carried out with this baby boy. God was faithful to his promise to Simeon.

All of these stories of Mary and Joseph, the shepherds, and Simeon are related. The focus on Jesus Christ and his plan of salvation is your invitation to come to the party. What are you going to do?

December 27

Fingerprints

*For since the creation of the world His invisible attributes,
His eternal power and divine nature, have been clearly seen,
being understood through what has been made,
so that they are without excuse.*
Romans 1:20 (NASB)

A fingerprint is an impression left by the friction ridges of a human finger. All human fingerprints are detailed and unique to each individual. Fingerprints can reveal a lot about a person, like their intelligence, their personality traits, and their unique talents. Dermatoglyphics is a branch of science that is dedicated to the study of fingerprints. Fingerprints are used regularly by forensic scientists to identify people. I find it interesting that fingerprints cannot tell you what a person looks like physically, but they can offer many other clues about a person's inner characteristics. God's fingerprints reveal his invisible characteristics, as we see in this passage of Romans.

When God created the world, his fingerprints were all over it. His invisible attributes, his eternal power, and his divine nature are clearly seen. They are right there, staring you in the face. God is infinite, all-powerful, all-wise, and good. I understand these things when I see the power of a thunderstorm, the beauty of a flower, the song of a bird, and a little baby smiling. I know he is there when I hear an inspiring song that speaks to my heart. But God went even further when he revealed himself physically in his Son, Jesus Christ. People could see Jesus' face, touch him, and hear his voice. People wrote books about Jesus so we could know for sure that God exists and so we could trust our lives to him. God revealed himself clearly to mankind because he wants us to have a relationship with him. His invisible fingerprints reveal his heart for you.

December 28

The Longest Reign

The Lord reigns.
Psalm 93:1 (ESV)

When you think of political leaders in the twentieth century, whom do you think of? Churchill, Roosevelt, Mandela, Gandhi, or maybe Reagan? Let me suggest to you a female monarch who reigned for over seventy years as the Queen of the United Kingdom. Elizabeth Alexandra Mary reigned from 1952 until her death in 2022. She had the longest reign of any modern kingdom. Her accomplishments and devotion to the British people are unquestioned. But what I find most inspiring is her faith in God. She was a bold witness for Jesus Christ. In her Christmas message in 2000, she said, "To many of us, our beliefs are of fundamental importance. For me the teachings of Christ and my own personal accountability before God provide a framework in which I try to lead my life. I, like so many of you, have drawn great comfort in difficult times from Christ's words and example." This woman of faith was willing to set the example for her nation.

As I think about Queen Elizabeth II, I am reminded of a very important point: "The Lord reigns." Jesus Christ is our King. He is the sovereign ruler of the entire world. His reign began before creation and is happening right now. He is firmly in control, and there is no situation too difficult for him. Despite all the bad news we hear, our King is still sitting on his throne. He has not left. Yes, "the Lord reigns"!

As we end the year, I have only one question for you as we say goodbye. Who is your King? Whom do you serve? King Jesus has always been there waiting for you, and he will be there long after you and I depart. "The Lord reigns." This is the good news for all mankind! And for you, it is the best news you will ever hear.

December 29

Give Yourself Up

Therefore be imitators of God, as beloved children; and walk in love, just as Christ also loved you and gave Himself up for us, an offering and a sacrifice to God as a fragrant aroma.
Ephesians 5:1-2 (NASB)

Have you ever thought about what it means to give yourself up? According to several dictionaries, you "give yourself up" when you surrender yourself completely to another person or cause. We don't give ourselves up very often. In fact, one character in Leo Tolstoy's novel *Anna Karenina* makes this profound statement: "I imagine the mainspring of all our actions is, after all, self-interest." This statement rings true, doesn't it? Self-interest is the real driving force behind most of our actions. But self-interest runs counter to the message God gives us in the verse we are considering today. Let's take a look.

Children imitate their father, especially if they know their father loves them. This verse tells us that we are God's beloved children and admonishes us to imitate his love—to "walk in love." Our example is Christ, who loved us so much that he gave himself up for us as an offering and a sacrifice to God to pay the debt for our sins. Jesus' loving sacrifice for us is like a sweet-smelling aroma to God. Are you willing to seek the good of others even if it means great expense to yourself? Are you willing to give yourself up? Your sacrifices are also a sweet-smelling fragrance to God. Giving yourself up for others is what it means to "walk in love."

December 30

Come and See

> *Come and you will see.*
> John 1:39 (ESV)

My brother-in-law tells a funny story about the time when he got fired from his paper route. One day, in the middle of his job delivering newspapers, an emergency vehicle with all its lights and sirens blaring came passing by. In the midst of all of the excitement and chaos, he forgot what he was doing, dropped his bike, and ran after the fire truck to see what was going on. Isn't this typical of all of us? We are curious people, and we don't want to miss a thing! We go to where the action is because we want to get the real story. The verse for today is about two of Jesus' disciples who followed the action and got in on the greatest story ever told.

John the Baptist was telling everyone about the Lamb of God who would take away the sins of the world. This was big news! It sounded like the person John was talking about was the Messiah!

The next day, John pointed out Jesus to two of his disciples. "Look!" he said, "The Lamb of God!" Well, that was all they needed to hear. Those two disciples dropped everything to follow Jesus. They didn't want to miss a thing. They wanted to be with Jesus and get in on the greatest story ever told! They asked where he was staying, and he welcomed them. "Come and see," he said. He was inviting them to come with him, to spend time with him, and to become his disciples. And that's what they did! They spent that whole day with Jesus, and they did become two of his twelve disciples.

Jesus is inviting you to "come and see" too. This is a big deal! Don't turn down his invitation to *come* to him and *see* what he will do for you. Don't miss a thing! Become Jesus' disciple. You will never regret it. Jesus is the real deal!

December 31

A to Z

*I am the Alpha and the Omega, the First and the Last,
the Beginning and the End.
Come! Whoever is thirsty, let him come; and whoever wishes, let him
take the free gift of the water of life.*
Revelation 22:13, 17 (NIV)

If you have heard the phrase "A to Z," you know that it is not simply about the letters of the alphabet. A to Z refers to the full range of knowledge regarding a topic. This comprehensive knowledge includes everything about the topic from the beginning to the end. A to Z is what I thought of when I read these verses in Revelation. Jesus calls himself the Alpha and Omega, the first and last letters in the Greek alphabet. So why would Jesus identify himself this way?

Jesus was referring to himself as the full range of knowledge, "the first and the last, the beginning and the end," or the "A to Z." The first verse in the Bible says he was the beginning of everything. And the last verses of the Bible tell us he will be the end, the conclusion of human history. But Jesus doesn't just walk away from us in the end. Instead, he invites us to come with him. "Come!" Jesus says. "Whoever is thirsty, let him come; and whoever wishes, let him take the free gift of the water of life." In the end, Jesus offers us living water, the gift of life—with him—forever. This is incredible! If we accept his invitation, we get Jesus. If we get Jesus, we get everything, A to Z!

Acknowledgments

Nancy Lee is an editor and personal friend who deserves a special accolade for her skill as a wordsmith. Her understanding of the Bible and the gospel message is remarkable. She has taken my ideas and polished them into a finished product that simply presents God's invitation. It has been so much fun as we discussed and strategized the best way to share these stories and verses. Nancy has blessed my life in countless ways. If anyone is encouraged and challenged to experience Jesus Christ, then I have to thank Nancy for her tireless work!

What a blessing it is that my good friends Judy and Jerry Malone agreed to walk alongside me in this project. Their comments, encouragement, and prayers helped me to cross the finish line. I am totally indebted to you for your spiritual insights.

I am so thankful for Patti and Paul Quartuccio, my longtime friends who volunteered to review and offer suggestions for every one of my 366 devotionals. I am so grateful for our friendship all these years.

Special acknowledgment and thanks go to Kayla Dukes, Lynsey Ring, and Everardo Cortez, whose sketches made the words of this book come to life. What a joy and delight it was to work with each of you. May God richly bless your artistic talents and your faithfulness to Christ.

Many friends from my Chapelgate Men's Bible Study and neighborhood study group have contributed to this book with their many comments and ideas each week. Most of all, I am so grateful for their encouragement and prayers throughout the last several years.

I am also thankful to Josh Cooley, who provided me with so much good advice and challenged me with questions I had not even considered when writing this book. Many kudos to this incredible author.

Doug Lee is to be commended for the countless hours he contributed to his wife Nancy as they discussed all of these devotionals. Thank you for your godly wisdom and help during these last few years.

I take a bow to Believers BookServices for their guidance and assistance in making this book a reality. Dave Sheets, Marcus Costantino, and the team were absolutely a true joy to work with. And thank you to Mark and Penny Tuggle, who stewarded the editorial process with great care and respect for God, the reader, and me.

I am so thankful that God has blessed me with three awesome children and spouses: Lauren, Kevin, Doug, Penny, and Rachel. I am so grateful for each of them and am proud to be their Dad and father-in-law.

I also must recognize my seven incredible grandchildren who were included in many of the stories in this book. Their zest for life is a true joy and delight in my life. I love each one of them. Thank you, Kayla, Kolton, Brooklyn, Rylee, Max, Jace, and Emma!

My last thank you is for my beloved wife, Faith. She has been with me every day as we walked early in the morning, talking about a Bible verse or a story to be used in this book. What a blessing it is to have a woman of faith by my side, encouraging me in everything I do. She is my gal who has steadfastly loved me in spite of all of my flaws and the crazy idea of writing a book. I am truly blessed to be married to this wonderful woman!

About the Authors and Artists

Authors

Dennis Bilter grew up in a rural community in Ohio. After enlisting in the US Army, he attended West Point and graduated as an Infantry officer serving another nine years. His career included telecommunications executive positions in operations, marketing, sales, public relations, and employee communications. In his last job he founded a nonprofit charity named Mephibosheth Foundation, providing vocational training worldwide for young adults. Denny lives in Marriottsville, Maryland with his wife and best friend, Faith. They have been married for forty-eight years and have three adult children and seven awesome grandchildren. His hobbies include golf, reading, traveling, and playing the violin. He and his wife are followers of Jesus and are active in Bible studies, church activities, and encouraging all seven of their grandchildren who live nearby.

Nancy Lee has served as a Christian educator for over thirty years. After graduating from the University of Minnesota, she and her husband, Doug, studied under Francis Schaeffer at L'Abri Fellowship in Switzerland. While living in Atlanta, Georgia, she helped start two Christian schools while supporting her husband as a military chaplain and rearing four wonderful children. In 2002, she joined the staff of Belhaven University in Jackson, Mississippi to create an online dual-enrollment program teaching Christian worldview to high school students from around the world. She and Doug have been married for fifty-four years and have four grown children, fifteen grandchildren, and two great-grandchildren.

Artists

Everardo Cortez was born in Los Angeles, California, and is a Mexican-American graphic artist currently living in Baltimore, Maryland. "Change is the only thing that is permanent in life."

Kayla Dukes is a high school student who attends Chapelgate Christian Academy in Marriottsville, Maryland. Art has been a big part of her life since she was very young. She loves being around her family and playing basketball. Most importantly she is my oldest grandchild who loves Jesus.

Lynsey Ring studied Art at Houghton College and Oxford University, then achieved her MFA from the New York Academy of Art, Graduate School of Figurative Art, in New York, NY. She has exhibited in New York, San Francisco, and Baltimore, where she now resides with her family. Her work can be seen online at www.lynseyring.com.